SHAW'S GUIDE TO THE
COMMUNITY LAND ACT 1975

Shaw's Guide to
THE COMMUNITY LAND ACT 1975

by

HUGH ROSSI, LL.B., M.P.

A Solicitor of the Supreme Court (Hons.)
(a former Parliamentary Under-Secretary
of State for the Environment)

────────

LONDON:
Printed and Published by
SHAW & SONS LTD.,
Shaway House,
London, SE26 5AE
1976

Published   -   -   -   -   *January* 1976

ISBN 0 7219 0650 8

0721·906·508·8216

333 · 0026
R 73

IN 7836

DEDICATION

This guide is dedicated to—

—my colleagues on Standing Committee G—W. Benyon, Nick Budgen, Walter Clegg, Tony Durant, Michael Latham, Michael Morris, Graham Page, and Tim Sainsbury who sat with me in sessions lasting up to 27 hours at a stretch throughout a long hot summer term discussing over 1,000 amendments. The Act owes considerable improvement to their efforts.

—to my family who once more have tolerated a great deal to make my work possible.

H. R.

PREFACE

This book has been prepared in circumstances similar to those of my manual on the Rent Act 1974. Encouraged by the extensive take-up of that Shaw's Guide, I have followed the same format once again.

The General Commentary aims to give a comprehensive view and appreciation of the Act whilst the Commentary on Sections seeks to explain the intended meaning of its several segments and parts.

The principal feature of the Act is that it establishes a framework leaving the important detail to be filled in by Regulations or Ministerial directions. Therefore, I have drawn heavily upon our discussions in Parliament and Departmental explanatory memoranda to make available to the reader not only what the Act states but also how the Government intend it shall work.

HUGH ROSSI, M.P.

HOUSE OF COMMONS, S.W.1.

December 1975.

TABLE OF CONTENTS

A.—GENERAL COMMENTARY

[i]

B.—COMMENTARY ON SECTIONS

Part I.—Preliminary

Authorities for Purposes of the Act

SCHEDULES

C.—TEXT OF THE COMMUNITY LAND ACT 1975

For detailed Arrangement of Sections, *see* page 261.

SHAW'S GUIDE TO
THE COMMUNITY LAND ACT 1975

A.—GENERAL COMMENTARY

1. INTRODUCTION

The Community Land Act 1975 received the Royal Assent on the 12th November 1975. Different parts of it come into effect at different times.

Certain preliminary matters such as the preparation of Land Acquisition and Management Schemes and declarations of Disposal Notification Areas by local authorities may be embarked upon immediately after enactment. Part IV which stands by itself and deals, almost as an aside, with the compulsory purchase of unoccupied office premises, comes into effect one month after the passing of the Act.

The main scheme of the Act, providing for the public acquisition of all development land comes into operation in two phases. The first phase, which is a transitional period, starts on " the First appointed day " which is to be declared the 6th April 1976.[a] It ends on " the Second appointed day " when the scheme becomes fully operational and which will be declared by an order to be approved by both Houses of Parliament. Within the First phase those concerned with the Act will also have to contend with a " relevant date " as a series of orders are made translating a general power to acquire development land into a specific duty upon the authorities to do so. [b]

The avowed objectives of the Act as stated in the Government White Paper " Land " (Cmnd. 5730) are:—

a. to enable the community to control the development of land in accordance with its needs and priorities; and

---

(*a*) D. of E. Circular 121/75.
(*b*) *See also* the notes on s. 7.

b. to restore to the community the increase in value of land arising from its efforts.

This statement of objectives has met with general and popular approval. The delays and negative nature of our planning procedures have been the subject of mounting criticism over the years and led to the setting up of the Dobry enquiry in 1972. The sight of apparently unwarranted and excessive financial gains being made out of land on the grant of planning permission has long since been regarded as an " unacceptable face of capitalism ".

However, whether the Act is necessary in its present form to bring about the desirable objectives is another matter. Its impact upon planning owes very little to the Dobry Report and its fiscal objectives might be more efficiently obtained through the taxation system. Without a doubt it sets about its objectives by abrogating basic human rights of private ownership which hitherto have been regarded as invested with some sanctity under our system of law. As a cure for illness it might be said to prescribe decapitation for the relief of a headache.

The truth of the matter is of course that the underlying objective of the Act is other than the attractive statement of the White Paper. It is in fact the ultimate nationalisation of all development land.

As Mr. Secretary Anthony Crosland stated on one occasion " I have no doubt whatsoever that this will be the single most important and the single most Socialist measure to be implemented by this Labour Government ". Or as the Rt. Hon. John Silkin, the Minister for Planning and Local Government, stated on another " if all we were concerned about was to stop land speculation and to restore to the community the loss of development values, taxation would have been the way to do it. In our overcrowded island, where land is in short supply, we should now embark upon a total solution to the land question ".

2. THE LAND SCHEME

(a) Framework of the Land Scheme

The Act is essentially an enabling Act. The Secretary of State may require local authorities to do his bidding by making orders under at least thirteen of its provisions,[1] regulations under another eight,[2] directions under twelve,[3] and notifications under four.[4] Also his " consent ", " approval ", or " authority " is required at almost every turn. If all this proves to be inadequate for his purposes he may reserve all powers and functions to himself.

This Framework prompted the Administrative Law Committee of Justice, the British Section of the International Commission of Jurists, to comment in September 1975 " that the Community Land Bill in its present form is unacceptable from a constitutional point of view. For two reasons:— (1) because so much of major importance to the proposals is left to delegated legislation, and (2) because it confers such wide and unprecedented discretionary powers on local authorities and on the Secretary of State ".

Echoes come down to us through the years of the warnings given us by Lord Hewart in his constitutional essay " The New Despotism " when in 1929 he wrote that a Minister seeking autocratic powers would find " his course tolerably simple if he can

(a) get legislation passed in skeleton form;
(b) fill up the gaps with his own rules, orders and regulations;
(c) secure for them the force of statutes;
(d) makes his own decision final;
(e) arrange that the fact of his decision shall be conclusive proof of its legality;
(f) take power to modify the provisions of statutes; and

---

[1] Sections 2(1), 4(1), 5(1), 7(1), 10(4), 18(1), 26(3), 40(1), 48(2), 49(1), 50(1), Sch. 4, paras. 3 and 17(4).
[2] Sections 3(2), 14(9), 27(1), 46(1), 53(1), Sch. 4, paras. 11(4) and 21(5), Sch. 7, para. 8.
[3] Sections 8(3), 13(2), 16(7), 43, 44(1), (2), 45(1), Sch. 4, paras. 4(1) and 9(3), Sch. 5, paras. 1 and 3, Sch. 6, para. 1.
[4] Sections 13(2)(a), 21(3), Sch. 7, para. 2(2) and Sch. 8.

(*g*) prevent and avoid any sort of appeal to a court of law.

I am indebted to my friend and colleague Walter Clegg, M.P. who caught these echoes in committee and demonstrated how every one of the former Lord Chief Justice's criteria for despotism are faithfully followed in the Community Land Act.

(b) Outline of the Land Scheme

Within this framework, the Act sets out to ensure that, ultimately, virtually all development takes place on land which is in, or has passed through, public ownership.[1]

This land is to be brought into public ownership at a price which denies to the owner its development value. During the transitional period (between the first and second appointed days), this is achieved by enabling public authorities to purchase at market price less the amount of the development land tax that will be payable if the land changes hands privately. This tax is to be introduced in a second Act but it is understood that it will be initially 80% of the development value rising over a period of time to 100%. After the second appointed day, the price changes to the current use value of the land.[2]

To facilitate the identification of land suitable for development and accordingly for public acquisition, the local authorities have power to suspend every application to them for planning permission whilst they consider whether they require the land for themselves.[3] To overcome the obstacle of landowners being reluctant to put their heads into this noose, the authorities may come to development arrangements with third parties who identify the land of others as suitable for development and acquisition.[4] Additionally the authorities are able to declare Disposal Notification Areas in which no private sale of land (other than of a house on up to one acre) may take place without their being informed and given an opportunity of stating if they wish to acquire the property.[5]

So that the scheme is not subject to unreasonable delays or stubborn resistance, the private citizens' rights of objection to a compulsory purchase order or to demand a public enquiry are severely curtailed.[6]

---

[1] Sections 18 and 22.
[2] Section 25.
[3] Section 20 and Sch. 7.
[4] Schedule 6.
[5] Section 23.
[6] Schedule 4.

Once the land is in public ownership, the authorities may either develop it themselves, or make it available for development by others.[1] No disposals of the land, whether developed by them or undeveloped, may be made by the local authorities without the consent of the Secretary of State.[2] However, it is envisaged by the Act that disposals will take place since there is provision for negotiation of terms of disposal to either the original owner or to the applicant for planning permission with the owner's consent.[3] Moreover the authorities are ultimately expected to make a profit out of land transactions and divide the proceeds with the Exchequer.[4]

The net effect of this aspect of the scheme is that the land owner seeking to develop his own land will be obliged to sell it to the local authority less its development value and then acquire it back on terms reflecting the full development value before he can lay a brick, unless he falls within one of the exceptions to be laid down in regulations made from time to time, or contained in the Act.

There is of course no guarantee that the authority will be prepared to dispose back the land to him or if it is that the Secretary of State will permit this. Even where it happens the owner will not be certain of acquiring back the same interest in land that was acquired from him. Indeed it is evident from Ministerial Statements that regulations will provide that disposals of freeholds will only be permitted in the case of residential premises. Industrial or commercial development will be on a leasehold disposal with special consents being necessary for terms of more than 99 years.[5]

The injury and economic damage that these proposals can cause to those privately owning land are so evident as not to require comment. Indeed, so alarmed were church leaders of these effects that within a matter of days of publication of the Bill, they secured an interview with the Prime Minister and after mounting a nationwide campaign were granted special exceptions from the full operation of the land scheme in respect of the land holdings of churches and charities.[6]

---

[1] Section 17 and Sch. 6.
[2] Section 42.
[3] Schedule 6, para. 2.
[4] Section 44.
[5] D. of E. Circular 121/75.
[6] Pages 35-38 below.

The managers of pension funds affecting some 12 million pensioners or prospective pensioners with some £1,500m. invested in realty sought similar exceptions but were denied these.

It is a curiosity of the Act that it has to set up a hardship tribunal to mitigate the results of its own enactments.[1]

(c) Operation of the Land Scheme

In England, and Scotland, the operation of the scheme is in the hands of local authorities and new town corporations. Both county and district councils are " authorities " for the purpose of the Act: and so are the Peak Park Joint Planning Board and the Lake District Special Planning Board.[2]

They will all have to reach agreement between them in each area by the end of 1975 " or such later date as the Secretary of State may agree " on the division of functions between them. These agreements will be formalised in Land Acquisition and Management Schemes which are to be prepared jointly by all authorities in each county area.[3] In devising these schemes and allocating functions between themselves the local authorities must take into account such practical matters as the resources, staff and experience available to each of them.[4] Joint Boards comprising two or more authorities may be set up by the Secretary of State to manage schemes[5] and ultimately he may transfer functions to himself or a specially constituted agency if the local authorities in any area fail to operate a scheme.[6]

In Wales, a New Land Authority has been constituted which will exercise all the functions conferred on local authorities in England and Wales. It is not however a planning authority in its own right and may use local authorities as its agent where they have the resources to act.[7]

(d) Phasing of the Land Scheme

It is abundantly clear that the authorities do not possess the resources nor staff to embark immediately upon the wholesale

---

[1] Section 27.
[2] Section 1.
[3] Section 16.
[4] Schedule 5.
[5] Section 2.
[6] Section 50.
[7] Part II, ss. 8-14.

identification, acquisition, management, development, and disposal of land within their areas. Indeed the current need to curtail public sector borrowing argues, apart from every other consideration, a very gradual programme of public acquisition and development. It is for these reasons, no doubt, that the Secretary of State retains the right to trigger-off the two phases by declaring the first and second appointed days.

Within those two phases there are in fact three separate stages whose tabulation is helpful in obtaining a perspective of the Act. For this I am indebted to the very helpful consultative documents issued by the Department of the Environment in March 1975. The table is as follows[1]:

PHASE 1. TRANSITIONAL PERIOD (1st-2nd Appointed Day)

Stage A. (Before Full Duty Imposed in any Area)

(i) General Duty	on all authorities to consider desirability of bringing development land into public ownership[2] (other than exempt and excepted development—under s. 3).
(ii) Powers	for all authorities to acquire land suitable for development[3] (other than that exempt under s. 3).
(iii) Planning Applications	for relevant development made subject to procedure giving authorities an opportunity to consider acquisition[4] (other than exempt and excepted development under s. 3).
(iv) Price	market value net of Development Land Tax (80% rising to 100%).[5]

Stage B. (When Full Duty Imposed in an Area)
(1) In All Areas (Full and Non Full Duty)

(i) General Duty
(ii) Powers   } remain as in Stage A.
(iv) Price

---

[1] *See also* Sch. 2 and D. of E. Circular 121/75.
[2] Section 17.
[3] Section 15.
[4] Sections 19, 22.
[5] Development Land Tax Act (to be enacted).

(2) In Non Full Duty Areas

(iii) Planning Applications	remain as in Stage A.

(3) In Full Duty Areas

(v) Full Duty	to acquire all land suitable for all classes of relevant development designated in the Order imposing the Full duty[1]—prohibition against such designated relevant development on any land not in public ownership.[2]
(vi) Planning Applications	for such designated relevant development subject to procedure whereby planning permission (if granted) is suspended until land publicly acquired.[3] Note: Exempt and excepted development will not be subject to the Duty.

PHASE 2—PERMANENT SCHEME

Stage C.—(After 2nd appointed day)

(i) General Duty (ii) Powers	}Remain as in Stage A.
(iii) Planning Applications	For Exempt and Excepted Development remain as in Stage A. For designated relevant development continue as for Full duty areas in Stage B (and by Stage C all relevant development will have become designated).
(iv) Price	Current Use Value.[4]
(vi) Full Duty	already operating in all areas in respect of designated relevant development and by Stage C all relevant developments will be designated.

---

[1] Section 18.
[2] Sections 21 and 22.
[3] Section 21.
[4] Section 25.

3. DETAILS OF THE LAND SCHEME

Helpful as it may be in giving a perspective to the operation of the Act, the foregoing table introduces a number of terms and concepts which require more detailed explanation to make it meaningful. The remainder of this part of the commentary attempts to give that explanation following the table's sequence to facilitate reference back.

PHASE I.—TRANSITIONAL PERIOD

STAGE A.—BEFORE FULL DUTY IN AN AREA

(i) The General Duty of Local Authorities

This is threefold. From the first appointed day all local authorities will have a general duty:—

(a) to have regard to the desirability of bringing development land into public ownership, and

(b) to either develop that land themselves or to make it available for development by others, and

(c) to have regard to the desirability of securing the proper planning of their areas (s. 17(1)).

The last part of the duty was introduced at a late stage of the Act and is in effect a qualification of the first two parts which we shall treat separately.

(a) To consider desirability of bringing Development Land into Public Ownership

It must be noted at the outset that this duty relates to " development land ". This is defined as " land which in the opinion of the authority concerned is needed for relevant development within 10 years from the time they are acting " (s. 3).

The definition itself falls into two parts " in the opinion of " and " relevant development ", each of which requires separate consideration.

" In the Opinion of ". These words would seem to give the authorities virtually an unfettered discretion in deciding what is development land and consequently what they may consider desirable for public acquisition. However, in exercising this discretion the authorities are required to act within the planning framework. Thus the last part of the general duty ((i)(c) above) requires them to secure the proper planning of their area.

In considering what is development land, the authorities are therefore required to have regard to the provisions of the development plan so far as it is material, whether planning permission is in force or has been refused, and any other considerations which on an application for planning permission for any relevant development would be material for the purpose of determining that application (s. 17(2)).

This planning framework within which the authorities are free to decide what is development land constricts also their power to acquire land under section 15 and to declare disposal notification areas under section 23. The imposition of this framework seeks to meet the considerable criticism which was raised in Committee against the seemingly arbitrary and un-fettered powers being given to the authorities. Nevertheless, it must be remembered that the acquiring and developing authorities in most cases are also the planning authorities and as such make the very framework which is designed to contain them.

To obviate the dangers of this situation, the Government has made it known that central control will be exercised through financial requirements. Although the definition of " development land " speaks in terms of the authorities having regard to the needs of relevant development 10 years ahead they will not be required to acquire land up to 10 years ahead of their own needs. Far from it.

The local authorities will be required to prepare 5 year rolling programmes of their anticipated expenditure on development land, and these will be approved annually by the Department of the Environment as a basis for borrowing approval. The programme will not contain detailed lists of sites to be acquired but will need to be supported by reference to the planning basis on which the authorities are operating. This means that the programme must be prepared in the context of a regional strategy which has been endorsed by the Government, a structure plan, a local plan or non-statutory plan or policy adopted by the local authority and which is publicly available.[1]

It of course remains to be seen how this broad form of financial control can effectively curb arbitrary action by a local

---

[1] *See also* D. of E. Circular 121/75, paras. 69-73.

authority as regards an individual parcel of land in private
ownership.

We now turn to the second part of the definition of " development land ".

" Relevant Development ". This will, in the main, be
defined by regulation to be made by the Secretary of State who
thereby retains in his hands the key to the operation of the
whole Act.

" Relevant Development " is given a meaning by section 3,
namely, " any development except development—

    (*a*) of any class specified in Schedule 1 of the Act,
    (*b*) consisting exclusively of the building of a single
        dwelling house, and
    (*c*) of such class or classes as may be prescribed by the
        Secretary of State by regulations ".

The first category of development excluded from the definition
of relevant development and specified in the 1st Schedule is
known as **Exempt Development** and is completely outside the
scope of the acquisition powers and duties of the authorities.

The second two categories (*b*) and (*c*) are known as **Excepted
Development** and remain within the acquisition powers but
outside the duties and land scheme procedures for relevant
development.

Of these two categories (*b*) is self-explanatory and of a
limited nature but (*c*) gives the Secretary of State a great deal
of flexibility in regulating the operation of the land scheme by
bringing different kinds of development in and out of the
definition of " relevant development ".

Underlying the Government's thinking in making the distinction between **" Exempt "** and **" Excepted "** Development
was the contrast in their mind between " the scope of the land
scheme " and " the scope of the new powers of public
acquisition ".

This is best explained by way of example. It is intended
that a change of use of land to recreational use, together with
any necessary ancillary buildings, should generally be outside
the scope of the scheme. That is to say, if a sports club want
to lay out some land for a sports ground, and if they already

own the land or can arrange to buy it from the landowner, the Government does not intend for an authority to step in. So such development will be defined as Excepted Development by the regulations. However, it does not follow from this that recreational development is outside the scope of the acquisition power. The new acquisition power is available to authorities and could be used to facilitate the carrying out of the private recreational development, *e.g.* where the acquisition by an authority would be the only means by which a sports club could obtain the necessary land.

Applying this example, it will be seen that the Government's desire is to have only a very limited category of development outside " the scope of the acquisition power "—this is the Exempt Development. The other concept Excepted Development is concerned with exemption from " the scope of the scheme " only.

Great objection has been made both within and without Parliament that the Government should leave so much of the key definition to the whole Act to be dealt with by regulation. The objections have been raised on the grounds that this method (1) creates uncertainty making it difficult for private individuals to order their affairs properly in advance, (2) leaves too much power in the hands of the Secretary of State since regulations and their alteration are not subject to the same Parliamentary scrutiny, debate and control as are Acts of Parliament and amending legislation.—*See* Lord Hewart and Justice argument.[1]

However, apart from a small concession of writing the definition of the very limited exempt development into the Act the Government has resisted all requests that relevant development be defined in precise statutory terms on the grounds that they must retain a high degree of flexibility in the light of experience and as circumstances change.

It is therefore not possible at this stage to state with any precision what will be the major exceptions from relevant development which will in any case be changed from time to time. However, from the consultative documents which have been issued by the Government it would seem that the exclusions will follow broadly the following lines:—

---

[1] Pages 3 and 4 above.

EXCEPTED DEVELOPMENT PROPOSALS[1]

1. *White Paper Day Land*

(*a*) Development in accordance with an extant planning permission which was in force on 12 September 1974 or was granted after that date on appeal where the original planning decision was on or before that date.[2]

(*b*) Any development carried out on land which was in the freehold ownership of a builder, or of a residential or industrial developer, on 12 September 1974. This exception will continue if the land is subsequently sold to another builder or developer. Entitlement would depend on registration of a claim within a prescribed period.[2]

(*c*) Development consisting exclusively of the erection of an industrial building (including ancillary uses) where a material interest in the land was owned by an industrial undertaker on 12 September 1974. This exception will continue if the land is subsequently sold to another industrial undertaker.

2. *Minor Development Projects*

(*a*) Any industrial development where the total floor space created does not exceed 15,000 sq. ft. This is designed to cover small industrial buildings or extensions. (Extensions to large buildings will fall within para. 8 below.)

(*b*) Any development (other than industrial development) where the total floor space created does not exceed 10,000 sq. ft. This exception is designed to cover a very wide range of development, whether as a single unit or a number of separate units, including:

> Small-scale housing development (this would cover development of the order of 10-12 houses or up to 20 flats).
>
> Small commercial buildings.
>
> Most recreational buildings.
>
> Other small buildings, *e.g.* churches, meeting halls.
>
> A wide range of extensions to buildings of all types.

---

[1] Reproduced from Annex B to D. of E. Circular 121/75. These proposals now appear as draft Regulations laid before Parliament which are set out at the end of this book, p. 365, *post*.

[2] It is suggested that the Secretary of State will not normally entertain C.P.O.'s where planning permission was obtained or builders bought land before 12th November 1975 provided good progress is made with the development (*ibid.*, paras. 56 and 57).

It will also cover cases of mixed use, for example, shops with offices or flats above them.

3. *Special Categories of Development*

(*a*) *Changes of Use*

Any material change of use in land or buildings together with the erection of ancillary buildings within paragraphs 2(*a*) or (*b*) above, as appropriate. Amongst other things, this would cover the restoration of mineral workings, the deposit of refuse or waste materials, and most recreational development not already covered by paragraph 2(*b*) above, leaving only major recreational facilities within relevant development.

(*b*) *Rebuilding and Enlargement*

Rebuilding or enlargement of a building existing on 12 September 1974 or erected later so long as the floor space in the building as rebuilt or enlarged does not exceed by more than 10% the floor space in the building before rebuilding or enlargement. (Some extensions will already be within exempt development by virtue of Schedule 1 of the Act. Other extensions will be covered by paragraphs 2(*a*) and (*b*) above.)

(*c*) *Mineral Extraction*

Development consisting exclusively of the winning and working of minerals (including ancillary operations), together with the erection of ancillary buildings within paragraph 2(*a*) above. Works in connection with treatment and disposal of minerals so far as they are effectively industrial processes will fall within the treatment of other industrial development.

(*d*) *Agriculture and Forestry*

All development for the purposes of agriculture and forestry on land used for this purpose, which is not within exempt development or which is not excluded elsewhere (*e.g.* by virtue of the inclusion in paragraph 2(*b*) above of small development projects).

NOTES.[1]

1. It is to be noted that what is excepted from the Scheme is development not the land. The development

---

[1] Not part of D. of E. Circular 121/75, Annex B.

set out in the regulations will be able to take place without
the land needing to come into public ownership for that
purpose. However, the authorities may require the land
for more comprehensive development and so may nevertheless exercise their powers of acquisition of the land.

2. The Government have also indicated that the
making of excepted development regulations will not
remove the need for administrative guidance on the sorts
of development which, although they are not strictly
excepted development, should be allowed to go ahead
without public ownership. This applies especially to the
phasing-in of the scheme, but there may also be types of
development which, because of definitional problems, cannot be dealt with in the regulations and will remain to be
excepted by administrative action.

3. Although Excepted Development remains within
the scope of the acquisition powers under the Act, it does
receive a great deal of special treatment under the Act:—

    (i) it is outside the scope of the general duty under
section 17 to consider the acquisition of development land.

    (ii) it is not possible to include it in an order under
section 20 imposing the full duty to acquire for
designate types of development.

    (iii) it is outside the scope of the new compulsory
purchase procedures in Schedule 4, paragraphs
2-4 (*i.e.* the grounds of objection that the acquisition is unnecessary or inexpedient remain and
there is no power to dispense with a public
enquiry).

    (iv) it is outside the provisions of sections 19-22 and
Schedule 7 which enable the suspension of
planning permissions.

**(b) To Develop the land themselves or make it available for
development by others**

In exercising this part of their general duty, local authorities
are expected to pay full regard to the needs of all sections of the
community. Therefore the 6th Schedule requires them to have
regard to a number of factors. These include the needs of

people living in or wishing to live in the area; of industrial or commercial concerns carrying on business in the area, or wishing to do so; of builders and developers; of parish councils and of statutory undertakers; of charities. Finally, the Secretary of State may direct the authorities to have regard to such other matters as he may from time to time consider relevant.

Where an authority decides that the land should be made available for development by others priority must first be given to the owner of the land and then to a person who has applied for planning permission and was acting with the owner's written consent. (Schedule 6, paragraph 2.) However, this requirement does not prevent a developer making a planning application without the owner's consent and then, having identified the land for the authority, taking an equal chance with other developers of securing the right to develop. (*See also* discussion on Prior Rights, pages 30-32, below.)

(ii) Powers to Acquire Development Land
To enable them to fulfil their general duty which requires them to buy development land on a wide scale, the Act confers on the authorities new powers of land acquisition.

The authorities are given the power to acquire by agreement any development land in their areas (*i.e.* the land in their opinion suitable for development). There is also power to acquire such land by compulsory purchase, subject to confirmation of the Secretary of State. (Section 15.)

Some of these acquisitions will be in fulfilment of the authorities' five year rolling programmes (*see* page 10, above), others may arise on an *ad hoc* basis as the result of planning applications. However they may arise, and whether the acquisitions are by agreement or compulsory purchase, they will have to take place within the planning framework previously described. This is because the only land the authorities may acquire must be development land which is defined in relation to that framework.

The planning backing supporting the acquisition may take the form of a plan adopted or approved or which has passed through adequate public participation procedures. Alternatively it may derive from the grant of suitable planning permission.

Suitable planning backing for the acquisition would be provided by an approved structure plan, if sufficiently precise in detail; a local plan; a draft local plan which has been subject to public participation under section 12(1) of the Town and Country Planning Act 1971 if it conforms with the structure plan; a non-statutory plan or policy which has been adopted and agreed by the local authorities concerned subject to public participation as above; an existing planning permission; a planning application to be considered by the Secretary of State concurrently with the proposal for acquisition.

Exemptions and Exceptions to Powers of Acquisition

In our discussions of Exempt and Excepted Development we have already seen that Exempt Development as set out in Schedule 1 provides a very limited exclusion and is the only category of development outside " the scope of the acquisition power ".   (Page 11, above.)

Although Excepted Development remains within the scope of the acquisition power, it is, however, intended by the Government that this power will not normally be used to acquire land for Excepted Development.   It is understood that the Secretary of State will be issuing guidance by circular as to the circumstances in which he will be prepared to entertain compulsory purchase orders for Excepted Development.   The kind of cases where this might be appropriate include—

    (i) to facilitate development through acquisition of land where this could not be achieved by agreement by the individuals or bodies concerned (the sports club example, pages 11 and 12, above).

    (ii) for reasons of positive planning.

    (iii) to ensure comprehensive development of an area or to stop evasion by the breaking down of a large site into individual plots.

The treatment of the different classes of development which we have been discussing so far may be best summarised in the following Table:—

TREATMENT OF CLASSES OF DEVELOPMENT

Category of Development	Treatment by Act
1. Exempt development. Defined in Schedule 1.	Development outside the scope of the acquisition power under section 15.
2. Excepted development. Defined by regulations under section 3, with the addition of the single-dwelling plot.	Development— (a) within the power but permanently outside the normal scope of the scheme. (b) outside general duties under section 17 and section 18 duty. (c) outside special compulsory purchase procedure, Schedule 4. (d) outside provisions for suspension of planning permission, sections 19-22 and Schedule 7.
3. Relevant development. Defined by exclusion of exempt and excepted development.	Development within the power and ultimately to be brought within the full duty.

Compulsory Purchase Powers

So far we have discussed the principles which will underly public acquisition of land under the Scheme whether it be by agreement or compulsorily.

However, it is anticipated by the Government that its " total solution " to the land question will meet with less than enthusiastic co-operation from the private citizen faced with dispossession of his property at less than market value. Hence alterations have been made to the compulsory purchase system to make it easier and quicker for the authorities to enforce the take-over of development land.

Having overcome the hurdle (which mostly they will have constructed themselves) of establishing a planning background for designating and acquiring development land, the authorities may then proceed uninhibited by some of the protections afforded to the private citizen by the existing compulsory purchase code.

In general terms the procedures of the Acquisitions of Land Acts will apply to compulsory purchases under this Act (section 15(3)) save for important modifications introduced by the 4th Schedule.

The modifications are:—

(a) the Secretary of State may dispense with a public enquiry into a compulsory purchase order[1] where:—

(i) there is in existence a planning permission for relevant development granted by the Secretary of State after an opportunity had been given for a public local enquiry; or

(ii) there is an adopted or approved local plan and the grant of planning permission for relevant development on the land would be in accordance with the provisions of that plan; or

(iii) there is no adopted or approved local plan, but the grant of planning permission for relevant development of the land would be in accordance with either—

(a) the provisions of the development plan (*i.e.* an old-style plan consistent with an approved structure plan if one exists); or

(b) a draft structure or local plan has received what, in the Secretary of State's view is adequate public participation in the light of the requirements of sections 8(1) and 12(1) of the Town and Country Planning Act 1971; or

(c) a non-statutory plan which has received similar public participation and which has been accepted as a basis for planning decisions in the transition period to the

---

[1] Schedule 4, para. 2.

new development plan system in accordance with paragraph 11 of the memorandum attached to Circular 144/71.

Unless these requirements are met, an
enquiry or hearing into the compulsory purchase order has to be held, subject to the special
procedures to be mentioned next.

The Secretary of State may bring in procedures under which
he will be given an unfettered discretion as to whether to hold
an inquiry or hearing. This procedure could only be used if
it appeared to the Secretary of State to be in the public interest,
subject to Parliamentary approval, and for a limited life of 5
years. The enquiry or hearing could not be dispensed with as
against a residential occupier.[1]

These conditions under which the Secretary of State may
dispense with an enquiry or hearing are an improvement on
the proposals contained in the Bill as originally introduced
which allowed the Secretary of State to dispense with a public
enquiry into a compulsory purchase order wherever he " considers it expedient to do so ".

However, it still falls short of affording a private citizen
adequate protection. The object now is to dispense with a
compulsory purchase enquiry where there has already been
some form of public planning enquiry. This ignores the
tendency of the average citizen to lead his everyday life without
seeking the esoteric pleasures of studying planning proposals
and attending long and interminable planning enquiries at his
town hall. It is a different matter when a compulsory purchase
order falls on his doormat one dismal morning. He may feel
not a little aggrieved to then discover that he has lost his right
to a public enquiry into something which directly touches and
concerns him because he did not engage counsel to advise him
on a general planning enquiry some years previously. Not
surprisingly the Government has had some trouble with the
Council for Tribunals over these proposals.

(b) the Secretary of State may disregard objections to a
compulsory purchase order which are made on the

---

[1] Schedule 4, para. 4.

grounds that the acquisition is " unnecessary or inexpedient ".[1]

This removes the commonest ground of objection. It simply leaves " prematurity of acquisition " and " personal hardship ", other than that relating purely to terms of compensation. However this does not exclude objections on the ground that the ' development ' for which the land is required is unnecessary or inexpedient.

(c) the Abolition of Special Parliamentary Procedure.[2]

This relates where one public authority makes a compulsory purchase order on the land owned by another (including the land of parish and community councils and statutory undertakers). However, the procedure as it applies to special categories of land such as commons, open spaces and land held inalienably by the national trust remains unaffected.

(iii) Planning Applications

The authorities will be primarily engaged under the scheme in identifying development land for themselves. They will be doing this on the formulation of the new five year rolling programmes. However, it will be some time before they have the machinery, staff, and expertise to do this in a sufficiently comprehensive and at the same time detailed manner.

Therefore, the Act gives the authorities an opportunity to acquire development land which is identified to them by private individuals making planning applications. The assumption is that the grant of a planning permission is a clear indication of the suitability of the land for development and that the owner will wish to know at the outset whether an authority will desire to acquire it.

Permissions on or before 12 *September* 1974

We have already seen (page 13 above) that where planning permission has been granted on or before the 12 September 1974 (including refusals at that date subsequently reversed on appeal) regulations will treat the development as Excepted Development with the consequence that the local authority will not be normally allowed to acquire the land in question.

---

[1] Schedule 4, para. 3(5).
[2] Section 41.

Permissions after 12 *September* 1974

The Act deals with varying circumstances which arise where the planning permission is granted after the 12 September 1974. Here we are concerned for the moment with the situations which arise where the planning permission is granted in Stage A of Phase I that is to say during that stage of the Transitional period before full duty is imposed on an area. We will look at the subsequent situations when we come to consider the full duty (page 25 below).

During the period we are now considering, the Act deals with two separate situations:—

    (*a*) where planning permission was granted after the 12 September 1974 on an application made **before** the first appointed day.[1]

    (*b*) where planning permission was granted after the 12 September 1974 on an application made **on or after** the first appointed day.[2]

In case (*a*), there is a right to serve a 'notice of election' on one of the authorities in whose area the land lies that is to say either the district or the county authority. The notice may be served by the owner or someone with a contract to purchase. The effect of the notice is to suspend the planning permission consideration of which proceeds in the ordinary way. All the authorities concerned have three months to decide whether or not they wish to acquire the land. If the authorities decide not to acquire the land or, having served a notice of intention to acquire within the 3 months fail to take the first step in the acquisition before the end of 12 months from the date of their notice, then the suspension of the planning permission is lifted. Furthermore the authorities are debarred from acquiring the land by compulsory purchase for 5 years from the date of their decision or their failure to act.

In case (*b*), there is no right of the owner to serve a notice of election. The planning permission is however automatically suspended. Each authority within whose area the land lies is required to serve within the time laid down for giving a planning decision a notice stating whether or not, in the event of that

---

[1] Section 19.
[2] Section 20.

planning permission being granted, they intend to acquire any or all the land in question. Where no notice is served within the prescribed time limit this will be treated as a deemed notice of no intention to acquire.

Where no acquisition is proposed the suspension of the planning permission will be lifted and all the authorities concerned lose their powers to acquire for 5 years and the owner may proceed with his own development.[1]

Where acquisition is proposed then again there are certain time limits within which the authorities must proceed with the acquisition in the ordinary way or lose their rights to do so for five years leaving the owner free to proceed.[1]

Conditional Notices

The authorities are empowered to attach conditions to notices of non intention to acquire.[2] If these conditions are breached the powers of compulsory purchase are revived.[1]

(iv) Price

In the transitional period which we are still considering, the price that local authorities have to pay for land will be the market price reduced by the amount that the vendor would be liable to pay in development land tax if he sold privately.

Therefore the rules for ascertaining market value contained in the Land Compensation Acts 1961 and 1973 continue to apply and all rights to compensation such as home and farm loss payments remain.

The development land tax is not dealt with in the Act but is to be the subject of a separate enactment which is still to be introduced.

The Act does contain modification of the procedures governing the grant of Certificates of Appropriate Alternative Development under section 17 of the Land Compensation Act 1961.[3]

The modifications are that in future:—

(*a*) a local planning authority must not specify any class of development in a certificate unless it is completely certain it would have granted planning permission for

---

[1] Schedule 7, para. 1.
[2] Schedule 7, paras. 7 and 8.
[3] Section 47 and Sch. 9. *See also* D. of E. Circular 115/75. These changes take effect from 12 Dec. 1975 (s. 47(6)).

that class of development had it not proposed to acquire the land.

(b) the onus is placed on the applicant to give his grounds for believing that the class or classes of development specified in his application would be appropriate.

(c) the applicant would be enabled to apply for a " nil " certificate giving his reasons for believing that no development would have been appropriate other than that proposed to be carried out by the acquiring authority.

The object of these modifications is to reduce the compensation payable where there would in reality be little prospect of obtaining a planning permission for the suggested alternative development.

STAGE B.—FULL DUTY IN AN AREA
(v) The Full Duty

Throughout Stage A the local authorities are expected to build up their resources and their ability to handle all development land in their areas on their own. The speed at which this happens will vary from area to area.

Therefore the Secretary of State is able to make orders applying to each area separately, as it becomes ready, the full duty to ensure that virtually all development takes place on land which is in, or has passed through public ownership.[1] The date on which full duty order comes into force is known as " the relevant date ".[2]

Designated Relevant Development

This full duty will not necessarily apply to all relevant development. The orders may impose the full duty to designated classes of relevant development—" designated relevant development ".[3] This enables the full duty to be imposed in an area stage by stage as the resources of the local authority concerned continue to build up. For instance the full duty might, initially, apply only to land for housing and extend later to other types of development.

Once the full duty is imposed in respect of any class of relevant development, it will be obligatory on the authority

---

[1] Section 18(3).
[2] Section 18(6).
[3] Section 18(1).

subject to the order to acquire the land before that kind of development takes place.[1]   Conversely there is a prohibition against carrying out any designated relevant development other than on land which has been in the ownership of a local authority.   This means that such development cannot be carried out by a private individual or company unless the land has been made available to him by the local authority for that purpose.[2]

Excepted Development

We have already seen that for the purposes of the land scheme some types of development will never need to be designated either during Stage B of Phase I in the transitional period or after the second appointed day.   In effect there will be a permanent category of Excepted Development to be brought in by regulations made under section 3.

The development coming within this category will never be subject to the full duty to acquire and the associated prohibition will never apply to it.   However, the excepted development will remain within the powers of acquisition under section 15.

(vi) Planning Applications

We have already considered the effect of the Act upon a planning permission granted after the 12 September 1974 but before the relevant date under a section 18 full-duty order.

Now we have to consider the effect upon planning permissions granted after a relevant date.

A distinction has to be drawn between non-designated relevant development and designated relevant development. Non-designated relevant development is not a term of art used by the Act since it is intended that the regulations defining Excepted Development will cover all categories of relevant development which are not to be designated under section 18. However, the full duty is to be phased in by fitting the extent of designation in each area to the resources of the authorities concerned.   Thus for a period, which will vary in the different areas, categories of relevant development will exist which are not excepted by the regulations yet will not be designated by a

---

[1] Section 18(3).
[2] Section 21(4).

section 18 order because the resources do not exist to tackle all relevant development.

This non-Excepted relevant development outside the terms of the Order must by definition be unaffected by the relevant date. Therefore the procedures discussed under Stage A (pages 21 and 22 above) continue to apply and there will be a suspension of the planning permission, with a possibility of the lifting of the suspension, and no duty to acquire.

With regard to " designated relevant development " all planning permissions are automatically suspended if made on or after the relevant date.[1] There is no provision for the lifting of this suspension and the only way in which the planning permission may be implemented is for

(a) the development to be carried out by a public authority, or

(b) for the land to have passed through public ownership and made available for that development by the authority concerned.

PHASE II—THE PERMANENT SCHEME

The transitional period which we have been discussing so far comes to an end on the second appointed day. This will be not earlier than the first date upon which full duty orders apply to all relevant development in all areas, *i.e.* all relevant development has been designated everywhere throughout England, Scotland and Wales.[2]

The main significance of the Second Appointed Day is that it is the point in time at which there is a change in the basis of compensation to be paid for land by the authorities.

We have seen that during the transitional period the local authorities will pay the market price calculated under the Land Compensation Acts reduced by the development land tax. Also during the transitional period the development land tax will move from the initial 80% of development value towards 100% as the second appointed day approaches. The combined effect of the 100% tax and of the growth of local authority

---

[1] Section 21.
[2] Section 7(3).

activity in the land market (leading to a near monopoly buyer situation) will be that the cost of land to local authorities will progressively depreciate to current use value.

Therefore on the second appointed day the compensation code changes so that all the public authorities would actually pay is current use value. The rights to compensation or other payments not based on the value of the land such as home or farm loss payments remain unaltered.

Current Use Value does include some development value, that is to say the prospect of development included in Schedule 8 of the Town and Country Planning Act 1971 (Schedule 6, Scottish Act 1972) or the General Development Order for the time being in force. It also includes the value of Exempt development as defined by Schedule 1, of this Act.[1]

The kind of development value that is to be included in current use therefore is value attributable to the rebuilding or enlargement of a building so that the cubic content is not exceeded by 10% or in the case of a house by 1,750 cu. ft.; changes of use within the same use class; building (other than dwellings) on agricultural or forestry land.

Financial Hardship Tribunals. When the basis of compensation is changed to current use value the Government anticipates that some cases of difficulty will arise. Therefore the Act provides for the setting up of Financial Hardship Tribunals which will consider claims of hardship and have power to require the acquiring authority to pay up to a maximum of £50,000 over and above the current use value for any one claim.[2]

4. ANCILLARY MATTERS

(i) Disposal Notification Areas

In order to make it easier for them to acquire land in areas where they are considering acquisition, public authorities may declare such areas to be disposal notification areas (D.N.A.s).[3]

The purpose is two fold. First to enable authorities to find out about impending private transactions in the areas where

---

[1] Section 25(3).
[2] Section 27.
[3] Section 23.

they are considering acquisition. Secondly to warn prospective purchasers that acquisition by an authority is imminent.

It is the Government's intention that a D.N.A. should be declared only where there is development land although land not to be developed may be in the area. The D.N.A. is to be prepared within the framework of the rolling programmes and consistent with the planning backing relating to the definition of development land.[1]

The authorities may declare any area a D.N.A. and the declaration does not require the Secretary of State's consent. However, he may veto or amend a D.N.A.[2] •

Once declared a D.N.A. must be registered as a charge in the local land charges register.[3]   Thereafter anyone intending to enter into a binding contract to dispose of a material interest in land (other than in owner-occupied residential premises of up to one acre)[4] must give notice thereof to the local authority.[5] This gives the right to the authority to serve a counternotice within 4 weeks stating whether or not it wishes to acquire the land or any part of it.[6]

The counternotice does not act as a notice to treat and the vendor may still proceed with his original transaction if his purchaser is not put off by the knowledge that the authority will acquire sooner or later.   The vendor (if he is a residential or agricultural owner-occupier with certain rateable value limits) then has the right to serve a blight notice on the authority requiring it to purchase from him immediately.[7]   The vendor of owner-occupied residential premises of not more than one acre need only give notice of his intended disposal if he wishes, e.g. presumably where he finds the D.N.A. has destroyed the private market and he wishes to use the blight provisions.

Failure to serve notice on a local authority of an intended sale of land within a disposal notification area is an offence subject to a fine.[8]

Therefore it will be necessary for every vendor to make a local land changes search before entering into a contract for

---

1 And see D. of E. Circular 121/75, para. 28.   5 Section 23(5).
2 Schedule 8, para. 2.   6 Section 23(7).
3 Schedule 8, para. 1.   7 Section 23(8).
4 Section 23(6) and Sch. 8, Part III.   8 Section 23(9).

sale, and then if he turns up a D.N.A. to wait for 4 weeks before he can sign and exchange.

The obvious consequence of D.N.A.s will be to depress the price of land within them thereby reducing the base value for development land making it cheaper for authorities to buy.

(ii) Blight

We have just seen that the blight provisions of the Town and Country Planning Act 1971 have been extended to apply to properties falling within D.N.A.s.[1]

A similar extension is made where planning permissions are suspended under sections 19-21 so as to enable an owner-occupier, falling within the 1971 Act categories, to serve a blight notice compelling the authority concerned to buy his interest.[2]

However, the rights of an authority to resist a blight notice have also been enlarged so that a counternotice may now be served on the grounds that the authority do not intend to acquire the land within 10 years[3] (previously 15).

(iii) Management and Disposal of Land

Under the scheme it is intended that land will be bought for fairly early development. However, it is evident that some land will have to be held some time awaiting development especially where purchase is the consequence of D.N.A. blight procedures. Local authorities are required to make proper arrangements for the management of this land. This under existing legislation.

The disposal of land brought into public ownership is subject to the consent of the Secretary of State. This applies not only to land acquired under the Act but that acquired under any other enactment. The control is absolute and overrides the provisions of section 123 of the Local Government Act 1972.[4]

It is understood,[5] however, that the Government intend to issue general consents for disposals which will enable them to go ahead without specific reference back to the Secretary of State. The scope of these consents is still under consideration but it is understood they will follow the broad principles that:—

(i) disposals shall be on the best possible terms obtainable.

---

[1] Section 23(8).
[2] Section 22(6).
[3] Schedule 10, para. 6(3).
[4] Section 42.
[5] And see D. of E. Circular 121/75, paras. 39-42.

(ii) disposals of land for house building for owner occupation will be generally of the Freehold. Authorities will be encouraged to release land to builders by means of building agreements so that the freehold is conveyed direct to the purchasers of the houses with the builder paying for the right to carry out the development rather than for the land.

(iii) disposals for any other kind of development will normally be leasehold with regular rent reviews.

Originally it was announced that the length of leases will be restricted. This has, however, caused considerable disquiet amongst developers because the Finance institutions have indicated they are reluctant to make funds available for development on this basis. Therefore after reconsideration it has been announced that leases will be permitted of up to 99 years without special consent.[1] (*See also* First Report of the Advisory Group on Commercial Property Development—the Pilcher Report, November 1975.)

Guidance notes will be issued by the Department of the Environment to local authorities on disposal policies and procedures early next year. The notes will deal in some detail with arrangements for building agreements which will have to be such as to enable builders to finance their operation without any land to offer as a collateral security to their bankers. Also detailed guidance will be given on management after disposal of leasehold interests of commercial and industrial property. Significantly guidance will also be given on how to encourage developers to identify other peoples' land for acquisition and development.[2]

(iv) Prior Right Procedure

Special considerations arise where public authorities have acquired land from an owner who wishes to develop it for himself, or, following the making of a planning application, by an applicant who is not the owner.

The Act recognises the special position of former owners and also of those developers who have identified a site for development by applying for planning permission. Industrialists in particular need assurance that they will have an

---

[1] D. of E. Circular 121/75, para. 39(*b*).
[2] *Ibid.*, para. 42.

opportunity to renegotiate a lease on sites acquired from them. Also whilst building up their own resources and machinery public authorities will rely heavily upon private sector developers using their expertise and entrepreneurial skills to identify development land. Therefore an incentive has to be given to such developers.

Accordingly, the Act requires authorities to give prior rights to former owners and planning applicants on land disposals.[1] The procedure, however, applies only when an authority does not intend to develop the land itself or allow another authority to develop it but to make it available for private development. To give a measure of protection to land owners from unfair arrangements made between local authorities and developers identifying development land for them the developer will only qualify in a prior right situation if his application is accompanied by the written consent of the owner.[2] There is nothing to stop a developer making an application and taking his chance in competition with other developers who may or may not be interested.

Some indication has been given by the Government in their consultative document of May 1975 as to how they intend the prior rights procedure to operate as regards various categories of development.[3] Formal guidance is to be given early next year.[4]

Dwellings

Where land owned by a builder is acquired to enable a comprehensive development to take place, the Government in its guidance to public authorities may suggest that the builder be given a prior opportunity to carry out part of the development unless the authority is to do it all itself for its own use.

Industrial Development

The guidance may make it clear that land already held for development by an industrialist which passes into public

---

[1] Schedule 6, paras. (2), (3).
[2] Schedule 6, para. 6.
[3] It will also be noted that many of these categories will fall within the definition of Exempt Development in the proposed regulations (*see* page 11, above).
[4] D. of E. Circular 121/75, para. 42.

ownership, that industrialist shall be given a prior right to negotiate a leaseback of the site. Again there is the proviso that this will not apply if the authority requires the land for itself.

Commercial Development

The position will be similar to that of the industrialist.

Agriculture

Where an authority buys land for agricultural development which is relevant development (*e.g.* the erection of farm cottages) the prior right procedures will apply as in the other cases.

Mineral Development

Whenever an authority exercises its right of acquisition in order to make a site available for mineral development, a private mineral operator will be given a prior opportunity to negotiate a lease for exploiting the mineral deposits if the site was owned or identified by that operator.

(v) Financial Arrangements

The Government have promised that the scheme will not in any way add to the rate burden of local authorities. Hence the whole of it is to be financed out of capital borrowing. All expenditure including purchase price for land, administration and management costs, and the charges for servicing the loans will be financed out of the borrowing.[1] This will include all expenditure incurred in 1975/6 in preparation for the land scheme, *e.g.* staff time engaged in setting up the L.A.M.S. even before the Royal Assent.[2] The hope is that the borrowing will be eventually paid out of receipts from land disposals.

The borrowing for land acquisition will be a new key sector.[1] Control is to be exercised through approval of the 5-year rolling programmes of expenditure. Also the use of the receipts from land disposals will be strictly controlled centrally.

---

[1] D. of E. Circular 121/75, para. 44.
[2] *Ibid.*, para. 74.

The authorities are required by the Act to keep special accounts and records of all land transactions.[1]   The Secretary of State may direct what items must be credited and debited to the accounts.[2]   It has already been made clear that off-site infrastructure costs will not be debited to the account and must be borne separately by the authorities, *i.e.* not out of this new key sector.

With regard to expenditure, we have seen already that the 5-year rolling programmes will have to be submitted annually by the local authorities probably on a county basis to the Department of the Environment.   The programmes are to be prepared in accordance with agreed planning policies for the area and authorisation of expenditure would be on the basis that all individual purchases were in accordance with the programme although the authorisation itself will be a block loan sanction.   The Department will of course keep the overall borrowing limits in line with the national economic requirements of the day.

The authorities are being asked to submit their first 5-year programme by May 1976 to commence in 1977/8.   A system of individual loan sanctioning will operate for 1976/7.[3]

With regard to receipts, the Act again for these to be dealt with in directions to be given by the Secretary of State.[4]   The Government have announced that it is intended that when an individual land account comes into surplus this surplus will be divided between the authorities and central government. 40% of the annual surplus, if any, will be payable to the Secretary of State for the benefit of the Consolidated Fund. The remaining 60% will be available for the authorities but divided so that one half is retained by the individual authority in whose account the surplus arises and the other half goes into a pool to help out those authorities whose land account shows a deficit.[5]   The retention by the individual local authority

---

[1] Sections 43(1), 45(1).
[2] Section 43(2).
[3] D. of E. Circular 121/75, paras. 71/2.
[4] Section 44.
[5] D. of E. Circular 121/75, para. 45.

of its 30% of the surplus will of course be subject to any sharing arrangement it has made with other authorities in its area under the Land Management and Acquisition Schemes.

The surplus accruing to any local authority must be used by it for repayment of debt, to finance expenditure on a key sector project within the agreed programme, and to finance expenditure within the locally determined sector on the basis that the agreed level of borrowing for this sector was reduced *pro tanto*.

(vi) Reserve Powers

Throughout the discussion of the scheme it will have been noted that the Secretary of State retains effective control in his hands. He determines what is relevant development thereby defining the land the authorities have power to acquire; he determines the designated relevant development to which the full duty to acquire applies; he may veto disposal notification areas; he must approve the 5-year expenditure programme; he can control actual acquisitions by refusal to confirm individual compulsory purchase orders; no disposal of land may take place without his consent or on terms and in conditions laid down by him.

The authorities therefore are effectively the tools or agents of the Secretary of State in his strategic objective of bringing development land into public ownership.

To emphasise this state of affairs he retains the power to transfer all the functions of an authority under the Act to himself, or to another authority, or to any new body he may set up for this purpose.[1] Thereby he hopes by threat of use of this ultimate sanction to ensure a swift progress towards public ownership of land; subject of course to prevailing economic conditions and availability of resources. It is of course also an interesting speculation as to whether the Department of the Environment could cope with the work load thrown upon it if enough local authorities found they could not proceed as swiftly and enthusiastically towards the public ownership of land as the Government would desire.

---

[1] Section 48.

5. SPECIAL CATEGORIES

We have seen in our consideration of the concepts of relevant development, designated relevant development, and the prior rights on disposals, that the Government intend special treatment for dwellings, industrial development, commercial development, recreational buildings, agriculture and forestry and mineral working. This special treatment has not been fully defined since it is to be given by way of regulations which still have to be made under the Act and which will be varied from time to time. The special treatment, however, will take the form of varying degrees of exception for the categories of development mentioned from the full impact of the scheme.

As well as these exceptions the Act confers exclusions from the full impact of the scheme on particular kinds of persons in varying respects. These persons are:—(i) single plot owners, (ii) churches and charities, (iii) parish and community councils, (iv) statutory undertakers. We shall look at each in turn.

(i) Single Plot Owners

The one statutorily defined exception from relevant development is development consisting exclusively of the building of a single dwelling house.[1] Although defined by the Statute it is no different in status under the land scheme to any other kind of Excepted Development which is to be defined in regulations under section 3(2)(c).[2] It is outside ' the scope of the scheme ' but within ' the scope of the new powers of acquisition '.

(ii) Churches and Charities

Perhaps nothing did more to draw public attention to the possible impact of the Act than the fact that in the Bill as originally drawn no exemption was made for Churches and Charities. If this situation had remained then the financing of the reconstruction of churches or their new building in areas to which there had been shifts of population would have been seriously or possibly fatally undermined. Also the provision of old people's homes, houses for the physically and mentally handicapped, youth and community centres and similar

[1] Section 3(2)(b).
[2] See page 11, above.

charitable activities would have been jeopardised. The reason
is that much of this activity has been financed by the mixed
development on existing sites or by the disposal for development at full market price of redundant churches and sites in
inner-areas. The prospect of disposal of outmoded Victorian
church properties at current use value and the purchase of new
development land from local authorities at full market price
or on leases at rack rents filled the churches and charities with
dismay.

The Act now gives special privileges to churches and charities
in respect of land which they held on the 12 September 1974.

(a) during the transition period under the scheme (*i.e.*
until the second appointed day) or for a period of
eleven years, whichever shall be the longer, such land
may be disposed of at full market value. That is to
say if it is acquired by public authorities, those authorities will not be able to deduct the amount of development land tax.[1] With regard to private sales, the
Development Land Tax Act will provide that no
development land tax will be payable by churches and
charities.

(b) where relevant development of such land is proposed
by the church or charity, an authority will not be
expected to use its acquisition powers although these
powers will remain to be exercised where the authority
requires the land for itself. It has been made clear
that " the Secretary of State will not expect to confirm
any compulsory purchase orders for such land unless
there are special planning reasons for doing so ".[2]

(c) where the full-duty applies churches and charities will
be able to proceed with designated relevant development without the authorities being required to fulfil

---

[1] Section 25(6).
N.B.—The special treatment for charities is achieved in the various sections
quoted because land held by a charity is regarded as not subject to an " outstanding material interest"—s. 4(1)(b) and *see* p. 39, below.
[2] Rt. Hon. John Silkin, M.P. Hansard, 11 Nov. 1975. Vol. 899, No. 197,
Col. 1189.

their duty of ensuring the land passes through public ownership.[1]

(*d*) the provisions for suspension of planning permission will not apply to land owned by a charity for any kind of development.[2]

(*e*) after the second appointed day when current use value will apply to all land acquired by an authority, in so far as church and charity land is concerned that current use value will be the prevailing use of the locality in which the site is situate.[3] Thus the current use value of a redundant church in a predominantly commercial area will not be the value of an unused church but of a commercial site. Prevailing Use Value will also apply to land which comes into a charity's ownership **after** 12 September 1975 so long as it has been in continuous charity ownership and use for at least seven years. It is immaterial whether or not there is any building on the land.

Other minor benefits which apply to charities alone under the Act are:—

(i) the authorities will have to have regard to the needs of charities when exercising their functions.[4]

(ii) the special provisions (*a*) to (*e*) above will apply even though the land changes hands from one charity to another.[5]

(iii) in the case of direct testamentary bequests the date when ownership of the land transfers to

---

[1] Section 21(2).
[2] Section 22(8).
[3] Section 25(5).
[4] Schedule 6, para. 1(1)(v).
[5] Section 25(6).

them will be the date of death of the testator
and not the later date of the legal assent of the
land.[1]

(iv) in other cases the time will be the date when
the charity enters into a binding contract to
acquire the land.[2]

(v) when a church acquires land for a place of
religious worship it will be able to do so freehold. This will be provided for in the arrangements for general consents under section 42.

(vi) it is expected that the excepted development
regulations to except development of under
10,000 sq. feet will permanently exclude most
church buildings from the acquisition duty.

These modifications of the land scheme still leave the
Churches and Charities in the unhappy position of having to
contemplate the payment of development land tax at the end
of the 11 year moratorium. However, the Government view
is that this period is sufficient time for the Churches and
Charities to order their affairs and dispose of their land holdings.
Nevertheless, the consequential depreciation in the values of the
land holdings retained after the eleven year period will seriously
affect borrowings against the security of such land. Also the
Churches and Charities regard as unnecessarily restrictive the
qualification that most of the modifications in their favour of
the land scheme shall apply only to land which they held on
12 September 1974. It will hamper considerably their practice
of exchange of lands with private owners, if the modifications of
the scheme do not apply to land which so vests in them after
12 September 1974.

(iii) Parish and Community Councils

There are some 8,000 parish and community councils representing some 13 million people in England, Scotland and

---

[1] Section 25(7).
[2] Section 25(7)(a).

Wales owning many thousands of acres of allotment land, village greens, open spaces, playing fields, cemeteries, public halls and other public buildings.

Such public authorities are not authorities within the meaning of the Act[1] and have none of the powers, duties and functions conferred upon such authorities by it. Therefore in the absence of special provision the land of parish and community councils would be subject to the Act and the activities of the authorities in the same way as all land in private ownership. Many situations arise which these councils need to apply for planning permission, as for example the erection of a sports centre, the extension of a public hall, with the consequential risk of losing the land to an authority as defined in section 1.

To obviate this risk of transferring land from one kind of public ownership to another and creating local public ill-feeling in the process, the Act provides that the full-duty shall only apply to land not in public ownership. This is done by defining the interests in land which are subject to acquisition under the Act.

The power of acquisition under section 15 relates to any land which in the opinion of the authority is suitable for development.

The duty to acquire applies to all " outstanding material interests ".[2] An " outstanding " material interest is defined *inter alia* as one which is not " owned by a parish or, in Wales, a community council ".[3]

The effect of these provisions is that land owned by parish or community councils is subject to the powers of acquisition by local authorities (for example where they need it in further-ance of their planning proposals for an area) but not to the full-duty. Thus parishes can apply for planning permission to carry out designated relevant development without losing the land to an authority.

---

[1] Section 1.
[2] Section 18(2).
[3] Section 4(1)(*a*).

(iv) Statutory Undertakers

Land owned by statutory undertakers which means the whole range of nationalised bodies is in public ownership. Therefore a similar situation appertains as with parish councils.

The full-duty does not apply to the operational land of statutory undertakers.[1] Also the provisions relating to the suspension of planning permission do not apply to the operational land of statutory undertakers or what will become such land once the development which is the subject matter of the planning permission has taken place.[2]

The acquisition powers of local authorities and the general duty to consider acquisition for development apply to all land in the ownership of statutory undertakers. Acquisition will be at market price less development land tax during the transitional period and at current use value after the second appointed day. The objective will be to sort out statutory undertakers holding the land surplus to its actual operational requirements.

6. UNOCCUPIED OFFICE BUILDINGS

Power is given to the Secretary of State to acquire (by compulsion if necessary) buildings containing more than 5,000 metres of office accommodation where at least 75% of that accommodation has remained empty for two years or more.[3] The price will not exceed the value of the building at the time it was constructed.[4]

This power is not necessary to the main scheme of the Act, namely, the bringing of all development land into public ownership. In fact it is irrelevant to it. Its inclusion is simply to appease public opinion in respect of the situation where office buildings have been put up and apparently kept empty deliberately so as to enable their capital value to increase as current market rents rise in an inflationary economic situation.

---

[1] Section 18(4)(*d*).
[2] Section 22(8)(*b*).
[3] Section 28.
[4] Section 29.

The same objective could be obtained by the penal rating of empty office property, but acquisition is far more dramatic. It is to be assumed that the Secretary of State will not use these powers and spend public money to acquire what has proved to be a ' white elephant ' and thereby indemnify a rash developer from the loss he would otherwise suffer from his speculation.

The problem was essentially a central London problem, but the provisions are of general application. Curiously enough the powers have been brought in after a slump in office rents and capital values. (*See* Pilcher Report, November 1975.)

7. EXTENT OF THE ACT.

Apart from the additional rights conferred upon the Crown to acquire land for public service, the Act does not apply to Northern Ireland. The main scheme only affects England, Scotland and Wales.

* * * * *

B.—COMMENTARY ON SECTIONS

PART I—PRELIMINARY

Part I of the Act deals with definitions and other preliminary matters. The most important definitions are:—

(a) **" Authorities "**. This defines the authorities who are to exercise functions under the Act—*i.e.*, in general, local authorities in England and Scotland and the Land Authority for Wales (sections 1-2);

(b) **" Relevant development "**. This is development within the scope of the major provisions in sections 17-24. Section 3 provides for certain development to be either " exempt "—*i.e.* outside the scope of the acquisition power in section 15 and within the definition of current use value in section 25—or " excepted "—*i.e.* outside the normal scope of the scheme. Exempt development is set out in Schedule 1; excepted development is to be defined in regulations made under section 3.

(c) **" Outstanding material interests "**. These are defined broadly as interests in land not owned by local authorities, parish councils, charities or other bodies which may be specified by order. When the full duty in section 18 is operating, interests not owned by these bodies (namely, the ' outstanding material interests ' which are, broadly speaking, private interests)—will need to be acquired by an authority before development can take place.

(d) **" Operational land of statutory undertakers "**. Development may be carried out on such land without intervention by the authorities exercising functions under the Act. (Section 5.)

In addition, there are included in this Part provisions concerning commencement, and definitions of the first appointed day, the relevant date and the second appointed day, which are the key dates for the bringing in of the scheme. (Section 7, together with Schedule 2.)

SECTION 1.—DEFINITIONS

Subsection (1) defines the meaning of the word ' **authority** ' throughout the Act and thus determines the authorities which will exercise functions under the community land scheme. In England and Scotland, these are **local authorities** (as defined in section 6); **new town authorities** (as defined in section 6); and the two National Park Planning Boards established under section 1(2) of the Town and Country Planning Act 1971 to exercise planning powers in the areas of the Peak Park and the Lake District National Parks (the **Peak Park Joint Planning Board** established under S.I. 2061 of 1973, and the **Lake District Special Planning Board** established under S.I. 2001 of 1973). In Wales, the functions will be exercised by the **Land Authority for Wales** to be established under Part II of the Act, and by new town authorities.

Except in Wales, the authorities concerned are those which exercise planning functions. The Lake District and Peak Park Planning Boards, as reconstituted by the two orders made under the Local Government Act 1972, exercise virtually all the functions of a county and district planning authority under the Town and Country Planning Act 1971 within their respective areas. Therefore they are given the same powers in their areas as are given to local authorities under the scheme. No special provisions are needed for National Park Committees. Although they exercise the functions of planning authorities (with the exception of development plan preparation, and the control of development which either conflicts with the plan or straddles the park boundary), they do so as committees of the counties concerned. As such, they will be able to exercise the powers of local authorities under the Act.

Although new town development corporations do not have the same general planning functions as local authorities, they do have their own planning powers, they are therefore given the new powers and duties within their areas.

One result of giving functions to local authorities is that, in virtually all areas, there will be concurrent powers resting with two authorities. In some areas (*e.g.* in new town designated areas and of the Lake District and Peak Planning Boards)

even more authorities will be involved.   Consequently, provision is made, in section 16, for Land Acquisition and Management Schemes under which all the authorities in each county
area will be required to make arrangements for the exercise
of functions under the Act.   There is also power, in section 2,
for the setting up of joint boards to operate the scheme, where
this is appropriate.

In Wales the Act gives the Land Authority for Wales the
functions of acquiring, managing and disposing of land which
are in England and Scotland to be carried out by local authorities.   The Government's reason for proposing a different
system in Wales is partly because the small size of the country
and its population lessen the risk of remoteness and lack of
local knowledge which would otherwise be disadvantageous in
a central agency; partly because of the widely varying abilities
of Welsh local authorities to undertake the full range of
functions under the Act quickly.   The Government is considering devolving executive powers in the fields of housing and
planning to an elected Welsh Assembly and is considering
future links between the responsibility for the land scheme and
the powers of the Authority.   The relationship between the
Land Authority and an Assembly has however still to be
worked out.

The Land Authority will not be the only public body in
Wales acquiring, managing and disposing of development land.
Local authorities in Wales lose none of their existing powers to
carry out these functions.   New town development corporations will enjoy the same powers as the Land Authority.

The Land Authority will have no planning powers but is
expected to work in close collaboration with local planning
authorities to achieve the objective of positive planning
throughout the Principality.   Powers are contained in section
14(4)-(7) for Local Authorities to act as agents of the Land
Authorities.

Subsection (2) defines the area

(a) of a **new town authority,** as that designated by an
order under section 1 of the New Towns Act 1965 or
under section 1 of the New Towns (Scotland) Act
1968 as the site of the proposed new town (this includes

extensions to designated areas made by a subsequent order);

(b) of the **Land Authority for Wales,** as the whole of Wales;

(c) of the two **Park Planning Boards** as the area of National Park for which each is responsible, as defined in article 2(1) of the order setting up each Board.

Subsection (3) defines which are the relevant authorities to exercise functions under the community land scheme in respect of any particular piece of land. They are those within whose area the land is situated. Except in Wales, there will normally be two, and sometimes three, such authorities (county and district, with or without a New Town or Park Planning Board) in respect of any particular piece of land.

The effect of this provision is to limit the exercise of powers by any authority under the Act to the authority's own area. The community land scheme is primarily aimed at strengthening the planning functions of local authorities and there is no need for any authority to have powers under the scheme to buy land for disposal to private development in areas outside its own boundaries. Where local authorities need to buy land outside their areas for existing statutory purposes, they can do this under their existing powers under other legislation. And where circumstances make this desirable (*e.g.* where a town's expansion area is outside its boundaries) an authority will be able to exercise functions under the scheme as agent for the authority in whose area the land lies, using the powers in section 101 of the Local Government Act 1972. Note should be made of paragraph 1(1)(iv) of Schedule 6 which ensures that local authorities when exercising their functions have regard to the need of other authorities to acquire land in their areas.

SECTION 2.—JOINT BOARDS

This section empowers the Secretary of State to set up joint boards to exercise the functions of two or more authorities under the community land scheme. This provision does not apply in Wales where the scheme will be operated by a separate Land Authority and not by local authorities.

Joint boards are already a well established feature of local authority practice. There is a precedent for their use specifically in relation to the planning of areas where local authority boundaries militate against the best overall arrangements in section 1 of, and Schedule 1 to, the Town and Country Planning Act 1971 (which in turn goes back to section 4 of, and Schedule 1 to, the Town and Country Planning Act 1947). The 1971 Act provides the broad model for the present section.

In Scotland, legislation in force from 16 May 1975 makes general provision for the discharge of local authority functions jointly.

At present, the Government do not foresee that wide use will need to be made of the power in this section, but the Act includes the provision just in case circumstances may arise requiring it, as for example where a growth area straddles a county boundary. The general intention remains that as far as possible the functions under the scheme be exercised by existing authorities with planning powers as described under section 1. Although formal power under the section rests with the Secretary of State, membership of a joint board would consist solely of local authority appointees, and it is not envisaged that a joint board would be set up except where the local authorities in an area (or at least a majority of them) wished it.

Subsection (1) provides that the Secretary of State may, if he considers it expedient, establish a joint board to exercise all or any of the functions under the community land scheme in the areas of two or more authorities, or in any parts of those areas. The Secretary of State is first required to consult the authorities concerned; he may then make an order setting up the board and determining its functions and its area.

Subsection (2) requires the Secretary of State to hold a public local inquiry before making an order which is contested by any of the authorities involved. The order will be subject to annulment by either House of Parliament thus giving a final right of objection to a non-consenting authority through Parliament.

This is standard form, *vide* section 1(2) and section 287(5)(*a*) of the Town and Country Planning Act 1971.

Subsection (3) enables the order to constitute any joint board from members appointed by the constituent authorities, the number of members being settled by the order in each case. The joint board is to be a body corporate.

This subsection parallels paragraphs 1 and 2 of Schedule 1 to the 1971 Act and paragraphs 1 and 2 of Schedule 1, Part II, of the Scottish Planning Act of 1972. Such bodies are invariably made bodies corporate to enable them to make binding corporate decisions, and to hold land in their own right. All the members of a Board are to be appointed by the constituent authorities; there is no power for the Secretary of State to appoint members of his own choosing.

Subsection (4) enables the order constituting the joint board, or any order revoking or amending the original order, to lay down procedural and related requirements to govern the conduct of the board.

This provision is in standard form and is similar to paragraph 3(*a*) of Schedule 1 to the 1971 Act or paragraph 2, Part II, Schedule 1 of the Scottish Planning Act of 1972. In relation to England it is without prejudice to section 241 of the Local Government Act 1972 which allows any order setting up a statutory joint board consisting of local authorities and discharging local authority functions to incorporate, with any necessary modifications, any of the provisions of the 1972 Act. The power to vary or revoke any order made under this section applies by virtue of section 53(4) of the Community Land Act.

Subsection (5) enables any order made under this section to make such incidental, consequential, transitional or supplementary provision as appears to the Secretary of State to be necessary or expedient, and in particular to provide for transfers of staff, property, and related matters, and to adopt or modify the Act or any other enactments relating to land acquisition.

These provisions are again generally in standard form (*see* for example paragraph 3(*b*) to (*d*) of Schedule 1 to the 1971 Act and paragraph 2(*b*) to (*d*) of Schedule 1, Part II, of the Scottish Planning Act of 1972), and are designed to ensure sufficient flexibility to enable the board to be set up in the way which allows it to operate most effectively. Sufficient powers are included to allow full protection for any staff transferred from authorities to a joint board, including the safeguarding of their salaries and pensions, or compensation for any financial loss or inconvenience which they might incur.

Subsection (5)(*b*) is not, however, precedented in the 1971 Act. The power to adapt or modify the provisions of the Community Land Act itself is included because the existence of a Joint Board, which could effectively be a single-tier authority for the purposes of the Act, would entail some changes, *e.g.* to preserve the position of the local authorities in the area acting in their own right. It also gives power to adapt or modify other legislation relating to the acquisition of land so as to ensure that the Joint Board would be in the same position as its constituent authorities. The need for this arises because authorities in operating the scheme will be able to use powers in other legislation as well as the new powers in the Act, and a joint Board might need the same powers.

It should be noted this power is a limited one. It can only be exercised where the provisions required would be incidental, consequential, transitional or supplementary to the main provisions of the order. In other words, the power can be used only to adapt or modify legislation so as to make it fit the circumstances of the Joint Board which is to be set up, and not as a general legislative amendment power in the hands of the Secretary of State.

Subsection (6) excludes Wales from the application of the section.

In Wales, functions under the community land scheme will not be exercised by local authorities, but only by the Land Authority for Wales and by new town development corporations (*see* Note on section 1). Accordingly there will be no need for any joint board to exercise the functions of authorities in relation to the scheme.

Subsection (7) prevents any order under this section from coming into effect until one month after Royal Assent. This is the standard period for the coming into operation of most Acts of Parliament. It is designed to allow time for copies to become available for study before any action is taken under the new legislation.

SECTION 3.—MEANING OF RELEVANT DEVELOP-MENT

This section defines two concepts, namely, ' development land ' and ' relevant development ' which between them regulate the entire operation of the land scheme.

The concept of ' relevant development ' in particular is the key to its operation in three respects:—

(1) the concept governs the new duties conferred on the public authorities by the Act. The general duty under section 17 requiring the authorities ' to have regard to the desirability of bringing into public ownership' relates to development land. Such land, in turn, depends upon its suitability for ' relevant development ' (section 3(1)).

Ultimately, when the compulsory duty to acquire is imposed upon the public authorities by the Secretary of State making orders under section 18, those orders will relate to designated kinds of ' relevant development '.

(2) the concept controls the handling of planning applications under the land scheme. The procedures in sections 19 to 22 and Schedule 7 (providing for the suspension of planning permissions) operate only on applications and permissions for ' relevant development '.

(3) the concept will regulate the basis of compensation to be paid for land acquired by the authorities after the Second Appointed Day. This basis, under section 25, will be on the assumption that planning permission would not be granted for that land in respect of ' relevant development ' unless that planning permission is already in force on the second appointed day or the development in question falls within Schedule 8 to the Town and Country Planning Act 1971 (Schedule 6 of the 1972 Scottish Act) or Schedule 1, paragraph 1, of the Act. The concept therefore generally sets a ceiling to the amount that the authorities will pay for the land after the Second Appointed Day.

Much of the criticism levelled against the unconstitutional nature of the Act derives from the definition of the two central concepts in section 3.

The definition of ' development land ' speaks of land " which in the opinion of the authority concerned is needed for . . . ".   This is regarded by some as an undesirably wide subjective discretion not capable of challenge in the Courts. It is on a par with the power under section 15 to acquire any land " which in their opinion, is suitable for development ".

However, it is the definition of relevant development which leaves the most effective control in the hands of the Secretary of State.   This is because, with some minor exclusions to be considered below, it is he who, by regulations, will determine what is not relevant development and therefore govern the entire operation of the land scheme in the three respects mentioned above.   The regulations require the approval of Parliament but the opportunities for Parliamentary discussion of regulations is very limited.   Hence the misgivings of Justice (*see* General Commentary, page 3).

Subsection (1) defines ' development land ' as land which in the opinion of the authority concerned is needed for relevant development within 10 years from the time at which they are acting.

The authority is therefore the sole arbiter of what is development land within the limits imposed by the concept of relevant development.

In practice the authorities' ability to look forward ten years will be restricted by the five-year rolling programmes they will be required to submit to the Secretary of State for borrowing requirement.   Nowhere does the Act speak of five-year programmes but this governmental requirement was made clear during its progress through Parliament.[1]

Subsection (2) provides that the term " relevant development " shall include any development other than—

    (*a*) that of any class specified in Schedule 1—to be known as ' Exempt Development ';

    (*b*) that consisting exclusively of the building of a single dwelling-house; and

---

[1] Now *see* D. of E. Circular 121/75, para. 1.

> (*c*) that of such class or classes as may be prescribed in regulations by the Secretary of State.

The exclusions from relevant development under (*a*) and (*b*) are very limited in extent relating either to very minor or specific kinds of development. The exclusions which may be made under (*c*) are limitless and therefore effectively regulate the entire meaning and effect of the definition of ' relevant development '.

It is this subsection which throws up the distinction between **Exempt Development** (*i.e.* (*a*) above as described in Schedule 1) and **Excepted Development** (*i.e.* (*b*) and (*c*) above—the single dwelling-house or exclusion by the regulations).

This distinction is of importance.

Exempt Development has two functions under the Act:—

> (i) by virtue of section 15(2) it is outside the scope of the powers of acquisition, *i.e.* the powers cannot be used to buy land which is suitable **only** for exempt development,
>
> (ii) by virtue of section 25(3) and (4)(*b*) the prospect of being able to carry out some exempt development is to be included in the current use value and will be therefore reflected in the compensation paid for land after the second appointed day.

Excepted Development remains within the scope of the powers of acquisition but will be normally outside the scope of the land scheme. This means that development can take place without the land concerned having to pass through public ownership. There will be no obligation upon the public authorities to acquire such land and excepted development will be outside the scope of section 18 orders. However, it must be emphasised that the powers to acquire under section 15 remain and may be exercised in order to ensure that a more comprehensive development or one in the interests of positive planning takes place. Thus the fact that small development projects (*e.g.* 15,000 sq. ft. industrial or 10,000 sq. ft. other development) may normally go ahead without public acquisition, does not mean that all small sites are free from that risk. It remains open to an authority to decide it can deal with the site better on a more comprehensive basis or that it is needed for other relevant development even where the private development proposals fall within the scope of excepted development.

The Government have indicated they will exercise a check administratively upon local authorities in order to ensure that there is some value in having an ' excepted development '. This check will be exercised through the Secretary of State's power to confirm compulsory purchase orders. However, it remains to be seen whether the inevitable delays and expense entailed in resisting compulsory purchase orders will make the exceptions of much value to the private sector.

The extent of the exceptions to be included in the regulations still remains to be seen. However, the Government's current thinking in this regard has been discussed under General Comments (pages 13-15 above).[1]

Subsection (3) provides that the definition of a single dwelling-house includes the construction or laying out of any garage, outhouse, garden, court, yard, forecourt or other appurtenance for occupation with, and for the purposes of a single dwelling-house. Thus ancillary development necessary for the enjoyment of a dwelling-house is brought within the exception to relevant development mentioned in subsection (2)(*b*) above.

Subsection (4) provides that regulations under this section shall not be made unless a draft of the regulations has been approved by a resolution of each House of Parliament.

SECTION 4.—OUTSTANDING MATERIAL INTERESTS

This section defines the circumstances in which material interests in land (*i.e.* freeholds or leaseholds with at least 7 years to run—section 6) are to be treated as ' outstanding ' for the purposes of the Act.

In very broad terms an " outstanding material interest " in land is a material interest vested in private ownership.

The definition is relevant to section 18(3) under which public authorities may be given a duty by Order to acquire all " outstanding material interests in land which is needed for the purposes of designated relevant development ". However, whilst only material interests which are " outstanding " fall within the **duty** to acquire, **all** material interests, whether

---

[1] *See now* the draft Community Land (Excepted Development) Regulations 1976, p. 365 *post*.

outstanding or not, fall within the scope of the **powers** to acquire under section 15.

The definition is also relevant to section 22(8)(*a*) by virtue of which the provisions for the suspension of planning permission do not apply where no material interest in land is outstanding.

Subsection (1) provides that a material interest in land **shall be** outstanding unless:—

(*a*) It is already in some form of public ownership.

The subsection specifically refers to the ownership of " an authority " (defined by section 1), " a local or new town authority, a parish or community council " (all defined by section 6), or, " in Scotland, the council of a district within the area of a general planning authority ". Statutory Undertakers are not mentioned in this subsection since their operational land is specifically excluded by virtue of section 18(4)(*d*) and section 22(8)(*b*).

or   (*b*) it is and has been in the ownership of a charity up to the date in question continually since the 12th September 1974 (White Paper day). It is not necessary that the material interest shall have been in the ownership of the **same** charity throughout the period.

This forms part of the limited relief from the land scheme which is being given to charities. Thus existing charity land may be used to best advantage without suspension of any planning application the charity may make and without attracting the public duty to acquire. This will enable a large partly-used chapel to be demolished and a smaller modern building put up financed out of mixed development on the same site. Other relief consists of special provisions relating to compensation contained in section 25 and those which will appear in the Development Land Tax Act.

The overall position of charities is discussed in the General Commentary at pages 35-38.

For the purposes of the Act a charity is defined (section 6) as having the same meaning as in section 360, Income and Corporation Taxes Act 1970, *i.e.* it is not limited only to ecclesiastical charities.

or (*c*) it is of a description specified in an order made by
the Secretary of State.

This will enable the Secretary of State to grant exemptions
to bodies of a kind similar to that granted to public authorities
and charities in respect of **all** the land owned by those bodies.

Contrast should be made with the power under section
5(1)(*c*) whereby the Secretary of State may specify any body
to be a statutory undertaker for the purposes of the Act.   This
would give such a body exemption under section 18(4)(*d*) and
section 22(8)(*b*) in respect of what falls within the concept of
" operational land " only.

Subsection (2) provides that ownership of a material interest
in land by any body specified in subsection (1) shall include a
contractual right to acquire the land or entitlement to the land
under a deceased person's will.

Subsection (3) provides that an order under (1)(*c*) extending
the exemptions of this section to bodies other than public
authorities or charities shall be subject to annulment procedure
in Parliament.

SECTION 5.—STATUTORY UNDERTAKERS

This section defines the meanings of " statutory undertakers " and " operational land " for the purposes of the Act.
These definitions are required primarily for the purposes of
sections 18(4)(*d*) and 22(8)(*b*), under which statutory undertakers and certain comparable bodies are able to acquire and
develop land needed for their statutory functions without the
intervention of authorities.

The definition of statutory undertakers is also relevant to
section 41, which excludes the operation of special parliamentary
procedure in certain cases of the compulsory purchase of land
by local authorities or statutory undertakers, and to certain
supplemental provisions in Schedule 4, Part III, concerning the
extinguishment of rights of way, and rights as to the apparatus
of statutory undertakers.

The underlying concept is that since statutory undertakers
are empowered by Parliament to provide certain services for
the community, they are free to carry out development in
pursuance of their statutory responsibilities (subject to the
grant of planning permission) without authorities under the
scheme having an obligation to intervene.

The duty to bring land needed for designated relevant development into community ownership imposed on authorities by order under section 18 will not apply to the operational land of statutory undertakers (section 18(4)(*d*)). By virtue of section 22(8)(*b*) planning permission granted in respect of the operational land of statutory undertakers (or land which would be operational land if it were used or held by statutory undertakers for the purpose covered by the permission) cannot be subject to suspension of the permission (*i.e.* to the prohibition which would otherwise apply if the land were not owned by, or made available by, an authority).

Subsection (1) defines three categories of " **statutory undertakers** ". *Paragraph* (*a*) is identical with the definition in section 290(1) of the Town and Country Planning Act 1971 and section 275(1) of the Scottish Act of 1972. *Paragraph* (*b*) specifically includes the British Airports Authority, the Civil Aviation Authority, Post Office and the National Coal Board and covers other authorities, bodies or undertakers which, although they may not be within the Town and Country Planning Act definition, have been given the status of statutory undertakers for the purposes of that Act under other specific legislation. *Paragraph* (*c*) enables the Secretary of State by order, subject to negative resolution procedure (subsection (6)) to specify as statutory undertakers, for the purposes of the Act, any other authority, body or undertakers.

The Government's intention is that the bodies specified by order under paragraph (*c*), and thus accorded statutory undertaker status for the purposes of the Act, will be strictly limited to those which are plainly comparable to statutory undertakers in general as having functions of a public nature. Section 4(3)(*c*) enables the Secretary of State to apply to other bodies similar exemptions as for statutory undertakers by declaring that their interests in land shall not be treated as outstanding.

Subsection (2) defines " **operational land** " in relation to statutory undertakers within subsection (1) and corresponds with the definition in section 222 of the Town and Country Planning Act 1971 and section 211 of the Scottish Act of 1972. This definition will not apply where operational land is defined in relation to particular undertakers by order under sub-section (3).

The question whether land is used or held for the purposes of an undertaking or is comparable with land in general rather than with land used for the purposes of the statutory under-taking—and is thus not " operational land "—is a question of fact.   " Land in general " would depend on particular cir-cumstances, but would often include premises such as offices, shops, showrooms and dwelling-houses, and in the event of a dispute the question falls to be determined by the Minister who is the appropriate Minister in relation to the undertakers (section 5(5), e.g. in the case of land used or held by the electricity or gas industries the Secretary of State for Energy.

The definition is not restricted in the manner of section 223 of the Planning Act which provides that land acquired on or after 6 December 1968 (or, under section 212 of the Scottish Act 1972, 8 December 1969) or held immediately before that date but not then operational is not to be treated as operational land unless a specific planning permission has been granted for development for the purposes of the undertaking, or the land was operational land when transferred from other undertakers under the Transport Act 1968.   This narrower definition is appropriate for planning control purposes but if applied to this Act would fail to recognise that statutory undertakers may need to acquire land some years in advance, when the precise form of intended development is not known, in order to ensure that land is available to meet their future commitments and responsibilities.

Subsection (3) enables the Secretary of State and the appro-priate Minister by joint order to define " operational land " in relation to specified statutory undertakers.   This definition would then replace the definition in subsection (2) in relation to those undertakers.

This provision is intended for use where the standard defini-tion of operational land is not appropriate having regard to circumstances of the particular undertakers, for example where the test of comparability with land held for the purposes of statutory undertakings would be too restrictive, or where, as in the case of the Regional Water Authorities, the undertaking does not include all the functions of the statutory undertakers.

Subsection (4)(a) gives to " the appropriate Minister " and any reference to " the Secretary of State and the appropriate Minister " the same meanings as in the Planning Acts, in relation to matters involving statutory undertakers who are also statutory undertakers for the purposes of those Acts. For any other statutory undertakers **subsection (4)(b)** provides that the meanings are to be given by an order made by the Secretary of State.

These definitions are required for the purposes of subsection (5) (Questions whether land is operational land) and of paragraphs 17, 18 and 19 (extinguishment of rights of way and rights as to removal or resiting of apparatus of statutory undertakers), of Schedule 4.

Subsection (5) provides (as does section 290(2) of the 1971 Planning Act) for the Treasury to determine, in cases of doubt, which Minister is the " appropriate Minister ", and the appropriate Minister to determine whether land of statutory undertakers is operational land or (for the purposes of section 22(8)(*b*)) would be operational land if used or held by statutory undertakers for the purposes covered by a planning permission.

Subsection (6) provides that an order made under subsection (1)(*c*), subsection (3) or subsection (4)(*b*) shall be subject to the negative resolution procedure.

SECTION 6.—INTERPRETATION

This section contains the interpretation of expressions which are used throughout the Act.

Much of the interpretation involves reference back to the Town and Country Planning Act 1971 and the Town and Country Planning (Scotland) Act 1972.

Subsection (1) defines a number of expressions which are common to the whole Act, mostly in self-explanatory terms. Attention may, however, be drawn to the following points:—

(1) " **building** "—this is the same definition as that used in the 1971 Act and its Scottish equivalent.

(2) "**development** "—has the same meaning as in section 22 of the 1971 Act and section 19 of the Scottish Act, where it is defined, subject to certain exceptions, as
" the carrying out of building, engineering, mining

or other operations in, on, over or under land, or the making of any material change in the use of any building or other land ".

The exceptions include such items of maintenance, improvement and alterations to buildings which do not materially affect the external appearance.

(3) **" development plan "**—this has the same meaning as in the 1971 Act or the Scottish Act. The term thus includes old-style development plans, as overlaid by an approved structure plan where there is one in existence, until a local plan for an area comes into force.

(4) **Local Authorities** are defined as being—

    (*a*) in England as county and district councils, and their equivalents for London—the Greater London Council, the London Borough Councils and the Common Council of the City. No definition of areas is needed: this is given by the Local Government Act 1972 and the London Government Act 1963, respectively.

    (*b*) in Wales as county and district councils.

Although local authorities in Wales are not " authorities " for the purposes of the Act a definition is needed for the purpose of some of the Act's provisions. For example, section 14(4) allows such local authorities, by agreement, to act for the Land Authority for Wales on an agency basis. Several sections of the Act also impose responsibilities and duties on them (*e.g.* sections 43 and 45), or require consultation with them. A definition is needed also because of the provisions of section 21(9).

    (*c*) in Scotland as regional, general or district planning authorities under the Local Government (Scotland) Act 1973. This is to ensure that district authorities within the area of general planning authorities, who have no planning functions, are not included. They are, however, included in the definition of " local authority " for the purposes of local government legislation.

Finally this definition of " local authority " applies the provisions of the Act to the Isles of Scilly as if the Council for the Isles were a county council. This is because the Council for the Isles is a single-tier authority and neither a county nor district council.

(5) **" New Town Authority "** means a development corporation established under section 2 of the New Towns Act 1965 or section 2 of the New Towns (Scotland) Act 1968.

Subsection (2) provides that for the purposes of the definition of " **material interest** " in subsection (1) it is to be assumed, as regards the length of a lease, that any option to renew or extend the lease is exercised and that any option to terminate the lease is not exercised. (This applies in both cases to any options other than one conferred by or under an Act of Parliament.) This is so provided to prevent evasion by the granting of leases for less than 7 years with substantial renewals or extensions guaranteed by the inclusion of an option provision, or of leases for longer than 7 years which contain an option to terminate. Statutory provisions (*e.g.* under the Landlord and Tenant Acts, the Agricultural Holdings Acts and the Law of Property Act 1925) are excluded because a statutory option is restricted in scope and clearly cannot be used as a method of evasion.

Subsection (3) provides that where a planning permission is granted on an appeal against a refusal (or deemed refusal) it shall be treated as having been granted on the date of that refusal (or deemed refusal).

There are various places in the Act where the date of the grant of planning permission is crucial, for example in section 21. Where such permission is granted on appeal the date of grant is, for the purposes of the Planning Act, regarded as being the date of the refusal (or the deemed refusal where section 37 of the 1971 Act applies). The subsection imports the effect of section 290(4)(*d*) of the 1971 Act.

Subsection (4) provides that references in the Act to planning permission for relevant development, or for any other kind of development, includes a reference to planning permission for any development which includes the kind of development specified. This means that a permission is still to be regarded as a permission for relevant development even though it covers not only relevant development but also some development which is not " relevant ".

Subsection (5) provides that the expression **" suspension of planning permission "** in the Act is to be read as referring to suspension under sections 19 to 22 of, and Schedule 7 to, the Act. These are the provisions which set out the procedure for handling planning applications for relevant development, under which authorities can ensure that any planning permission granted on such an application remains suspended if they wish to seek to acquire the land.

Subsection (6) provides that the expression " a notice to treat " is to be taken as including a deemed notice to treat (*e.g.* following a general vesting declaration or a purchase notice). (The date of notice to treat is relevant, for instance, for section 25 of the Act, which deals with the compensation payable where land is acquired compulsorily by a public authority following the service of a notice to treat on or after the second appointed day.)

Subsection (7) provides that references in the Act to any enactment are to be construed as references to that enactment as amended by this or any other Act unless otherwise stated.

SECTION 7.—THE APPOINTED DAYS, ETC.

This section sets out the principal commencement provisions of the Act and defines three different dates for implementing the scheme by stages. These are:—

    (i) the first appointed day;

    (ii) the relevant date;

    (iii) the second appointed day.

Part I of Schedule 2 sets out the main provisions of the Act for which each of these dates is significant.

The operation of the scheme depends on a phased introduction of the provisions of the Act in line with the ability of authorities to take on their new responsibilities. The **first appointed day** brings into operation the general duty on authorities to consider the desirability of bringing development land into public ownership (section 17), together with the wider powers to acquire land (section 15). From that date also new procedures apply, enabling authorities to consider acquisition on the making of a planning application for relevant development (section 20).

As authorities build up their resources and their ability to handle all development land in their areas, orders will be made (under section 18) applying to each area, as it is ready the full duty to acquire all land needed for such classes of relevant development as are designated in the order. The date on which such an order becomes effective is the " **relevant date** " for the area covered by the order. From the same date, such designated relevant development is prohibited from taking place in that area other than on land owned by a public authority or made available by an authority for the development in question. This is achieved by section 21 under which all planning permissions for such development granted on or after the " relevant date " are " suspended " until the condition of public ownership is satisfied.

Finally, when the full duty has been imposed in all areas in respect of all relevant development the **second appointed day** will be brought in. From that time the basis of compensation for all public authority acquisitions will, under section 25, become current use value. **The bringing in of the second appointed day does not, however, affect the powers or duties of authorities.**

Schedule 2 provides a useful summary of the main provisions of the Act coming into force on the respective dates and also requires the Secretaries of State to keep a register of the various " relevant date " orders.

Apart from the sections mentioned above all other sections of the Act come into effect either on Royal Assent, one month after Royal Assent or on the first appointed day. It was the Government's original intention to bring in the first appointed day soon after the Royal Assent. However, delays in the legislative programme and the postponement of the introduction of the Development Land Tax Bill which will materially affect the price at which the authorities will buy land have led subsequently to the suggestion that the first appointed day will be the 6th April 1976.[1]

---

[1] Now confirmed by D. of E. Circular 121/75, para. 1.

Subsection (1) defines the first and second appointed days as being such days as the Secretary of State may by order appoint. The subsection also defines the relevant date as being the date on which an order under subsection (5) of section 18 comes into force.

The first appointed day order will bring in the transitional arrangements under the scheme. The main sections concerned are listed in Part I of Schedule 2. The second appointed day order applies only to section 25 (which provides that the basis of compensation for all public authority acquisitions shall become current use value) and by implication, to the power in section 27, to set up Financial Hardship Tribunals to consider cases arising from the change made by section 25.

The appointment of the days by orders gives the Secretary of State considerable flexibility and control over the Staging of the land scheme. The First Appointed Day will be 6th April 1976, when the Development Land Tax will also come into effect, and current estimates are that the Second Appointed Day will be some ten years hence if the scheme survives that long.

The " relevant date " is significant for sections 18 and 21 and is defined in subsection (6) of section 18 as being the date on which an order under that section (imposing the full duty for classes of relevant development designated by the order) comes into force. The order also brings into force the prohibition (or automatic suspension of planning permission for the designated classes of development) provided in section 21, which is complementary to the imposition of the full duty in a particular area imposed by a section 18 order.

Subsection (2) precludes the first appointed day from being appointed before a draft of the Relevant Development Regulations (to be made under section 3(2)(*c*)) has been approved by Parliament. These regulations defining excepted development will lay down the categories of development outside the duties under section 17 and until they are in force there will be nothing for the new procedures under sections 19-21 to bite on. Hence these regulations have to be in force before the first appointed day.

Subsection (3) provides that the second appointed day shall not be brought in until orders have been made (under section 18) applying the full duty and the prohibition in respect of all relevant development to all areas in Great Britain. At this stage authorities will be in a near monopoly position as suppliers of land for relevant development and with DLT having moved to the maximum rate of 100% the effective basis of acquisition will be little more than current use value anyway.

Subsection (4) requires that the second appointed day order shall be subject to the affirmative resolution procedure in each House of Parliament. This is the normal parliamentary procedure for important legislative changes effected by Statutory Instrument, and gives Parliament a limited opportunity to debate the matter before any change can come into effect.

Subsection (5) applies the provisions of Schedule 2. Part I of the Schedule summarises the main provisions of the Act where the three starting dates are relevant. Part II requires registers to be kept of the various section 18 " relevant date " orders.

PART II—THE LAND AUTHORITY FOR WALES

Part II of the Act establishes the procedure for setting up the Land Authority for Wales and for the Authority's operations. It specifies the Authority's status and functions and requires them to comply with directions given by the Secretary of State. The reasons for the Authority's establishment are given in the notes on section 1(1) (*see* page 44 above).

Other matters covered by this Part of the Act are contingency arrangements for meeting the Authority's initial expenses; borrowing powers and guarantees; accounts and audit; annual reports and powers relating to the management, development and disposal of land, including powers for local authorities to act as agents of the Land Authority.

SECTION 8—THE AUTHORITY

This section provides for the setting up of the Land Authority for Wales and briefly specifies their status and functions and requires them to comply with directions given by the Secretary of State.

The Land Authority are to perform in Wales the functions of acquiring, managing and disposing of land for private development which are in England and Scotland to be carried out by local authorities.

However, the Land Authority for Wales will not be the only body in Wales performing these functions. Local authorities already have similar powers under existing legislation and these powers are not to be affected. New town development corporations will enjoy the same powers as the Land Authority (section 1(1)(*c*)) and by administrative arrangement will alone exercise powers under the Act within the designated areas of Welsh new towns, the Land Authority not operating within such areas.

Subsection (1) sets up and names the Authority and specifies that their functions are to be those assigned to them under the Act.

" Functions " are defined in section 5 as including powers and duties. The functions in respect of land are set out more particularly in section 14, Part III, and Schedules 4 and 6 of the Act. Financial functions and duties are set out more particularly in the remainder of Part II of the Act and in sections 43 and 44.

The functions of the Land Authority for Wales follow as closely as possible those conferred on local authorities in England and Scotland and on new town development corporations in England, Scotland and Wales (*see* definition of " authority " in section 1(1)). The Authority are given no planning responsibilities, these still being exercised by local planning authorities in Wales. The Authority are to be a land authority only. Their powers to carry out works are limited to works considered expedient to the subsequent disposal of land (section 14(3)); with the consent of the Secretary of State, to works, which no other authority has power to carry out (Schedule 4, paragraph 9(1)); and to the repair and maintenance of buildings or works on land which they have acquired (Schedule 4, paragraph 9(4)).

Subsection (2) applies to the Authority the provisions of Schedule 3 which deals with the way in which members of the Authority and their staff are to be appointed, the fixing of their conditions of service, and the conduct of the Authority's business.

Subsection (3) requires the Authority to comply with directions given by the Secretary of State. Section 54 provides that a direction (or consent) given under the Act may be general or limited to any particular case or class of case, may be addressed to any particular authority or class of authority, and may be unconditional or subject to any conditions. In addition to this general power of giving directions the Act contains six other provisions for the Secretary of State to give directions to the Authority. One is in section 13(2) dealing with the contents of the Authority's annual report; one is in section 43 and two are in section 44 all dealing with the keeping of accounts and records; one is in Schedule 6, paragraph 1, dealing with matters to be taken into account by authorities in exercising their functions in relation to the ownership and development of land.

Finally, one is in Schedule 4, paragraph 9(3) dealing with the advertising by the Authority of an intention to carry out, with the Secretary of State's consent, works on land which they own. The Authority are required under section 13(2)(a) to include in their annual report any directions given to them by the Secretary of State unless the Secretary of State notifies them that disclosure would be against the interests of national security.

The Secretary of State's power to issue directions to the Authority gives him substantial control over the working of the Authority. Under section 14 and Part III however, the Authority are given very wide discretion in the purchase, management and disposal of land. This discretion, however, must be exercised in accordance with planning policy, as determined at local planning authority and Government level. For this purpose directions of a general character only, would not be sufficient and particular direction may require the Authority to concentrate on buying or selling land in a certain locality. In addition, local authorities will continue to exercise their existing statutory powers to acquire land, for public and private development. It may therefore be necessary for the Secretary of State to use this power of direction to avoid unnecessary conflict and to channel the activities of the Authority towards certain localities. It is the Government's intention to use the power of direction to ensure that the Land Authority do not operate within the designated areas of new towns, where powers are to be exercised solely by the development corporation. Other issues where the Secretary of State might use his power of direction are:—

    (a) disputes with local authorities as to the disposal of land owned by the Land Authority;

    (b) proposals by the Land Authority to acquire by agreement land which the Secretary of State considers should be left in existing ownership (proposals to buy such land by compulsory purchase order can be controlled by the Secretary of State not confirming the order). Some disputes between the Authority and local authorities will be settled as part of the normal statutory process.

These are:—

    (a) a local authority refusing a planning application submitted by the Land Authority. This would be dealt with as a normal planning appeal;

    (b) Objections by a local authority to a Land Authority compulsory purchase order. The Land Authority will be required to notify local authorities of proposals to make compulsory purchase orders (Schedule 4, paragraph 6), and local authorities will have statutory objection rights. It is not proposed to impose reciprocal duties on local authorities.

Subsection (4) provides that the Authority are not to be a Crown body. This recognises the fact that their responsibilities will be similar to those of local authorities who will be carrying out the same functions in England and Scotland. They will have to apply for normal planning permission before developing any land; they will pay local rates on property which they occupy; and they will have to comply with building regulations like any private developer.

SECTION 9.—THE INITIAL DEBT

This section provides that the Land Authority for Wales shall on their establishment assume an initial debt, to be determined by the Secretary of State with Treasury approval, not exceeding £100,000. The debt will provide the machinery whereby the Secretary of State will be able to recover the expenses which he will incur in establishing the Authority.

Items on which the Secretary of State might wish to incur expenditure on the Authority's behalf are staff accommodation, furniture and stationery.

Expenditure will also be incurred on advertising for staff; interviewing applicants for appointments; and possibly in seconding civil servants for a time to work for the Authority before they have engaged their own staff.

The establishment of an initial debt is a common procedure in legislation setting up statutory authorities.

Subsection (1) provides that the Land Authority for Wales shall on their establishment assume an initial debt to the Secretary of State. The amount of the debt will be determined by the Secretary of State with the approval of the Treasury and must be notified to the Authority in writing.

Subsection (2) authorises the Secretary of State to meet the expenses which he will incur in establishing the Land Authority for Wales including expenses in connection with the provision of accommodation and the payment of salaries and expenses of members and officers of the Authority. These expenses will arise before the Authority are able to borrow the money to enable them to take on these responsibilities themselves. The subsection also provides that the funds required by the Secretary of State are to be provided by Parliament. This provision is necessary to authorise making funds available to the Secretary of State. The Secretary of State announced during the Second Reading of the Bill that he proposes to draw on the Contingencies Fund for this purpose.

Subsection (3) sets a limit of £100,000 on the amount of the initial debt, which was the estimate of the Secretary of State's expenses to be incurred up to the coming into existence of the Authority.

Subsection (4) empowers the Secretary of State, with the approval of the Treasury, to determine the terms of the debt and in particular the rate of interest, and the repayment of the debt.

Subsection (5) provides for the Secretary of State to pay into the National Loans Fund sums which he receives from the Authority by way of interest on or repayment of the initial debt.

SECTION 10.—BORROWING POWERS

This section deals with the borrowing powers of the Land Authority for Wales.

The Authority will not be set up with any initial capital or other financial resources. As with local authorities in England and Scotland the whole of their activities during the first few years will need to be financed by borrowing. The main heads of their expenditure will be:—

    (a) their own operating costs;

    (b) the purchase of development land;

    (c) preparing the land for disposal;

    (d) interest on their borrowing.

The largest item of expenditure by the Authority will be on the purchase of development land. This expenditure probably will rise year by year as the Authority either by engaging staff themselves or by using local authorities as agents under the provisions of section 14 become more able to buy land on a widening scale. Initially the Authority will only be required to have regard to the *desirability* of bringing development land into public ownership and of developing the land themselves or of making it available for development by others (section 17). The Authority will not in practice themselves take a direct financial interest in property development and the Secretary of State will exercise control over the Authority to ensure that development which they carry out under section 14(3) is limited to what is necessary to prepare land for disposal. Eventually, however, a duty will be placed on the Authority and on Welsh new town development corporations (where their respective areas are involved) to see that all outstanding material interests in land needed for designated relevant development in Wales are owned by the Authority, or by a local authority, or by a development corporation (section 18). The major duty to acquire land for private development will undoubtedly then fall on the Authority. The price the Authority pay for land they acquire will initially be market value less development land tax, but will become current use value on the second appointed day (section 25).

The expectation is that the Authority will eventually recover their expenditure through the price they charge on disposing of land. That price will be based on market value.

The Authority's borrowing limit is set at £40m, though this may be increased by order made by the Secretary of State with Treasury approval to £60m (subsection (4)). This will provide a margin for inflation or for the initial recovery of expenditure to be at a slower rate than has been forecast.

The principal source of the Authority's borrowing will be the National Loans Fund. The borrowing powers generally follow those conferred on water authorities and the National Water Council by Schedule 3 to the Water Act 1973 and those in the Maplin Development Act 1973, which themselves follow the general form of borrowing powers conferred by modern practice on statutory authorities. The powers should give the Authority sufficient flexibility to borrow money on satisfactory terms. There is one feature in which the Authority will have less flexibility than local authorities. This is that borrowing from United Kingdom sources in sterling of other than temporary loans may be only from the Secretary of State (*i.e.* the National Loans Fund). The Authority will thus not be able to go to the market for their borrowing. This follows precedent, and is in recognition of the fact that the Authority (unlike local authorities) have no power to raise revenue of their own (*e.g.* via the rates) so their ultimate security for borrowing will be their status as a public sector body. This is recognised in the power of the Treasury to guarantee their borrowing (section 11) which does not exist in the case of local authorities. A further factor is the need for central control of demands on the limited funds available for the gilt edged market.

Subsection (1) empowers the Authority to make temporary borrowings by overdraft or otherwise of such sums as they may require, either in sterling from the Secretary of State or with the specific consent or general authorisation of the Secretary of State (acting with the approval of the Treasury—*see* subsection (9)) in sterling or other currency from a person other than the Secretary of State.

The temporary borrowing powers will enable the Authority to obtain immediate finance for day to day expenses or unforeseen contingencies. Such borrowing would not remain outstanding for long periods. Where the object of the borrowing was a long term commitment the item would normally be refinanced by taking out a long term loan. The arrangements in this subsection are therefore primarily an administrative convenience. For normal temporary borrowing requirements within specified limits the borrowing would be approved by a general authorisation but major or unusual items would require the Secretary of State's specific approval.

Subsections (2) and (3) give the Authority their main borrowing powers as distinct from the temporary borrowing powers in subsection (1). **Subsection (2)** provides that they may borrow in sterling from the Secretary of State (*i.e.* from the National Loans Fund—subsection (8)); or with the consent of the Secretary of State (and approval of the Treasury) in a currency other than sterling from a person other than the Secretary of State.

Control by the Secretary of State is normal in the case of borrowing by publicly sponsored authorities and is particularly necessary in the case of borrowing in foreign currencies which has an effect on the country's balance of payments.

Subsection (3) authorises borrowing in any currency with the consent of the Secretary of State (and Treasury approval) and other than on a temporary basis from the Commission of the European Communities or the European Investment Bank.

It will be for the Land Authority to use their commercial judgment in deciding whether to seek approval for borrowing from these sources but should such borrowing be possible at favourable rates it is considered that the Authority should have power to take advantage of them.

The main sources of European Communities borrowing are the European Investment Bank and the European Coal and Steel Community, both of which make loans for industrial development. In both cases these loans are normally tied to specific development projects, which may include land purchase but only if it forms part of the scheme as a whole. Both these possibilities are remote at present, but powers are provided to enable the Authority to take advantage of possible future changes in the Community's policy which might have the effect of broadening the range of loans available.

Subsection (4) provides that the aggregate amount of the principal outstanding on the initial debt and any money borrowed under this section should not exceed £40m or such greater sum not exceeding £60m as the Secretary of State with the approval of the Treasury may specify by order.

Provisions of this kind are normally made for statutory bodies who will need to resort to extensive borrowing. The provision that the borrowing may need to be raised reflects the fact that the financial outcome of the Authority's operations at the outset cannot be accurately forecast. Much will depend on the speed with which they acquire land; the proportion of acquired land which is disposed of quickly or is kept in the Authority's ownership as part of a land bank; and the proportions in which land is disposed of by freehold sale, by leasehold at a single premium or leasehold at an annual ground rent. The Authority will at first incur an increasing debt which will not begin to fall until the receipts from disposals of land exceed overheads, the cost of further land acquisitions, the cost of preparing land for disposal and the payment of interest on the outstanding debt. The Government will exercise control of the Authority's financial and land acquisition programmes and will be able to control the extent to which receipts from disposals are used to redeem outstanding debts or to buy more land.

Subsection (5) provides that the draft of an order to raise the limit of the Authority's borrowing must be laid before the House of Commons and be subject to affirmative resolution procedure.

This is the normal procedure by which a change in a public body's borrowing limit within a ceiling incorporated in legislation is approved by Parliament.

Subsection (6) provides that the Authority shall not borrow money otherwise than as provided in this section.

The provisions in the section are sufficiently widely drawn to enable the Authority, with the Secretary of State's approval, to choose the most appropriate source of borrowing for particular functions and they will not be restrictive in a way which would be likely to put the Authority at any financial disadvantage.

Subsection (7) gives the Secretary of State power (i) to lend to the Authority any sums which they have power to borrow from him by virtue of this section; and (ii) to decide the conditions of loans which he makes under the section that is to say the rate of interest, the time at which the loan should be repaid and the method of repayment.

Provision (i) (with subsection (8)) is necessary to complete the chain of events by which funds flow from the National Loans Fund via the Secretary of State to the Authority. Provision (ii) is needed so long as the Authority are operating in deficit, *i.e.* before their accounts come into a cash surplus when the proceeds from disposals of land enable the initial loans to be paid off. It is normal for loans to be made for set terms and at known rates of interest. Should a loan have to be repaid before land profits are available to enable this to be done, the funds would have to be obtained from further borrowing.

Subsection (8) empowers the Treasury to issue out of the National Loans Fund to the Secretary of State sums to enable him to make loans to the Authority and provides that sums received by the Secretary of State under subsection (7) shall be paid into that Fund. These are the final essential steps in the flow of funds to and from the Land Authority.

Subsection (9) states that references in this section to the Secretary of State are references to him acting with the approval of the Treasury.

It is the normal practice where a Minister is given control over the borrowing powers of a public body that the approval of the Treasury should be obtained before the Secretary of State gives any consent or authorisation in connection with those powers.

SECTION 11.—GUARANTEES

This section empowers the Treasury to guarantee the principal and interest of any sums borrowed by the Land Authority for Wales from a person other than the Secretary of State and defines the procedures to be followed when guarantees are made or taken up.

Similar provisions are frequently found in legislation setting up statutory bodies. The main effect of a guarantee given by the Treasury is that it will enable the Authority, like other public bodies, to borrow at a lower rate of interest than they otherwise could. The Authority might be able to borrow from some sources at rates lower than those available through the National Loans Fund. For short term loan requirements advantageous rates of interest might be available from banks or other sources. In either case a guarantee would normally be required to secure the loan.

Subsection (1) enables the Treasury to guarantee repayment of the principal and interest of any loan raised by the Authority from a person other than the Secretary of State. This covers both the temporary and the long term borrowing permitted by section 10 within the limits laid down by that section.

Subsection (2) requires the Treasury to lay a statement of any guarantee before each House as soon as it is given. If any sum is issued in fulfilment of a guarantee, the Treasury must, as soon as practicable after the end of the financial year in which the issue took place, lay before Parliament a statement of the sums issued. Thereafter, the Treasury is required to lay an annual statement before each House until all liability in respect of principal and interest has been discharged.

It would be a serious matter if the Authority were unable to meet their liabilities in respect of a guaranteed loan and had to invoke the guarantee, and therefore Parliament must be told were this to happen.

Subsection (3) provides that payment in fulfilment of a Treasury guarantee shall be charged on and issued out of the Consolidated Fund. This is a necessary provision to enable funds to be made available.

Subsection (4) provides that if any sums are issued by the Treasury in fulfilment of a guarantee, then the Authority shall reimburse the Treasury as the Treasury may from time to time direct. The subsection also contains the power for the Treasury to charge interest on any sums from time to time being outstanding. These are normal conditions to ensure that the Treasury is fully reimbursed should it have to issue money under a guarantee of a loan to the Land Authority. The Land Authority would need to adjust the other borrowings and the land programme to enable them to meet the obligation under this subsection.

Subsection (5) provides that repayment to the Treasury by the Authority of sums issued in fulfilment of a guarantee and any interest on such sums shall be paid into the Consolidated Fund. This follows from the fact that, under subsection (3), the guarantee payments come out of the Fund.

SECTION 12.—ACCOUNTS AND AUDIT

This section provides for the keeping of financial accounts by the Land Authority for Wales and by the Secretary of State; for the accounts to be audited; and for the presentation to Parliament of the Land Authority's account and of the Secretary of State's account and of the Comptroller and Auditor General's report on each of these accounts.

The arrangements follow the general pattern which is normally required of statutory authorities and of Ministers responsible for making funds available to them. They need to be read with section 13 and with sections 43 and 44 which deal in more detail with the accounts and records of authorities generally (including the Land Authority for Wales). The complete pattern of actions and requirements is made up as follows:—

 (*a*) requirement on Land Authority to keep accounts and transmit them to Comptroller and Auditor General— (section 12);

 (*b*) requirement on Comptroller and Auditor General to examine and certify accounts under (*a*) and lay them and his report before Parliament—(section 12);

 (*c*) Secretary of State to keep account of his transactions with the National Loans Fund, and of the issue of loans to and repayment of loans by the Land Authority—(section 12);

 (*d*) audit by Comptroller and Auditor General of account under (*c*) and presentation to Parliament—(section 12);

(e) requirement on Land Authority to make annual report on exercise of their functions to Secretary of State and to attach a copy of their statement of accounts to the annual report—(section 13);

(f) Secretary of State to lay report on exercise of functions (excluding the statement of accounts) before Parliament—(section 13);

(g) Land Authority (in common with other authorities) to keep accounts and records as directed by the Secretary of State (with Treasury approval) and to supply Secretary of State with information—(section 43);

(h) Land Authority (in common with other authorities) to make payments out of surpluses to the Secretary of State as directed by him—(section 44);

(i) accounting by Secretary of State for share of surpluses received by him under (h) including payments to authorities out of surpluses—(section 44);

(j) audit by Comptroller and Auditor General and presentation to Parliament of accounts under (i)—(section 44).

There are thus two provisions requiring the Land Authority to keep accounts—a general provision to keep proper accounts in section 12 and a more precise provision to keep community land Surplus accounts in sections 43 and 44. There is provision in section 43(2)(a) for the Secretary of State, with Treasury approval, to direct what items should be shown in community land Surplus accounts. Since the Land Authority's functions are exclusively related to the acquisition, management and disposal of land for private development there is not likely in practice to be any great difference between the Authority's general accounts and their land surplus accounts. The Act nevertheless makes separate provision to cover the possibility that the community land surplus accounts will not always cover all those aspects of the Land Authority's operations on which accounts will be required.

Surpluses on the Land Authority's community land surplus account will, as in England and Scotland, be distributed between the Government and local authorities on a 40%/60% basis—*see* Note on section 44.

Subsection (1), paragraph (*a*), requires the Authority to keep proper accounts and records. Paragraph (*b*) requires the Authority to prepare for each accounting year (which is not specifically defined in the Act but which could most conveniently coincide with the financial year commencing on 1 April and is a matter on which the Secretary of State could if necessary give the Authority a direction under section 43) a statement of accounts in a form required by the Secretary of State with the approval of the Treasury. The statement must show the profit or loss of the Authority. It will also include the community land surplus accounts to be kept under sections 43 and 44. Paragraph (*c*) requires the Authority to transmit the statement of accounts to the Comptroller and Auditor General by the 30 November following the end of each accounting year.

These are normal provisions dealing with the preparation of annual accounts and their being made available for audit.

The Comptroller and Auditor General is given this responsibility because of the large sums of public money which will be initially involved; the lack of experience of land operations on the proposed scale by a newly created body; and the key role which the Land Authority will play in making land available for the whole range of private development in Wales, which will frequently involve difficult choices as to who is to be allowed to undertake particular developments and the terms on which they are to be allowed to do so. While commercial judgement will be one of the main criteria to be adopted, the Authority will have to take into account planning considerations and directions or guidance given by the Secretary of State. The audit will therefore need to have regard to more than just financial propriety and accurate book-keeping. Hence the Comptroller and Auditor General has been chosen rather than allowing audit by approved private auditors which is permitted with some public bodies operating on commercial lines.

Subsection (2) requires the Comptroller and Auditor General to audit the Authority's accounts and to lay them with his own report before Parliament.

The audited accounts of statutory bodies are normally laid before Parliament and where the auditor is the Comptroller and Auditor General he normally makes a report on the accounts which is also laid before Parliament.

Subsection (3) imposes a duty on the Secretary of State to account in such form and manner as the Treasury may approve for sums issued to him from the National Loans Fund for loan to the Authority, and for sums including interest repaid to him by the Authority in respect of those loans and of the initial debt referred to in sections 9 and 10. These accounts will, in fact, be in respect of the normal financial year beginning on 1 April, but " financial year " is not defined in the Act.

The subsection also requires the Secretary of State to send a copy of the account to the Comptroller and Auditor General by the end of November; and the Comptroller and Auditor General is required to examine, certify and report on the account and to lay copies of it together with his own report before Parliament.

These are normal provisions for the types of transaction in question. The Comptroller and Auditor General invariably audits accounts of transactions involving a government department.

SECTION 13.—REPORTS

This section requires the Land Authority for Wales to present an annual report on the exercise of their functions to the Secretary of State, and prescribes matters which have to be included in the report. A copy of the statement of accounts for the accounting year must be attached to the report. The section also requires the Secretary of State to lay a copy of the report before Parliament.

These are normal obligations on statutory authorities and on Ministers to whom they make reports. With the financial accounts and the Comptroller and Auditor General's report on the accounts which are separately presented to Parliament under section 12(2) they will enable the Minister concerned and Parliament to form a complete picture of the Authority's activities. Attention can be directed to successes and failures and to the extent to which the Authority are fulfilling the purposes which they were set up to achieve.

Subsection (1) requires the Land Authority for Wales to make to the Secretary of State after each accounting year a report on the exercise of their functions during that year.

This is a general broad requirement. It will permit the Secretary of State to see how the Land Authority are carrying out their remit. The report has to be made as soon as practicable but this expression needs to be considered in relation to the further requirement in subsection (3) below regarding the statement of accounts.

Subsection (2) specifies matters which must always be included in the report for any year. Sub-paragraph (*a*) requires the report to set out any directions given to the Authority by the Secretary of State unless he notifies them that it should be omitted in the interests of national security.

The object of this provision is to indicate those instances where responsibility for an action taken or not taken by the Authority lies with the Secretary of State and where it lies with the Authority. A direction by the Secretary of State may have security implications which it would not be in the national interest to publish. In practice they would also no doubt wish to include, where they consider it necessary for a proper understanding of their activities, a reference to guidance of a more general nature given to them by the Secretary of State.

Sub-paragraph (*b*) requires the report to contain such information relating to the plans, activities and financial position of the Authority as the Secretary of State may direct.

Subsection (3) requires a copy of the statement of accounts to be attached to the annual report. This is a normal requirement. The Authority will also be required under section 12(1)(*c*) to transmit a copy of their accounts to the Comptroller and Auditor General (who will in turn transmit them to Parliament with a copy of his report) but the Secretary of State will obviously also wish to see the statement of accounts. No time limit is specified in subsection (1) above for the annual report and statement of accounts to be sent to the Secretary of State (other than that it should be as soon as practicable). The Secretary of State will probably receive the unaudited accounts for his own information at this stage. He does not (under subsection (4) below) have to present the accounts to Parliament.

Subsection (4) requires the Secretary of State to lay a copy of the annual report before Parliament.

Parliament will receive from the Comptroller and Auditor General a separate copy of the certified accounts of the Authority and of his report on the accounts (section 12(2)). The Secretary of State's presentation of the Authority's report on the exercise of their functions will presumably be timed to coincide with the presentation of the Comptroller and Auditor General's report.

The performance by the Land Authority of their functions is likely to be a matter of considerable public interest. Not only will comparisons be made between the Land Authority's performance and that of local authorities in England and Scotland but the public at large in Wales who own land or wish to develop land will wish to know how they are likely to be affected by the Authority's operations. Local authorities in Wales will also wish to follow closely the Land Authority's financial results because these will have a bearing on the availability of surpluses for distribution between local authorities in Wales.

SECTION 14.—MANAGEMENT, ETC. OF LAND HELD BY THE AUTHORITY

This section sets out the general functions of the Land Authority for Wales in respect of the management, development and disposal of land; it requires local authorities in Wales to provide the Authority with information they will need to carry out their functions and authorises the Authority to make agency arrangements with local authorities for the discharge of their functions by those authorities.

As a statutory authority the Land Authority for Wales may only exercise functions which they are specifically authorised to undertake. The main purpose of this section is to confer this power on the Authority. Details of how the power is to be exercised are contained in other parts (particularly Part III and Schedule 4) of the Act.

Subsection (1) requires the Authority to manage and turn to account land which they have acquired.

The power of acquisition is in section 15 of the Act. The Authority will hold land either for a comparatively short period where the object is to dispose of it as quickly as possible for a development which is considered desirable and which has been given or is likely to receive planning permission; or they may hold it for a longer period in their " land bank " until it is ready to be disposed of, with the land being let in the meanwhile, normally to the people who occupied it before the Authority acquired it. When the land is disposed of this may be either on a freehold basis (when the Authority's obligations under subsection (1) would cease) or on a leasehold basis when the obligation would continue indefinitely. While the Authority hold the land the subsection requires them to use sound commercial judgment (" turning to account ") in managing it in the most efficient way.

Subsection (2) authorises the Authority with the consent of the Secretary of State to dispose of a material interest or any other interest which they may hold in land.

" Material interest " is defined in section 6(1) as the freehold or a lease with at least 7 years still to run. The Authority will normally acquire only the freehold of land in exercising their functions, but occasions may arise (for example in connection with land which they wish to occupy for their own operational purposes) when they might acquire other interests in land.

Disposal of land for residential purposes will generally be on a freehold basis, whereas disposal for other purposes will generally be on a leasehold basis. The reference to the disposal of " any other interest " in land will include the situation where builders will be permitted to enter upon land under the terms of a building agreement with a view to the building of houses for owner-occupation.

The object of requiring disposals to be subject to the consent of the Secretary of State is to ensure that the Authority comply with Government policy regarding the public ownership of land. General consents to dispose of land will normally be given, specifying the circumstances in which land may be disposed of on various conditions. Cases which fall outside the scope of the general consents will be authorised on an individual basis.

Subsection (3) authorises the Land Authority for Wales to carry out building engineering or other works on land where they consider this will assist in the disposal of that or other land.

This power is drawn in wide terms, and the intention is that the Land Authority for Wales should be able to carry out works similar to those which an English or Scottish local authority may charge against their community land surplus accounts (defined in section 44). These will be confined to site works which increase the disposal value of the land (*e.g.* levelling, on-site roadworks, street lighting, on-site sewers, etc.).

A further subsidiary power, common to all authorities, to carry out works with the prior consent of the Secretary of State on land acquired under the Act is contained in Schedule 4, paragraph 9(1), but this power would apply only in relation to buildings or works the construction of which, whether by the Authority or any other body, was not authorised by any other enactment.

There is also power in Schedule 4, paragraph 9(4), to repair or maintain buildings or works.

The Land Authority will need any appropriate planning permission before carrying out any works as if they were a private individual.

Subsection (4) authorises the Land Authority for Wales to arrange for the discharge of any of their functions by a local authority (defined in section 6(1) as the Council of a county or district)[1] and authorises Welsh local authorities to enter into such arrangements.

This is a broad power covering the functions of the Land Authority generally. It is an application of the code introduced for local authorities by sections 101 and 102 of the Local Government Act 1972. This code is recognised as giving local authorities greater freedom over their internal organisation and the way they discharge their functions, and it is desired that the Land Authority should enjoy similar powers subject of course to direction by the Secretary of State where necessary.

---

[1] *See* p. 58.

In some instances it will be appropriate for the Authority to enter into formal agency agreements with local authorities. In other circumstances the arrangements may be more *ad hoc* in nature, and less formal than an agency agreement. However, no authority vested with powers and responsibilities under legislation can by an administrative arrangement divest itself of those powers and responsibilities in favour of another body. In practice, any arrangement made between the Land Authority and a local authority will contain a provision enabling the Land Authority to terminate the arrangement. Nevertheless the subsection makes it clear that the arrangement will not prevent the authority from discharging the functions themself.

The intention will be for the Land Authority to make arrangements with local authorities wherever the local authorities are capable of discharging the responsibilities under such arrangements efficiently, with a reserve power to terminate the arrangement if it is not working satisfactorily.

The details of suitable agency arrangements cannot be finally settled until the Land Authority can themselves negotiate with the Welsh local authority associations but it seems likely that the arrangements will cover matters such as land referencing in connection with the preparation of compulsory purchase orders; legal conveyancing work when land is disposed of; supervision of the estate before land is disposed of; the landlord's role when property is disposed of on lease; and works service preparing land for disposal. The Land Authority would reimburse to local authorities their administrative costs when acting on behalf of the Authority.

Arrangements under this subsection are not to be a means of permitting the operation of the land scheme in Wales to pass into the hands of local authorities. The Secretary of State will use his general power of direction to control the nature and extent of any arrangements under this subsection.

Subsection (5) requires every county council and district council within the county to send one another a copy of any agency agreements they may make with the Land Authority and to hold it available for public inspection.

The object is to obtain the maximum publicity for these arrangements.

It is to be noted however, that copies of the agency arrangements are not to be sent to the Welsh community councils who will have to apply to the Land Authority for any information they desire. This is somewhat different from the treatment of parish councils in England and Wales which will be sent copies of Land Acquisition and Management Schemes made between the County and District Councils in any given area.

Subsection (6) will, so far as the Land Authority agree, apply the provisions of section 101 of the Local Government Act 1972 to functions discharged by local authorities under arrangements made under subsection (4) as though they were functions of the local authority itself. Section 101 enables local authorities to discharge their functions through a committee, subcommittee or officer, through any other local authority. Two or more authorities may discharge their functions jointly and may set up a joint committee.

The wording of the subsection adapts the provisions of section 101 to the relationship of principal and agent which will exist between the Land Authority and local authorities by the inclusion of the words " subject to the terms of the arrangements ".

The provision provides a recognised chain of authority below the Secretary of State, who will be ultimately responsible for the operation of the land scheme in Wales.

Subsection (7) confers a power on local authorities to become agents of the Land Authority for the performance of any services or the execution of any works for the Authority and which the Authority could perform by virtue of the Act.

Subsection (8) confers power on the Authority to do anything which would facilitate or be conducive or incidental to the performance of any of their functions.

This is a wide general power which is commonly conferred on statutory authorities who may carry out only functions which they are specifically authorised to carry out. Since it is not possible to foresee from the outset exactly what may be required in all circumstances if the Authority are to be able to function efficiently, a power is taken to cover any minor activities which it might otherwise be doubtful whether the Authority had power to carry out.

Subsection (9) requires every local authority to supply information to the Land Authority. **Sub-paragraph (a)** empowers the Secretary of State to make regulations prescribing the information which local authorities will be required to provide for purposes of the section. It is considered that this wording is wide enough to embrace the supply of information necessary to the Land Authority for any of their functions under the Act. **Sub-paragraph (b)** provides for the Secretary of State to specify in the regulations what certificates local authorities should supply to the Land Authority supporting the information the local authority are required to provide.

This provision is included to assist the operations of the Land Authority by enabling them to obtain information which they will need to have to carry out their functions. It is expected that the information required will mainly be about the planning policies of the local authorities or the planning status of particular land so that the Land Authority can decide what land to buy and to whom land should best be disposed of. The Land Authority may also wish to know what proposals the local authorities have for public works in the area so that they can decide how to manage their estate. Certificates will be necessary where the information has to be presented as evidence at a public inquiry.

PART III—COMMUNITY LAND

This part of the Act contains the main provisions of the Land Scheme. Other important provisions dealing in particular with the land transactions of authorities, and the Secretary of State's reserve powers are to be found in Parts V and VI respectively.

1. On **the first appointed day** authorities will assume new duties and powers.

The new **power of land acquisition** is dealt with in section 15 which also applies the provisions in Schedule 4. Authorities are given power to acquire, whether by agreement or compulsorily, land which, in their opinion, may be suitable for development (other than the exempt development set out in Schedule 1). The procedures for the making, and consideration by the Secretary of State of Compulsory Purchase Orders are contained in Schedule 4 (Part III of which applies to land acquired under section 15 procedures, with modifications, which already apply to land acquired under the Planning Acts).

Section 17, with Schedule 6, deals with the **general duties** which exist **from the first appointed day.** Authorities will have a duty to consider the desirability both of bringing development land into public ownership and into development and of securing the proper planning of their area; and also duties relating to the disposal of land to meet particular needs. Development land is defined as land which, in the opinion of the authority concerned is needed for relevant development within ten years (section 3). The duties, and the identification of development land, will have to be carried out within the planning framework for the area concerned.

2. On **the relevant date** the Secretary of State will be able to bring in by order the " **full duty** " in section 18. An Order will apply to a particular area, and will designate the types of relevant development to which it is to apply. It will then be the duty of the authorities in that area to arrange between them for any outstanding material interests in land which is needed for the purposes of the types of relevant development designated in the Order to be brought into public ownership. This duty will not extend to the operational land of statutory undertakers or to land which is not needed for development within ten years.

This full duty under section 18 is backed up by the imposition of a **prohibition on** the types of **development** designated in a section 18 order taking place other than on land which is in, or has passed through, public ownership. Under section 21 any planning permission granted on or after the relevant date for designated relevant development is automatically " suspended " unless the land is either in the ownership of an authority, or has been made available for specified development by an authority. This provision does not apply to development on the operational land of statutory undertakers, or to land in which no material interests are outstanding.

3. From **the second appointed day** (which cannot be brought in until section 18 orders are operating for all relevant development in all areas) the **basis of compensation** for compulsory purchase is changed to **current use value.** This is achieved in section 25 by positing certain assumptions as to planning permission affecting valuation. In brief, the assumptions are that planning permission would not be granted for any development other than that which is either exempt development (as defined in Schedule 1), or falls within the definition of what is not " new " development in the Planning Acts (" Schedule 8 Development "), or is permitted by a planning permission which is in force and has not been suspended under the provisions of the Act. These assumptions only operate where compensation is based on the value of land and do not therefore affect the equivalent reinstatement basis of compensation, or provisions concerning disturbance, and other such payments— *e.g.* home and farm loss payments.

Section 27 enables the Secretary of State to set up **financial hardship tribunals** to consider cases of possible hardship arising from the change in the compensation code on the second appointed day.

4. Part III deals also with the following matters (which are relevant to the operation of the scheme from the first appointed day):—

    (*a*) The drawing up of **land acquisition and management schemes,** under which all the authorities in each county area will agree on the exercise of functions under the scheme (section 16 and Schedule 5);

    (*b*) The **handling of planning applications** for relevant development made on or after the first appointed day, and the suspension of planning permissions granted on such applications (section 20 and Schedule 7). (Section 19 enables planning permissions granted on applications made between White Paper day and the first appointed day to be brought within these arrangements, at the option of the owner of the land.) These provisions do not apply to development carried out on the operational land of statutory undertakers or on land in which there are no outstanding material interests.

(c) The declaration of **disposal notification areas** to enable authorities to obtain information about disposals of development land (sections 23-24 and Schedule 8).

(d) The basis of **compensation** for transactions in land between certain authorities after the first appointed day (section 26).

SECTION 15.—POWERS OF ACQUISITION AND APPROPRIATION

This section empowers authorities to acquire any land which in their opinion is suitable for development (other than exempt development), and any necessary adjoining land, by agreement or compulsorily. By means of Part I of Schedule 4 which are applied by the section, it also changes existing legislation governing compulsory purchase. However, these changes only apply to development land,[1] *i.e.* land which is being acquired as needed for relevant development (and therefore the changes do not apply to Excepted Development).

The basic intention of the Act is that all development land should either be in or have passed through public ownership before development takes place. To this end authorities are to be given both general duties under section 17 and, in due course, the full duty under section 18. This section gives authorities the acquisition powers necessary to enable them to carry out these duties.

Subsection (1) empowers an authority to acquire any land which in their opinion is suitable for development by agreement or compulsorily. Compulsory acquisition is to be subject to authorisation by the Secretary of State.

The acquisition power does not relate to development land but to " any land . . . suitable for development " and therefore extends to Excepted Development (but not to Exempt Development, *see* subsection (2) below).[2]

The section does not impose any restraints on the Secretary of State when he is deciding whether to confirm a compulsory purchase order. In accordance with normal practice he will

[1] *See* Sch. 4, para. 1(2)(a).
[2] *See also* p. 17, above.

require authorities, by administrative action, to justify their proposals in appropriate detail. Also he will be giving guidance by circulars on the way in which authorities are to support their contention that land is suitable for development and in particular on the limited cases in which he will be prepared to entertain compulsory purchase orders in respect of Excepted Development. (*See* general commentary, page 17 above.)[1]

Subsection (2) excludes exempt development (as specified in Schedule 1) from the meaning of ' development ' in subsection (1), and thus from the acquisition power.

Subsection (3) extends the acquisition powers to cover:—

(*a*) land adjoining development land acquired by an authority which is required for works to facilitate its development or use; and

(*b*) land to be given in exchange for open space land which has been acquired for development.

The scope of (*a*) is strictly limited. It is only intended to cover cases where land adjoining development land is unsuitable for development in itself, but might be needed to facilitate development of the main site; *e.g.* for visibility splays, or for access to the site. The test of whether such land is needed will be an objective one, and will not depend upon the opinion of the authority concerned. Compulsory acquisitions of such land will not be subject to the expedited procedure of Part I of Schedule 4.

On (*b*), the power to acquire land to be given in exchange for open space land is well precedented, viz. section 112(1)(*c*) of the Town and Country Planning Act 1971 (land required for the replacement of open space in the course of redevelopment or improvement).

This provision is designed to ensure that where the taking of public open space, etc., for development is justified on planning grounds, its replacement, where that is desirable and where suitable land is available, is not frustrated for lack of powers to acquire land for that purpose. It is frequently convenient, where the acquisition of exchange land is necessary, for the whole operation to be carried out under the same powers and sometimes in a single compulsory purchase order.

---

[1] Note: Guidance is given in Circular 121/75, para. 57, on land in the ownership of builders.

" Fuel or field garden allotment " has no meaning in Scottish legislation and is therefore omitted from the application of the power to Scotland.

Subsection (4) applies the Acquisition of Land Acts to compulsory acquisition by all authorities with powers under the Act.

Legislation governing compulsory purchase consists of the Acquisition of Land (Authorisation Procedure) Act 1946, the Land Compensation Acts 1961 and 1973, the Compulsory Purchase Act 1965 and section 30 of the Town and Country Planning Act 1968 and the equivalent legislation for Scotland. Subject to the modifications in Part I of Schedule 4, all these provisions apply to compulsory acquisition under this section, and this is achieved by applying the 1946 Act (and the Scottish Act of 1947) as if the Act were in force immediately before the commencement of that Act. The Land Authority for Wales, new town development corporations and the National Park Planning Boards are also deemed to be local authorities for the purpose of that Act. All the subsequent legislation then applies automatically.

Subsection (5) applies the provisions of Schedule 4 to the Act. The Schedule is in four parts:—

Part I makes substantive modifications in the Acquisition of Land Acts applied by subsection (4) above (the significant changes apply only to acquisition of development land);

Part II deals with the acquisition of land by agreement.

Part III contains detailed supplemental provisions in respect of land acquired under this section (the effect is that authorities can deal with such land as if it had been acquired under the power in the Town and Country Planning Acts);

Part IV deals with appropriation of land by local authorities.

Subsection (6) provides that the powers of compulsory acquisition under this section and of appropriation under Part IV of Schedule 4 shall not be exercised before the first appointed day.

SECTION 16.—LAND ACQUISITION AND MANAGE-MENT SCHEMES

This section, together with Schedule 5, provides for the exercise of functions under the community land scheme to be regulated (except in Wales and the Isles of Scilly) by **land acquisition and management schemes** (LAMS).

In **England** LAMS are to be prepared and revised jointly by all the authorities in each county area. Initial schemes are to be prepared by 31 December 1975 in England, unless the Secretary of State agrees to an extension of time in a particular area.

In **Scotland** these schemes are to be prepared and revised in the area of a regional planning authority by that authority, after consultation with district planning authorities and New Town Development Corporations; and in the area of a general planning authority, by that authority acting alone, there being no other authorities with planning functions in the areas of general planning authorities. In Scotland, schemes are to be prepared by a date to be specified by Order.

The Act places the operation of the community land scheme in England and Scotland in the hands of the authorities which exercise the major land use planning functions—local authorities, new town development corporations and the National Park Planning Boards. This is achieved by section 1. However, this means that in relation to any given piece of land, there will generally be at least two authorities involved (County and district in England, regional and district planning authorities in Scotland). This will increase to three where a development corporation or Planning Board is involved. It would produce an anomalous situation if more than one authority were to seek to acquire the same piece of land. The existence of a LAMS for each county area or region is therefore designed to make clear the respective functions of all the authorities in that area, and to resolve any conflicts.

It is the responsibility of the authorities concerned to devise the particular scheme that best suits their needs. Section 16 lays down the functions that are to be covered by a scheme. Schedule 5 sets out matters to be considered in preparing or revising a scheme and provisions which must be contained in each scheme. Beyond this, it is up to the authorities concerned. There is no power for the Secretary of State to approve a scheme—though he has default powers under Schedule 5 and can if necessary instruct the authorities concerned to revise a scheme.

It is intended that in England, the new acquisition powers and duties in respect of private development will so far as possible follow the split of planning functions. So both counties and districts have a role. As the structure planning authority a county council will have a strategic role to play in the planning of the way in which the new powers are used in their area. District councils, with their responsibility for local plans and day-to-day planning work, within the context of the structure plan, will also have a major role.

The question of which authority is to be responsible for the acquisition of land for private development (within the overall strategy to which both county and district will contribute) must be settled pragmatically with particular regard to the existing resources, qualifications and availability of manpower.

In Scotland likewise, the intention is that the division of duties between regional and district planning authorities should reflect the planning responsibilities of each. Regional planning authorities have a primary responsibility for the preparation of land acquisition and management schemes to ensure that these are made and revised appropriately in accordance with the objectives and priorities set out in Regional Reports and Structure Plans. District planning authorities have a contribution to make in the framing of land acquisition and management schemes because of their responsibility for local plans and also have a large responsibility for implementing them by the acquisition of land, since all planning applications will be referred to district planning authorities for decision in the first instance.

It might happen that effective arrangements cannot be made in particular areas. Then it will be remembered that under section 2 the Secretary of State has powers to set up joint boards to perform the functions of two or more authorities.

Subsection (1) provides that there shall be a land acquisition and management scheme covering the area of each county authority.

Subsection (2) provides that each scheme should be made (and revised as necessary) by all the authorities in the area of the county authority acting jointly. For Scotland the subsection, read along with subsection (11) places the responsibility for ensuring that the scheme is prepared on the regional planning authority after consultation with district planning authorities and New Town Development Corporations. General planning authorities act alone in preparing their schemes.

Subsection (3) requires that a scheme shall provide for the exercise of functions (whether under this or any other Act) relating to the acquisition of land either for development by the authorities and subsequent disposal or with a view to disposal for subsequent development by others; and for the exercise of any other functions under the Act, except those of Part IV (which deals with unoccupied office premises, and where the powers are exercised solely by the Secretary of State).

This provision covers all land acquired for subsequent disposal, whether the authority concerned develop it themselves and then dispose of it, or make it available to a private developer. The requirement needs to extend to action under other legislation because local authorities will be able to use existing Housing and Planning Act powers to buy land for private development, and because land management will be carried out under existing powers. The provision also covers other functions of authorities under the Act, *e.g.* the declaration of disposal notification areas (*see* section 23).

Subsection (4) provides that in England, schemes shall be prepared not later than 31 December 1975, though it empowers the Secretary of State to agree to later preparation in any particular case.

Local authorities in many areas have anticipated the Royal Assent and proceeded with the preparation of LAMS without authority. However, the delays in enacting the Act have rendered the 31 December as legally impractical and there may be local problems to resolve, so provision is made for extension of time. Where there are serious problems, the Secretary of State will be able to exercise his default powers under paragraph 4(3) of Schedule 5, and make a LAMS himself. The date of 31 December 1975 relates to the actual making of a LAMS, and not to its subsequent sending to the Secretary of State under paragraph 4(1) of Schedule 5.

Subsection (5) provides in Scotland for the Secretary of State to determine the date for preparation of schemes by order.

Local government reorganisation in Scotland is following a year behind the reorganisation in England, and this must affect the date by which schemes can be worked out. For Scotland, the end of 1975 is an even less realistic timetable. Hence the power to set the date by order, which will be used to ensure the making of schemes by the earliest realistic date. By virtue of section 53(2)(*a*), the order will be made by statutory instrument, but will not be subject to any Parliamentary procedure.

Subsection (6) attracts the provisions of Schedule 5 to the Act, which deals with the making, revision and contents of the schemes.

Subsection (7) provides that land acquisition and management schemes shall not create any obligations enforceable in law, except and insofar as the Secretary of State, on the application of all the authorities in a county area, directs to the contrary.

LAMS are designed to be practical working arrangements between authorities and not to provide the basis of legalistic argument that a particular local authority is acting *ultra vires*, in any particular acquisition or other action. So generally, LAMS should not create any obligations which are legally enforceable. In any event, the Secretary of State, through his control of acquisition programmes, CPO authorisations and disposal policy can ensure that, as between the authorities themselves, the provisions of the LAMS (which might be one made or revised by the Secretary of State himself) are adhered to.

Subsection (8) provides that references in this section or Schedule 5 to the functions of any authority shall where appropriate include references to functions under other enactments.

This is to ensure that schemes can cover arrangements for the exercise of functions relating to the acquisition of land for private development under other enactments (*e.g.* the Planning Acts), as well as under the Act, and also to ensure that they cover the powers of management and disposal which, in the case of local authorities, are contained in the Local Government Act 1972.

Subsection (9) defines the terms used in this section and in Schedule 5.   In particular, it defines what authorities are to be regarded as county authorities.

Subsection (10) provides that for the purpose of preparing schemes, the Peak Park Joint Planning Board shall be regarded as an authority in each of the six county areas of which it forms part.   This is because it is the only authority which straddles a county boundary.

Subsection (11) provides that, for the purposes of application of section 16 and Schedule 5 to Scotland, references to a regional planning authority acting jointly with authorities in its area shall be construed as references to that authority acting after consultation with all other authorities in its area, and references to a general planning authority acting jointly shall be construed as references to such an authority acting alone.

Subsection (12) provides that the clause shall not apply to Wales or the Isles of Scilly.   LAMS are not needed in Wales because functions there will rest only with the Land Authority and new town development corporation, and it is intended to deal with the division of responsibility between these administratively.   The Council of the Isles of Scilly is a single-tier authority, so that no LAMS is required there.

SECTION 17.—GENERAL DUTIES OF AUTHORITIES

This section sets out the general duties which are to rest on every section 1 authority.

The section deals also with the way in which authorities are to approach the task of deciding what is " development land " a matter which under the definition in section 3 is left to the judgement of the authority concerned in each case. Authorities are requested to have regard to the development plan, any relevant planning decision, and any factors material to a planning decision.

The section also applies the provisions of Schedule 6 which makes further provision concerning general duties, with particular reference to the disposal of land.

Subsection (1) sets out the duties which are to be laid on authorities from the first appointed day. (For definition of " authorities ", *see* Note on section 1.) These general duties are that in exercising their functions (as defined in subsection (6)) authorities must have regard to the desirability of bringing development land into public ownership with a view either to developing it themselves, or making it available for development by others and of securing the proper planning of their area.

It should be noted that, unlike the full duty provided in section 18, there is no absolute requirement on authorities to acquire all or any land. In the early stages of the scheme, many authorities will not have the resources to attempt ambitious acquisition programmes and the subsection therefore gives them a discretion. The general duty in this subsection is framed in terms of development land generally. This means that it covers land required for public as well as for private development. Thus the subsection refers to development by the authority as well as to the making of land available for development by others. In relation to land for their own development authorities will be able to fulfil the duty either by the use of their existing powers or by using their new powers under the Act. The requirement for authorities to have regard to the desirability of securing the proper planning of their area is intended to govern the exercise of all their functions as defined in subsection (6).

Subsection (2) sets out the factors which authorities must have regard to in determining whether land is development land. These factors are: the provisions of the development plan, whether a planning permission for relevant development for the land is in force, or has been refused, and any other considerations which would be material in determining a planning application for the land in question.

The object of this subsection is to ensure that in considering whether land is development land, authorities have regard to all the proper planning considerations that might affect their decision. However, it remains to be seen whether the profit motive in development will override pure planning criteria. Much criticism has been levelled at the Act because the development authorities are to be one and the same as the planning authorities.

The subsection makes specific reference to the provisions of the development plan, which includes structure plans, local plans and old style development plans. The subsection also states that the authority must have regard to whether planning permission for relevant development on the land is in force or has been refused. The refusal of planning permission does not in itself preclude an authority from buying the land particularly if it can say it wants the land for some different development (*e.g.* flats instead of houses, or to merge it with other land for a more comprehensive development) and may have refused the planning application for this reason. This power will no doubt cause many difficulties between authorities and private citizens. Finally the authority must have regard to any considerations which, on an application for planning permission for relevant development on the land, would be material for the purpose of determining the application. This means that an authority should take into consideration, in addition to the matters mentioned above, such factors as informal and non-statutory plans, where relevant. The wording used here means that an authority will need to have regard to the same factors that would be relevant if they were determining a planning application—*see* section 29 of the 1971 Act.

Subsection (3) provides that in considering whether any land in Wales is development land, the Land Authority for Wales shall consult the district and county councils concerned, except where a planning permission for relevant development is already in force in respect of the land.

In Wales the functions of acquisition and disposal of land under the Act are given to the Land Authority for Wales and not to local authorities. Planning functions however remain with the local authorities and therefore these authorities are to be consulted by the Land Authority on what land is to be regarded as development land (though the decision will remain the responsibility of the Authority). Such consultation will not however be necessary where a planning permission for relevant development on the land is in existence as its status as development land will already have been established.

Subsection (4) applies the provisions of Schedule 6. The Schedule spells out the matters which authorities must take into account in fulfilling their acquisition and disposal functions. (*See* Note on that Schedule.)

Subsection (5) defines functions for the purposes of the section and Schedule 6 as meaning not only functions under the Act but also:—

(*a*) in the case of local authorities, new town authorities and the two National Park Planning Boards, their functions under the Planning Acts, and

(*b*) in the case of new town authorities, their functions under the New Towns Act 1965 (and the equivalent Scottish Act of 1968).

The effect of this subsection is to ensure that in exercising their functions under the Planning Acts and the New Towns Acts (as well as under the Act), the appropriate authorities have regard to the objectives of the community land scheme. The functions under the other Acts to which the general duty applies is limited by the wording of the subsection to functions concerning acquisition, management and disposal of land.

SECTION 18.—COMPREHENSIVE ACQUISITION OF DEVELOPMENT LAND

This section provides for the " **full duty** " which the Secretary of State can bring in by order when the authorities in an area are ready to take it on. The date on which a section 18 order comes into force is called the " **relevant date** ".

F

The bringing in of the full duty will be progressive in two senses:—

> (a) orders bringing in the duty will be made area by area;

> (b) the orders will " designate " the types of relevant development to which they apply.

So the full duty could be brought in within, say, the area of a single district or county council and, say, for housing development only.   Development which is designated within an area will also be subject to the " prohibition of development " (section 21).   Relevant development which is not for the time being designated will remain within the power of acquisition in section 15 and the procedures for handling planning applications in section 20.

The full duty will rest jointly on all the authorities in the area to which an order applies.   As, however, the full duty (unlike the general duty in section 17) requires specific action on the part of the authorities and as the Secretary of State might need to enforce such action, one authority will have a residual duty to act where other authorities have not done so.

The full duty is expressed as a duty to acquire all outstanding material interests.   Such interests are defined in section 4.

The full duty will not apply to land which is not needed for development within the next 10 years.   Nor will it apply to development on the operational land of statutory undertakers (so that such development will always be able to go ahead without intervention under the scheme, though the power for an authority to intervene will remain).   The bringing in of the full duty will not supersede the general duties in section 17 and Schedule 6.   These provisions will continue to apply, and will govern the way in which authorities continue to act when the full duty is in operation.

An order bringing in the full duty will be made by statutory instrument, and will be subject to the negative resolution procedure in either House of Parliament.   By virtue of paragraph 1 of Part II to Schedule 2 the Secretary of State is required to keep a register showing the extent to which " full duty " orders have been brought in.

Subsection (1) enables the Secretary of State to make orders imposing on authorities the duty to acquire all land needed for relevant development of the kinds " designated " in the orders.

Orders will need to be made in stages as individual authorities build up their resources and their ability to handle all development land in their areas (*see* introductory note to this section). Eventually orders will cover all areas and be in respect of all relevant development.

Subsection (2) requires the Secretary of State to consult all the authorities whose areas include land to which an order will apply before making such an order. This is to ensure that the authorities are able to handle the development land before the duty is imposed and to identify that upon which the ultimate duty to acquire will fall under subsection (5) below in accordance with the arrangements made between themselves under subsection (3) below.

Subsection (3) defines the nature of the duty to be imposed on authorities by an order under subsection (1). This is that all outstanding material interests in land (as defined in section 4) which are **needed** for designated relevant development in an area to which the order applies must be acquired by one or other of the authorities in whose area the land is situated. The subsection provides that the authorities concerned shall arrange between them who is actually to acquire the land and this will be dealt with in their Land Acquisition and Management Schemes (*see* note on subsection (3) and section 16).

The authorities on whom the full duty rests are those in section 1. In England and Scotland the duty will be automatically satisfied in relation to land for relevant development which is to be carried out by local authorities (*e.g.* local authority housing). But unless special provision were made, land for local authority development in Wales would have to be acquired by the Land Authority or by a new town development corporation. To avoid this subsection (3) provides that, for the purposes of this section authorities are to include local authorities in Wales.

The duty is imposed on all authorities in the duty area in terms of **arranging** for the acquisition of land. This is in line with the general intention that the scheme should be operated jointly by counties and districts. But there must be a final duty actually to acquire land which can be imposed on only **one** of the authorities; this is dealt with in subsection (5).

It will be noted that the **duty** is in respect of land **needed** for **designated relevant** development and is thus narrower than the **power** which is for all land **suitable** for development, *i.e.* including " excepted development " (*see* note on section 3).

Subsection (4) requires authorities in carrying out their duties under the section to have regard to the Land Acquisition and Management Scheme for the county area.

Section 16 and Schedule 5 provide for Land Acquisition and Management Schemes to be prepared for each county area; and Schedule 5 (paragraph 3(1)(*a*)) particularly specifies that one of the matters which must be covered in a Scheme is arrangements for co-ordination of action by authorities. The arrangements for acquiring land for designated relevant development referred to in subsection (3) of this clause must therefore be in accordance with the LAMS.

It also excludes from the full duty:—

(*a*) land which is not needed for designated relevant development within the next 10 years;

This 10 year period is a limitation on the scope of the duty, not a target. It does not mean that authorities must at once set out to acquire all the land that will be required within the 10 year period.

(*b*) land in respect of which all the authorities have lost their powers of compulsory purchase under the Act (by virtue of sections 19(5) or 20(2));

Under the provisions of sections 19 and 20 (which operate only until the bringing in of the duty in relation to a particular type of development in an area) authorities lose their powers of compulsory purchase under the Act for five years if, in certain circumstances they do not pursue the acquisition of land which is the object of a planning application or permission, for relevant development. It would put authorities in an impossible position if the bringing in of the full duty required them to acquire such land which they had already decided should not be acquired. It would also create uncertainty for landowners which the arrangements concerning the loss of powers are intended to remove.

(c) land which has already passed through the hands of an authority;

Without this subsection an authority would in theory be under a duty to re-acquire land which they had just disposed of, and this would obviously be an absurdity.

(d) the operational land of statutory undertakers.

Statutory undertakers and their operational land are defined in section 5 in respect of which development is allowed to go ahead without the intervention of authorities. Therefore authorities are not placed under a duty to acquire land for this purpose. (See also section 22(8).)

Subsection (5) provides that an order under the section shall designate one authority on whom will fall the duty to acquire all the outstanding material interests in land needed for designated relevant development which are not acquired by one of the other authorities.

As already seen, all the authorities concerned will be required to **arrange** between themselves for the necessary land to be acquired. They could not all have a duty actually to **acquire**, as this could lead to administrative chaos.

It is expected that the authority to be designated for the purposes of this subsection will be the authority which is most active in the acquisition of land for private development.

For the reasons explained in relation to subsection (3) it is provided that the designated authority in Wales (i.e., generally, the Land Authority) will not have the duty to acquire land which has already been acquired by a district or county council.

Subsection (6) defines the " relevant date " as meaning the date on which an order under this section is made in respect of designated relevant development in each particular area. Thus

there may be different relevant dates for different kinds of
relevant development in each area to which the duty is applied.
These relevant dates also dictate the date on which the section
21 prohibition of development except on land owned by or
disposed of by authorities, is imposed.

As there are likely to be a considerable number of relevant
dates covering different kinds of development in different areas
the Act provides that registers, showing the dates and extent
of all orders under this section, shall be kept by the respective
Secretaries of State in Cardiff, Edinburgh and London (*see*
Schedule 2, Part II).

Subsection (7) provides that no order is to be made under
this section before a LAMS has been prepared for the area,
nor before the first appointed day. *It also provides that such
orders shall be subject to the negative resolution procedure.

Until the authorities in a county area have agreed their
LAMS they will be in no position to take on the full duties
imposed by this section. And it would clearly be impossible
to bring in the full duty in an area before the necessary powers
and procedures have been brought into force by a first
appointed day order.

Subsection (8) excludes subsection (7)(*a*) from Wales and the
Isles of Scilly. This is because, by virtue of section 16(12),
there will be no Land Acquisition and Management Schemes
there.

Subsection (9) defines " county authority " (which appears
in subsections (1)(*a*) and (7)(*a*)) as having the same meaning
as in section 16.

SECTION 19. — PERMISSION BEFORE RELEVANT DATE: APPLICATIONS BEFORE FIRST APPOINTED DAY

This section, with Schedule 7, provides a procedure enabling
persons with a material interest in land who **applied for planning
permission** for relevant development **before** the first appointed
day, but whose permission was not granted until after 12
September 1974 (the date of the White Paper), to serve a

" notice of election " on any authority with powers under the Act asking them whether or not they propose to acquire their land. By Serving such a notice an owner will be able to discover whether that authority or any other authority with powers under the Act are going to seek to acquire his land on the basis of the planning permission which has been granted; but in so doing he will in effect elect to bring his planning permission within the procedures (including the " suspension " of planning permission) which will apply to planning applications for relevant development made after the first appointed day.

On receipt of the notice the planning permission concerned will be " suspended " and the authorities will have 3 months in which to decide whether or not to acquire. If the authorities decide not to acquire the land, the suspension of planning permission will be lifted, and the authorities will be debarred from acquiring the land (using their compulsory powers under the Act) for 5 years from the date of their decision. Where an authority decide to acquire, the permission will remain suspended until the authority either acquire the land or fail to pursue acquisition in the circumstances described in Schedule 7.

The procedure is a modification of that laid down in section 20 and Schedule 7 (which deals with the situation where an application for planning permission for relevant development is made **after** the first appointed day) and reference should be made to the notes on that section and Schedule.

Where planning permission for relevant development was granted after 12 September 1974, the owner of a material interest may wish to know, when the scheme comes into operation, whether or not he is free to undertake the development without the intervention of an authority; and the section enables him to put the question beyond doubt. It does not, however, cover planning permissions which were in force on 12 September 1974 because it is intended to treat development in accordance with such a permission as Excepted Development and thus be outside the normal scope of the scheme (*see* General Commentary at page 13).

Subsection (1) states that the section applies to planning permissions for relevant development granted after 12 September 1974 (the date of the White Paper) but before the relevant date (defined in section 18(6)), where the application for permission was made **before** the first appointed day. The section only applies, however, where an election is made under subsection (2).

It will be seen that section 20 deals with the situation of planning applications made on or after the first appointed day. With regard to planning permissions in respect of 'designated' relevant development granted on or after the relevant date (*i.e.* the date when the section 18 duty and the section 21 prohibition come into operation), these are automatically suspended until the land in question is brought into public ownership, and there can be no question of authorities deciding whether or not to exercise their powers.

Subsection (2) enables a person who has a material interest in the whole of the land covered by the planning permission and is entitled to possession of the land as against every other owner of a material interest in the same land to serve a notice of election in the prescribed form on any of the authorities concerned. The subsection also provides that the authority on whom notice is served shall send a copy to each of the other authorities concerned.

Although the notice need only be served on one of the authorities, this is regarded as service on all of them. There it is further provided that the authority receiving the notice send a copy to the other authorities concerned so that they can decide whether or not they wish to acquire the land. It is expected that provision will have been made in the relevant LAMS for only one of the authorities to take action.

The intention behind the subsection is that only a person with a freehold or a lease with more than 7 years unexpired and is entitled to possession at the time as against any other holders of material interests shall be entitled to serve the notice of election. This is because such a person is the only one in a position to carry out the development covered by the planning permission and therefore needs to know where he stands. Conversely it prevents someone with a material interest but not entitled to possession from making an election and thus suspending the planning permission and frustrating the development.

Subsection (3) enables a person with a binding contract to acquire a freehold or lease for at least 7 years to qualify to serve a notice of election under the preceding subsection. It also includes a crofter or landholder in his croft or holding in relation to Scotland.

Subsection (4) states that a notice of election under subsection (2) shall not be served either before the first appointed day or before the date the planning permission is granted.

The new acquisition power does not become available until the first appointed day so there is no need for a person to serve a notice of election before then. Also the need for a person to find out whether acquisition is intended does not arise until there is in existence a planning permission for relevant development.

Subsection (5) provides that if an authority abandon their power to purchase—in the circumstances set out in paragraph 1 of Schedule 7—they shall lose their powers of compulsory purchase under the Act for a period of 5 years, calculated in accordance with paragraph 1 of the Schedule.

This is similar to the provision in section 20(2).

Subsection (6) provides that when a notice of election is served the planning permission in question shall be suspended from the date of service of the notice until the end of the period prescribed by paragraph 2 of Schedule 7, *i.e.* when all the authorities concerned have abandoned their powers to purchase the land or when any of them purchases the land, whichever is the earlier.

This is similar to the provision in section 20(3).

SECTION 20.—PERMISSIONS BEFORE RELEVANT DATE: APPLICATIONS ON OR AFTER FIRST APPOINTED DAY

This section together with Schedule 7, deals with the situation where an **application for planning permission** for relevant

development is made **on or after** the first appointed day and
the permission is granted before the relevant date (as defined
in section 18). (Section 19 has dealt with the situation where
the application is made before the first appointed day and
section 21 deals with that where the permission is granted on
or after the relevant date.)

Under the scheme any application for planning permission
for relevant development raises the question of acquisition by
one or other of the authorities concerned. So section 20
provides for " **suspension** " of planning permissions mentioned
above until **either** public acquisition of the land has taken place
or the authorities concerned have abandoned their power to
purchase the land compulsorily. The mechanics whereby this
is achieved are set out in Schedule 7.

The essential features of the procedures are that:—

> (*a*) they give authorities an opportunity to acquire
> development land brought to their attention by
> planning applications, and prevent development being
> started under the planning permission in the meantime;
> and

> (*b*) they enable owners, and applicants, to ascertain
> whether the land is to be acquired on the grant of the
> planning permission or whether they are to be free to
> carry out the development themselves.

Subsection (1) states that the section applies to planning
permission for relevant development granted before the relevant
date on an application made on or after the first appointed
day. The effect of this is that such planning permissions may
be suspended in accordance with subsection (3). (*Cf.* section
19.—Applications before first appointed day; section 21—
permissions after relevant date.)

As the new powers of acquisition are not available until the
first appointed day there will not have been an opportunity
for an authority to consider acquisition on an application
made before that day.

Once a relevant date order has been made planning permissions for the types of development designated for that particular area are automatically suspended until the land has been acquired by an authority so the provisions of section 20 and Schedule 7 will no longer be needed in relation to those types of development (though they will still apply to applications and permissions for relevant development—which is not yet designated).

Subsection (2) provides that where planning permission is granted and where an authority abandon their power to purchase the land in the circumstances set out in Schedule 7, paragraph 1, the authority concerned shall lose their powers of compulsory purchase under the Act for a period of 5 years (calculated in accordance with paragraph 1 of the Schedule).

The circumstances in which an authority lose their powers are laid down in Schedule 7: broadly speaking this occurs when an authority say they do not intend to acquire the land or when they fail to pursue their intention to do so. This enables the owner to undertake the development himself within the 5 year period without having to worry about the possibility of the threat of acquisition re-appearing (e.g. owing to a change of mind on the part of the authority).

Subsection (3) provides that where a planning permission covered by the section is granted before the period prescribed in Schedule 7, paragraph 2, it shall be suspended until that period ends.

The subsection is drafted so as to make it clear that the suspension only operates where planning permission is granted before acquisition has taken place or before all the authorities have abandoned their powers to purchase.

The object of suspension is to give the authorities time to consider acquisition of land before development covered by a permission is started. In normal circumstances it is expected that decisions on acquisition and on planning applications will be made at the same time. However, it would be pointless to suspend where the acquisition decision has already been taken.

SECTION 21.—PERMISSION GRANTED ON OR AFTER RELEVANT DATE

This section operates where a section 18 order has been made imposing the full duty to acquire land on an authority with a view to their developing it themselves or disposing of it to others to develop. The section prohibits relevant development of the kinds designated in the order taking place, other than on land owned by an authority or made available by them for that purpose. The prohibition is achieved by providing for an automatic suspension of any planning permission for such development within the area concerned until the land has been acquired by an authority.

Because of the exclusion provided in section 22(8) the prohibition does not apply to land in which there are no material interests outstanding or to the operational land of statutory undertakers. Nor does it apply to relevant development which is not designated within the area concerned; these types of development will continue to be governed by the provisions of sections 19 and 20.

Subsection (1) states that the section applies to planning permission for relevant development granted on or after the relevant date, whatever the date of the application.

Although this section refers simply to " planning permission for relevant development ", by virtue of the definition of relevant date in section 18(5) the provisions will in fact apply only to the designated relevant development specified in the appropriate relevant date order. Under Part II of Schedule 2 the Secretary of State is required to keep a register of relevant date orders so that owners and others with an interest in development in an area will be able to find out whether orders have been made and if so, what development has been designated under them.

Subsection (2) provides that planning permissions to which the section applies shall be " suspended " unless either (*a*) the land on which the development allowed by the permission is to be carried out is in public ownership (*i.e.* there are no outstanding material interests) **and** the development is carried out by or on behalf of an authority; **or** (*b*) the conditions set out in subsections (3) or (4) are met.

The subsection ensures firstly that planning permission is not suspended where the development to which it relates is carried out on land in public ownership for or on behalf of an authority.

Secondly, it covers development carried out by private developers who have obtained land from an authority. Thus the suspension ensures that all land for development covered by the relevant date order is in or first passes into the ownership of an authority. However, land held by a charity from the 12 September 1974 or land belonging to parish or community councils is exempt from this suspension by section 22(8) below.

Subsection (3) provides that where the Secretary of State decides not to confirm a compulsory purchase order after the relevant date for designated relevant development the suspension of the planning permission for such development shall be lifted if the Secretary of State so directs.

This is a limited power to cover special situations where the Secretary of State might decide to allow the development to proceed without public ownership. No indications have been given so far as to when this power might be exercised, save for hardship, but given the philosophy underlying the Act it is a power not likely to be used frequently.

Subsection (4) defines the conditions (referred to in subsection (2)(*b*)) to be met before the suspension of planning permission under this section is lifted. These are:—

(*a*) that a material interest in the land (defined in section 6 as the freehold or a lease with less than 7 years unexpired), has been disposed of by an authority, and that immediately before the disposal there were no material interests outstanding;

(*b*) that the authority in question have approved the carrying out of the development in accordance with the planning permission;

(*c*) that the authority have issued a certificate in the
prescribed form stating that conditions (*a*) and (*b*) are
met.

The suspension remains in force until all these conditions
are met.   (Section 22 deals with the position where the development is carried out while the permission is still suspended.)

Subsection (5) deals with the situation where the land was
disposed of by an authority before the first appointed day and
makes it clear that the conditions mentioned in subsection (4)
can be regarded as satisfied if the authority have since approved
the interest which they disposed of as being an interest appropriate for the purposes of the section and have issued a certificate
under subsection (4)(*c*) confirming this.

Where an authority have disposed of land before the provisions of the Act have come into force the interest they disposed
of may or may not have satisfied the land scheme.   If it did,
there is no reason to require the land again to come into the
ownership of an authority.   If it did not, this subsection enables
the authority to stop the planning permission from becoming
unsuspended until the authority have acquired the land again.

Subsection (6) states that the certificate given under subsection (4)(*c*) shall be conclusive evidence of the facts stated in
it.   The purpose of this provision is to ensure that successors
in title to the person named in the certificate do not need to
seek confirmation of the facts from the authority concerned.

Subsections (7) and (8) require an authority issuing a certificate as above shall send a copy to every other authority in
whose area the land is also situate unless those other authorities
have indicated there is no need.   These subsections are
primarily to assist district councils which are most concerned
with enforcement of planning control and therefore will require
to know if a permission is still suspended.   However, they are
widely drawn so the information will be made available to
other authorities in the area if they require it.

Subsection (9) states that in applying the section to Wales
" authority " includes a local authority whose area includes the
land. Although the powers and duties under the Act in Wales
are to be exercised by the Land Authority for Wales and not
by the local authorities, the latter will still be developing land
for their own use and also disposing of some land for private
development. This subsection operates so that planning permissions for their own development are unsuspended under
subsection (2)(*a*) and so that they can lift the suspension of
planning permission on disposing of land for private development through the procedure in subsection (4). Local authorities in Wales acting outside their own areas are covered by
the fact that interests which they hold are not defined as " outstanding " in section 4. The difference between the two situations is that a local authority in Wales inside its own area
can either develop land itself or make it available for private
development outside the scope of the section 21 prohibition;
but Welsh local authorities acting **outside** their areas are only
given protection so far as their own development is concerned.

SECTION 22.—SUSPENSION OF PLANNING PERMIS-
SION: SUPPLEMENTAL

This section contains supplementary provisions concerning
the suspension of planning permissions under sections 19 to
21 (" the previous sections "). It deals principally (in subsections (1)-(5)) with the situation where relevant development
covered by planning permission is carried out at a time when
the planning permission is suspended, and provides that the
suspended permission shall be disregarded for the purposes of
the enforcement of control provisions of Part V of the 1971
Town and Country Planning Act (and the Scottish Act of 1972)
and that in determining the amount of any compensation
payable in respect of the land any development carried out
while the permission was suspended shall be ignored. The
section makes it clear that these provisions apply also to planning permissions granted under sections 32 and 88 of the 1971
Town and Country Planning Act (and the equivalent sections
of the Scottish Act)—that is to say permissions to retain

development carried out without prior permission, and permission granted following the quashing of an enforcement notice.

The section also relieves land already in some form of public ownership including land owned by parish councils or by charities on the 12 September 1974 from the suspension provisions of the preceding sections.

Subsection (1) states that if relevant development is carried out while planning permission is suspended under the previous sections, that planning permission shall be disregarded in applying the enforcement of control provision of Part V of the 1971 Act and the Scottish Act of 1972. This means that any relevant development carried out while the suspension of planning permission is in force will be development carried out in breach of planning control and thus subject to the enforcement provisions of the Planning Acts.

The main instrument for securing compliance with the provisions suspending planning permissions no doubt will be the threat of acquisition by an authority at a price which excludes the value of the development carried out while the permission was suspended (subsection (2)). However, enforcement under the Planning Acts will possibly arise where development carried out in accordance with a suspended planning permission is not in accordance with the development which the local authority seek to secure after acquiring the land. The enforcement machinery provides the means of securing removal of the offending development, if necessary, by the local authority in default of the owner, and provides them with power to recover their costs.

Subsection (2) provides that, where relevant development is carried out while the planning permission is suspended, the value of such development covered by the planning permission and actually carried out while it is suspended shall be ignored for the purpose of calculating the compensation to be paid on the acquisition of the land in question.

The mere power of enforcement, with the limited penalties available under the Planning Acts, are not considered a sufficient deterrent. So a stronger sanction is achieved by excluding from the compensation payable on compulsory acquisition the value of such unlawful development as has taken place.

Subsection (3) provides that where any development is carried out without planning permission and planning permission is subsequently granted under:—

(*a*) Section 32 of the 1971 Act (section 29 of the 1972 Scottish Act)—which deals with planning permission for the retention of development already carried out, or

(*b*) Section 88 of the 1971 Act (section 85 of the Scottish Act)—planning permission given by the Secretary of State on appeal against an enforcement notice,

it shall be regarded as carried out after the grant and while the permission is suspended.

This effectively treats these categories of permissions in the same way as if they had been granted on a normal application. Otherwise persons wishing to avoid suspension and the penal provisions would simply start development without planning permission. Subsection (4), however, enables an authority to disregard the penal provisions of subsection (2) in relation to development covered by a section 32 or section 88 planning permission.

Subsection (4) provides that where planning permission is granted under sections 32 or 88 of the 1971 Act (or sections 29 or 85 of the Scottish Act of 1972) the person granting that permission may, if he thinks fit, direct that the provisions of subsection (2) shall not apply.

These sections of the Planning Acts relate to cases where development has already been carried out without planning permission having first been obtained, and enable the authority concerned (or the Secretary of State on appeal) subsequently to grant permission for the retention of that development. The development may have been commenced by someone who genuinely did not know that planning permission was needed for the works he carried out. In cases of this sort the authority (or the Secretary of State) may well think it reasonable that the penal provisions of subsection (2) should not apply and subsection (4) gives them this power.

Subsection (5) requires that, except in the circumstances provided for in subsection (2), the suspension of planning permissions by virtue of the previous sections shall not affect the amount of compensation payable on compulsory purchase or any other compensation which depends on the value of land.

The effect of this is that for the purposes of assessing compensation on the compulsory acquisition of land covered by a suspended planning permission, the suspension is ignored and the value of the planning permission is taken into account. The same applies where, for example, the compensation is for severance from or injurious affection of other land held with the land which is to be purchased.

Subsection (6) provides that section 192(1) of the 1971 Planning Act and section 181(1) of the Scottish Act of 1972 (which deal with blight notices) shall have effect as if the land specified in these sections included land in respect of which planning permission, for relevant development, is suspended under the previous sections.

This provision safeguards residential and agricultural owner-occupier and owner-occupier of either property whose rateable value does not exceed £2,250. If they need to sell but find they cannot privately because the planning permission on their land is suspended they may serve a blight notice on the appropriate authority requiring that authority to buy the land.

Subsection (7) provides that any time limit imposed by a condition attaching to a suspended planning permission shall be extended for a period equal to the suspension.

Sections 41 to 44 of the 1971 Act (sections 38-41 of the Scottish Act) provide for conditions to be attached to planning permissions requiring the development to be begun (or, in the case of an outline permission, for approval of details to be sought) within a specified period. Where, however, a permission is suspended by virtue of the previous sections the owner of the land may well be unable through no fault of his own to comply with the condition. The subsection therefore provides that the specified period shall be extended for a period equal to that of the suspension.

Planning permissions may also be granted for a limited period—for instance, the use of land for a particular purpose might be permitted for 5 years from the date of the permission; here again it would not be right for the period to begin until the permission became effective.

Subsection (8) provides that sections 19-21 shall not apply to planning permissions granted in respect of:—

    (*a*) land in which no material interests are outstanding.

The concept of outstanding material interests is defined in section 4 and the effect of this provision is to exempt land owned by an authority, local or new town authority, a parish or community council, or in Scotland the council of a district within the area of a general planning authority, or, by a charity since before 12 September 1974, from the " suspension " procedures of sections 19-21.

    (*b*) the operational land of statutory undertakers or land which would be operational land if the development for which planning permission has been sought were to be carried out.

This (together with section 18(3)(*d*)), enables statutory undertakers to acquire and develop land needed for their statutory functions without the intervention of local authorities.

Subsection (9) makes it clear that references to planning permissions in sections 19-21 includes permissions regarded as granted on a deemed application under section 88(7) of the 1971 Act or the equivalent section 85(7) of the Scottish Act of 1974.

The purpose of this subsection is to ensure that deemed applications for planning permission made under section 88 of the 1971 Act (and the equivalent Scottish provisions) are treated for the purposes of the previous sections as if they had been made in the usual way. Such permissions will therefore be subject to the suspension provisions of those sections.

SECTION 23.—DISPOSAL NOTIFICATION AREAS

This section enables authorities to declare certain areas to be " **disposal notification areas** ", (D.N.A.s), as a means of obtaining information about disposals of development land.

The provisions are based on those in section 47 and Schedule 4 of the Housing Act 1974 relating to Housing Action Areas. Anyone proposing to dispose of a material interest in land has to inform the authority concerned before entering into a binding contract. The authority then have to say whether or not they wished to acquire the land. They have no power to stop the intended transaction going ahead, but they would be in a position to attempt to negotiate with the vendor or if necessary to make a compulsory purchase order.

Although the procedures are borrowed from the Housing Action Areas, the concept is quite different. Housing Action Areas are decayed urban residential areas where the properties are in such poor condition and of so little value that private capital is unlikely to be spent in bringing them up to good standards. They are small in extent comprising not more than 300-400 houses. A D.N.A. has no geographical limitation provided it contains development land and it is created in order to pre-empt private development.

Under the D.N.A. procedure a vendor, whose private sale has been frustrated by an authority stating that they intend to acquire his land, may require that authority to do so. This is achieved by applying the blight provisions in the Planning Acts.

The declaration of a D.N.A. will not in any way affect the rights of objection to a compulsory purchase order, or, by virtue of section 9 of the Land Compensation Act, the price that an authority will pay for land which it acquired.

However, it is evident that in practice the declaration of a D.N.A. is bound to depress the value of all property within that area. Private purchasers will be reluctant to proceed when they discover that an authority has indicated they would like to acquire a property or, even when they do not, that it is near property that is to be subject to public acquisition and development. This depression of values in an area will facilitate acquisition by an authority particularly where the effect of a D.N.A. is to place them in the position of monopoly buyers by frightening off private buyers.

The Government has indicated they will not allow authorities to abuse these powers and they will only be allowed to exercise them where there is a planning justification. Also an option is given to the owner-occupier of residential premises.

Although D.N.A.s do not require the approval of the Secretary of State, he has the power to modify or veto them under Schedule 8, paragraph 2.

Any authority (as defined in section 1) can declare a disposal notification area within its own area. It is expected that responsibility for such areas, and arrangements for necessary consultation will be dealt with in Land Acquisition and Management Schemes under section 16.

Subsection (1) states that an authority may if they wish exercise the powers given by the section for the purpose of obtaining information about intended disposals of development land.

It is to be noted that a D.N.A. may be declared only where there is some " development land "—*i.e.* land needed for relevant development within 10 years. However, as will be seen from the following subsection there is no limitation on the size of the area within which the development land is situate.

Subsection (2) enables an authority to declare **any** land in their area to be a disposal notification area by passing a resolution to that effect. The Land Authority for Wales are required to consult each local authority whose area is affected by a D.N.A. before passing the resolution.

The local authorities in Wales will, as planning authorities, be concerned with the Land Authority's acquisition proposals and therefore they are to be consulted before a D.N.A., embracing part of their area, is declared.

Subsection (3) provides that the effective date for a D.N.A. must be specified in the authority's resolution.   The date must not be earlier than three months from the passing of the resolution, nor earlier than the first appointed day.

By virtue of Part II of Schedule 8 a person proposing to dispose of land must give at least 4 weeks' notice to the authority concerned.   The 3-month time limit therefore leaves two months for the intending vendor to be made aware of the declaration of the D.N.A. and to give timely notice of the sale. This section comes into effect as soon as the Act receives Royal Assent.   So authorities will be able to begin the procedure for declaring a D.N.A. straight away.   But, by virtue of **subsection** (3)(b) the notification provisions cannot become operative until after the first appointed day when authorities assume their main powers under the Act.

Subsection (4) applies the provisions of Part I of Schedule 8 (which govern the publicity procedures on declaring a disposal notification area and the function of the Secretary of State) after an authority have passed a resolution.

Subsection (5) requires anyone proposing to dispose (or to enter into a binding contract to dispose) of a material interest in land in a D.N.A. to give notice to the appropriate authority in accordance with the procedure laid down in Part II of Schedule 8.   The purpose of such a notification is to enable the authority to decide whether or not to seek to acquire the land.

The requirement to notify in effect binds a prospective vendor the moment he places his property in the hands of an estate agent to find him a purchaser.   It, moreover, applies to material interests in **all** land[1] and not only in development land; presumably because private vendors are not in a position to judge in all cases whether their land is development land. The service of a notice does not given an authority a pre-emptive right to acquire the land and the vendor could in theory proceed with a private sale.   But no doubt intending purchasers will ask to see the authority's counter-notice and promptly lose interest when local land charges searches reveal the property is within a D.N.A.

---

[1] But *see* Sch. 8, para. 4, and subsection (6) below.

Subsection (6) exempts the following categories of transaction from the notification requirements:—

(*a*) a disposal in performance of a contract of which notification has already been given under subsection (5). The authority will already have reacted to the first notification so any further notification is superfluous.

(*b*) a transaction taking place before the effective date specified in the resolution. However, the notice is required if the disposal takes place after the effective date if in performance of a contract entered into before the effective date and so not notified. This should be contrasted with (*a*) above.

(*c*) a transaction which is not for valuable consideration. This means that gifts do not have to be notified to the authority.

(*d*) a disposal or contract for a disposal to any authority or to the Crown. The acquisition powers do not extend to Crown land so there is no need for authorities to be notified of any disposal by a private vendor to the Crown. Of course, the Crown itself does not have to give notice of its disposals even without this subsection as the section does not in any event bind it. Similarly disposals to a public authority are excluded as the intention is to obtain information of transactions in the private sector to enable the public sector to step in.

Subsection (7) requires an authority who have received a notice under subsection (5) as soon as practicable to acknowledge receipt of the notice (specifying the date it was received) and within four weeks to serve a counter notice in the prescribed form stating whether or not they propose to purchase all or part of the land in question.

The authority have only four weeks to make up their minds whether or not to acquire, but this should not present them with any great difficulty given that they will have settled the broad lines of their intentions before declaring the D.N.A.

It should be noted that " purchase " in this subsection covers purchase under **any** powers; it is not restricted to the acquisition powers in the Act.   If an authority having said they do not intend to purchase subsequently attempt to do so compulsorily, it is expected that in the transitional stage the Secretary of State would decline to confirm the c.p.o. if opposed on these grounds.

Subsection (8) provides that the blight provisions of section 192(1) of the Town and Country Planning Act 1971 (and section 181(1) of the Scottish Act of 1972) shall apply where an authority either serve a counter notice stating that they intend to acquire the land or fail to serve any counter notice. This enables a vendor within the qualifying categories—(*see below*) to require the authority to purchase his land, and this is achieved by inserting amongst the grounds on which a blight notice can be served under the Planning Acts sub-paragraphs (*a*) and (*b*) of this subsection.

The sections of the Planning Acts mentioned above set out a number of grounds on which certain persons can claim that their land has been blighted by the prospect of public acquisition.   Where such persons can show that despite reasonable endeavours they have been unable to sell their property except at a substantially lower price than they would otherwise have received they may serve a notice on the authority requiring them to purchase their land.   The authority must then either buy the land or declare that they do not propose to do so: in the latter event the blight will be removed and normal market conditions will prevail.   Subsection (8), by including in this category land in respect of which an authority have served a counter notice stating that they do intend to purchase—or in respect of which no counter notice has been served—gives these classes of persons the same rights.

The vendors within the qualifying categories are residential and agricultural owner-occupiers and owner-occupiers of other premises with a rateable value not exceeding £2,250.

Subsection (9) provides for penalties on persons who, without reasonable excuse, fail to give notice of a proposed disposal under subsection (5) or deliberately make false statements in such notices.   These penalties are:—

(i) on summary conviction, a fine not exceeding £400.

(ii) on indictment, an unlimited fine.

Subsection (10) provides that the failure to give notice under the section shall not of itself invalidate the transaction of which the notice should have been given.   This emphasises that a counter notice under subsection (7) is not a compulsory purchase order or notice to treat.   The vendor even after a counter notice may proceed with a private sale if his purchaser is willing.

SECTION 24.—REVOCATION OF DUTY TO NOTIFY

This section is supplementary to section 23 and enables an authority which has passed a resolution declaring a disposal notification area to pass a further resolution to the effect that all or part of it shall cease to be a disposal notification area. This may be necessary when all the development land in that area has passed into their ownership or when, for example, a change in planning strategy indicates that development is not after all to take place in some part of it.

Subsection (1) states that an authority who have passed a resolution declaring a disposal notification area may at any time pass a further resolution terminating all or part of that area.   The effect of such termination would be that disposal of material interests in land in that area (or part of it) would no longer need to be notified to authorities.

Subsection (2) provides that, as with an original declaration of a disposal notification area in Wales, the Land Authority must consult the local authorities concerned before passing a further resolution.

Subsection (3) applies the provisions of Part IV of Schedule 8 (publicity arrangements) on the termination of all or part of a disposal notification area.   These arrangements are similar to those provided on the original declaration of an area under section 23.

SECTION 25.—LAND COMPENSATION

This is one of the key sections of the Act because it provides the means by which the final transition to current use value is effected for all land compensation.

The section comes into effect on the second appointed day, which by virtue of section 7(3) cannot be until all relevant development has been designated by orders made under section 18 in all areas of Great Britain.

The provisions apply not only to compensation for compulsory purchase but also to all other statutory compensation based on the value of land. This is a reversal of the trend of recent years culminating in the Land Compensation Act 1973 which is to provide more and more compensation for private individuals injured by community activity. Negotiated settlements will follow suit since authorities will offer the same amount as if the land were being acquired compulsorily.

Current use value (C.U.V.) is basically the value of the land shorn of any value attributable to the hope that development would be permitted. It includes, however, any value due to the hope that development of any class specified in Schedule 1 to the Act (Exempt Development) would have been permitted and also any value due to a positive assumption (not merely hope) that development of any class specified in Schedule 8 to Town and Country Planning Act 1971 (or Schedule 6 of the Town and Country Planning (Scotland) Act 1972) would be permitted (unless permission has actually been refused for such development and compensation paid).

If a planning permission is suspended (under the provisions of sections 19-21) at the time when the compensation is assessed it is to be assumed that it was not granted. Value attributable to any unsuspended planning permission which is in force at the time, however, is included in current use value. Such planning permissions included in C.U.V. comprise also pre-first appointed day permissions if still in force (*e.g.* where development has begun); permissions granted on applications made on or after the first appointed day but before the bringing in of the section 21 prohibition and unsuspended by the action of the relevant authorities; and any permission which has become unsuspended by the bringing of the land into public ownership (this provides the basis for authorities to dispose of such land at full market value).

Special provisions are made for **charity land**. Current use value does not apply to the assessment of compensation in respect of an interest in land owned by a charity when the interest in question was owned by a charity on 12 September 1974 and continued to be owned by any charity—until the second appointed day or for eleven years, whichever may be the later date. Furthermore an interest in land is deemed to have been owned by a charity if they had either before or during this period entered into a binding contract to acquire the land or from the date of death of a testator devising land to them.

Charities will therefore continue to receive compensation at market value for a minimum period of eleven years from 12 September 1974. After that period they will be entitled to claim prevailing use value (*i.e.* compensation based on the land use prevailing in the neighbourhood) in respect of functional land held by them for seven years whenever acquired.

Provision is also made for the setting up of **hardship tribunals** to make additional payments where personal hardship is suffered as a result of the switch to C.U.V.

Subsection (1) stipulates that the provisions which make current use value (C.U.V.) of land the basis of compensation on public acquisition shall apply—

(*a*) where a notice to treat is served on or after the second appointed day whether under this or any other Act of Parliament, and

(*b*) in every other case where statutory compensation is payable on or after the second appointed day based directly or indirectly on the value of an interest in land. This means that C.U.V. will also apply to compensation for injurious affection where no land is actually acquired and to compensation for various planning restrictions such as the revocation or modification of planning permissions. It will not, however, apply to home-loss payments.

Subsection (2) lays down the assumptions to be made when calculating C.U.V. and provides for modifications of these in respect of certain charity lands.

Sub-paragraph (a) states that it must be assumed in calculating the C.U.V. of an interest in land that planning permission would not be granted in respect of that land or any other land. This assumption is not to apply (i) in the case specified in subsection (3), *i.e.* in respect of Exempt and Schedule 8 Development (*see below*), and (ii) in the cases specified in subsections (5) and (6) relating to charity land.

The prospect of development on other land can be an important source of development value (particularly in the case of compensation for severance and injurious affection) and must therefore be disregarded in assessing current use value.

Schedule 1 (Exempt Development) to the Act specifies certain minor classes of development. These are to be completely outside the scope of the acquisition power in section 15 and within current use value. For the purposes of this section the significant paragraph in Schedule 1 is paragraph 1 which covers development for which permission is granted by a General Development Order. The other two paragraphs in the Schedule (which are needed for the purpose of defining the scope of the acquisition power) are taken from Schedule 8 and therefore covered separately in this sub-paragraph.

Schedule 8 of the 1971 Act (and Schedule 6 of the Scottish Act of 1972) specify a number of classes of development which are not new development, including rebuilding with a limited increase in size. These formed the basis of existing use rights under the Town and Country Planning Act 1947 (or the Scottish Act of 1947) and have remained a basic element of the compensation code since then. It is therefore right that they should be included within the definition of current use value. Inclusion in Schedule 8 does not necessarily mean that a particular class of development can be carried out without the need to apply for planning permission. Permission would for example be needed for rebuilding, but compensation is payable if the planning permission is refused and the land acquired. Since these provisions are cases " where the value of an interest in land falls to be determined on the assumption that planning permission would be granted for development of any class specified in Schedule 8 " of the 1971 Act, section 278 and Schedule 18 of that Act have effect and amend Schedule 8 accordingly. (The corresponding references in the Town and Country Planning (Scotland) Act 1972 are to section 263, Schedule 16 and Schedule 6 respectively.) The effect of these provisions—which derive from the Town and Country Planning Act 1963—is to qualify the 10% cubic capacity tolerance in the original schedule by providing that it is to be assumed that only a 10% increase would be permitted in floorspace in any case.

Sub-paragraph (*b*) states that it must be assumed that any planning permission, which is suspended when the compensation is assessed, has not been granted. This assumption does not apply to any other—*i.e.* unsuspended—planning permission in force at the time. The assumption does not apply either in the case set out in subsection (5) below.

Certain planning permissions for relevant development may be in force at the second appointed day without being suspended either because they were obtained before the relevant date and the authorities did not acquire the land, or because they were obtained after the relevant date and the land was bought from an authority. In both cases it is right that any value attaching to such permissions should be included in current use value, in the first instance because the authorities have had the chance to buy the land and have declined it; in the second instance because otherwise authorities will be unable to sell land at a price including development value. Any planning permission granted on the basis of an application made before the first appointed day which is still in existence on the second appointed day will also be included in current use value as will any permissions for excepted development (*see* note on section 3) because these permissions cannot be suspended.

Subsection (3) provides that the assumption in subsection (2)(*a*) above (*i.e.* that planning permission has not been granted in all cases where notice to treat was served after the second appointed day) shall not apply to:—

(i) Exempt Development as specified in the 1st Schedule of the Act;

(ii) Development which is not new development as specified in Schedule 8, Town and Country Planning Act 1971 (Schedule 6 of the 1972 Scottish Act).

It must be noted that by virtue of section 15(3) of the Land Compensation Act 1961 there is a positive assumption that Schedule 8 development will be granted (even if likely to be refused) unless planning permission has in fact been refused and compensation paid.

Subsection (4) provides that for the purposes of both subsections (2)(*a*) and (3) above no account is to be taken of the following changes effected on or after the second appointed day:—

(*a*) any change made by an order under section 22, Town and Country Planning Act 1971 (section 19, Scottish Act 1972) in the uses of land not involving development, or

(*b*) any change made by the making, variation or revocation of a general development order, in the kinds of development falling within paragraph 1 of Schedule 1 (Exempt Development) to this Act.

Provision is also made for cases where the interest in land is being compulsorily acquired. If the notice of the making or preparation in draft of the compulsory purchase order was first published before the second appointed day, no account is to be taken of any of the changes specified in (i) and (ii) above if those changes were made on or after the date when the compulsory purchase order was published.

Paragraph 1 of Schedule 1 (Exempt Development) says that any development permitted by the General Development Order shall be exempt development. Section 22 of the 1971 Act itself provides that changes of use within a use class in a Use Classes Order are not development at all, and will thus be within C.U.V.

In order to avoid doubts about the level of C.U.V. it is necessary to ensure that those factors which affect the definition are " frozen " on the second appointed day. The subsection therefore provides that no account is to be taken of any change in the Use Classes Order which would reflect back into the deemed permission granted by the 1971 Act (sub-paragraph (*a*)) or in the General Development Order (sub-paragraph (*b*)).

Provision is also made in this subsection for cases where land is acquired by compulsory purchase. A person could well be put at a disadvantage if he decided not to object to a compulsory purchase order which was first published before the second appointed day and had based that decision on the assumption that he would get a certain level of compensation only to find that because of one of the changes specified in this subsection, which he could not have anticipated at that stage, his compensation was less than he had expected. Therefore it is provided that any such change made on or after the date when the compulsory purchase order was first published shall be disregarded in assessing the compensation.

Subsection (5) introduces an assumption of prevailing use value into the compensation to be paid for charity land in certain circumstances.

It is provided that where, during the whole period of 7 years immediately preceding the date at which compensation is to be assessed,—

(*a*) the interest has been owned by a charity (not necessarily the same charity throughout the 7 year period) and

(*b*) the land (as distinct from the rents and profits) has been used wholly or mainly for the purposes of a charity

then it is to be assumed that planning permission would be granted for any uses corresponding with that prevailing in respect of neighbouring land.

This assumption applies only to functional as distinct from investment land and it does not apply if the charity has the benefit of the assumption made in the next subsection which applies where the land has been owned by a charity for the longer period of 10 years.

This " prevailing use value " is given to charities in place of C.U.V. to meet one of the particular difficulties otherwise faced

by charities under the Act.   It meets the situation of a sale of
a redundant church building in a declining inner-city area from
whence most of the population has shifted.   Obviously the
C.U.V. of a church which nobody wants *qua* a church is
negligible.   Its disposal would certainly not provide the means
of building a new church in a suburb or new town to which the
population has gone.   Hence this subsection enables the
church to sell its land (not merely a building) to a public
authority at a price based on the permitted use of adjoining
land, be this residential, commercial or industrial.   In many
cases this would mean that provided the conditions of the
subsection are complied with a local authority could expect to
pay full market price inclusive of development value on the
acquisition of such sites.

It is to be noted that in contrast to the next subsection the
charity land need not have been held by any charity on 12
September 1974, but may have been acquired at any time
later.   It must have been held by a charity however for at
least 7 years.

Subsection (6) displaces in favour of charities all the assumptions laid down in subsection (2) (disregarding grants of
planning permissions) and in subsection (5) (prevailing use
value).

In consequence it restores the normal full market price
payable under the Land Acquisition Acts to charity land falling
within its provisions.

The limitations on its operation are that the land must be
held continuously by a charity (though not necessarily the same
charity throughout) from 12 September 1974 until a date
mentioned in subsection (1)(*a*) and (*b*) above (*i.e.* where compensation arises on or after the second appointed date.   This
period, during which a full open market price is payable, however, cannot exceed eleven years beyond 12 September 1974
or approximately ten years from the passing of the Act.

This period is considered sufficiently long by the Government to enable charities to arrange their assets before their
lands can be taken from them at C.U.V.   Of course, at the end
of the period the prevailing use value under subsection (5) will
apply in appropriate cases.

However, the churches and charities feel that this subsection does not go far enough to give them proper relief. The ten year period from enactment is in their view far too short given the extent of their holdings and the time it takes to make proposals for land development. The present national economic situation makes such planning even more difficult. In addition, the prospect of the value of land holdings dropping from market value to C.U.V. in 10 years' time has an immediate effect on the valuations of such land. The value will decline steadily and progressively to C.U.V. over the period. This will be severely prejudicial to the borrowing power of charities most of which is arranged against the security of their land values. Thus many charitable activities are bound to suffer as a result of the Act.

Subsection (7) for the purposes of subsections (5) and (6) above (assumptions in favour of charities) the qualifying periods for ownership will remain satisfied if any part is made up by—

(a) time during which the charity has entered into a binding contract to buy land (*i.e.* ownership dates from signing of contract and not conveyance);

(b) time during which the charity benefits as from the date of death of a testator (*i.e.* ownership dates from the death and not from actual assent or conveyance by the personal representatives following the rule that a " will speaks from death ").

Subsection (8) provides that this section shall have effect notwithstanding any provision in any other Act. The effect is to override all other statutory assumptions as to planning permission; except where this would result in greater compensation being paid under this Act (*see* subsection (10), below).

Subsection (9) provides that the various planning assumptions contained in the Land Compensation Act 1961 (and the corresponding Scottish Act 1963) for the purpose of assessing compensation for compulsory purchase shall not have effect as regards planning permission for development. They will, however, continue to apply in the assessment of compensation as regards Exempt Development and Schedule 8 development (*see also* section 26(8)(*b*)).

Subsection (10) provides this section shall not apply in such a manner as to produce a higher compensation than would otherwise be payable under earlier statutes. This might otherwise be possible with regards compensation for depreciation in land value caused by public works under section 5, Land Compensation Act 1973 (and the corresponding Scotland Act).

Thus the effect of this subsection combined with subsection (1)(*b*) is that the Act not only enables public authorities to buy up private land cheaply but it destroys ' at a stroke ' the compensation provisions laboriously built up over the years in favour of private citizens injured by public authority activity. This is a far cry from ' returning to the community the value created by the community '.

SECTION 26.—COMPENSATION PAYABLE IN TRANSACTIONS BETWEEN CERTAIN AUTHORITIES

In the transitional period between the first and second appointed days the basis of compensation for land acquired compulsorily by authorities and by the Crown from the private sector or any other public body will continue to be market value, but the actual cost of land to the authorities will be reduced by enabling them to buy at a price which excludes the amount of development land tax which would have been payable had the vendor sold privately. Authorities will not themselves be liable to development land tax either on the carrying out of development or on the disposal of land. (These transitional arrangements will appear in the Development Land Tax Act.)

The Government has under consideration that this valuation basis which applies where an authority acquires land from the private sector should also apply to transactions between authorities, *i.e.* the purchasing authority will pay market value less an amount equivalent to the tax which would have been payable had the land been owned by someone not exempt from paying tax.

It is possible that the exercise of compulsory purchase powers by one authority against another, at present extremely rare, may become more frequent particularly as it is provided in section 41, compulsory purchase orders in such circumstances are no longer subject to special parliamentary procedure after confirmation.

If it is finally decided that the price for land transferred within the public sector is to be on the same basis as for acquisition from private owners it will be necessary for section 5 of the Land Compensation Act 1961 and section 12 of the Land Compensation (Scotland) Act 1963 to be modified in order that the rules for the assessment of compensation in the case of such transfers produce a " net of notional tax " result. These modifications cannot be spelt out in this Act because the final terms of the Development Land Tax Bill, on which the framing of those modifications depends, will not be settled until that Bill is enacted.   The modifications will also provide the basis for achieving the same result in the case of sales and purchases by agreement between authorities, the practice being to relate the consideration for such transfers to the compensation which would have been payable if the land were being acquired compulsorily.

Therefore this section provides a general power to modify by regulations the basis of compensation where land is acquired by one authority from another.

Subsection (1) provides that the section applies to compulsory acquisitions—

(*a*) where notice to treat was served on or after the first appointed day;

(*b*) the person from whom the interest is being acquired is a local or new town authority, the Land Authority for Wales, the Peak Park Joint or Lake District Planning Board or a joint board established under section 2 of the Act or a body specified in an order made by the Secretary of State; and

(*c*) the person acquiring the interest is a body mentioned in paragraph (*b*) or a Minister.

Subsection (2) empowers the Secretary of State to make an order modifying the rules in the Land Compensation Acts for the purpose of assessing compensation where the compulsory acquisition falls within this section. The modifications may be such as the Secretary of State considers it expedient to make.

Subsection (3) makes such an order subject to the consent of the Treasury and approval by both Houses of Parliament.

SECTION 27.—FINANCIAL HARDSHIP TRIBUNALS

This section contains the enabling powers for the Secretary of State to set up tribunals to consider cases of financial hardship arising from the change in the compensation code on the second appointed day.

Undoubtedly difficulties will arise from this change and individual cases of financial hardship are bound to result from the scheme. The compensation code was painstakingly built up over the years and modified as new circumstances of injustice to private individuals came to light as a result of public authority acquisition or works. This code disappears not only for acquisition but for incidental compensation such as injurious affection.

However, the Government is in a dilemma since to seek to alleviate hardship could result in the tribunals restoring indirectly development values and so derogate from the basic principle of current use value. A limit is accordingly set to the amount that can be awarded in any one case, £50,000 initially, but with provision for adjustment when necessary. The section is in fact very widely drawn so as to give the Secretary of State the greatest freedom of action in the light of experience.

Subsection (1) enables the Secretary of State to make regulations setting up a hardship tribunal or tribunals. This may be done either by constituting a new body or bodies or by conferring the functions of a financial hardship tribunal on an existing body or bodies. The regulation making power includes the power to specify the functions of the proposed tribunals. By virtue of subsection (10) any such regulations would be subject to affirmative resolution.

It will be seen that all the options are left open as to the type of body to be used to discharge the functions of processing individual hardship claims.

In particular, the Secretary of State will be able to consider whether an entirely new body should be set up or whether the functions might be conferred on an existing body or bodies with relevant experience. Tribunals could be nationally or locally constituted and separate tribunals could be set up for Wales and Scotland.

Subsection (2) enables the Secretary of State to make regulations providing for the membership and chairing of the tribunal and setting out the terms of appointment, pay, pensions, etc.

Subsection (3) provides that appointments are to be made by the Secretary of State and that he is to determine pay, pensions, etc., subject to the approval of the Minister for the Civil Service.

These are standard provisions for setting up bodies of this sort. By virtue of subsection (11) these regulations would be subject to negative resolution.

Subsection (4) provides the right to apply for the award of an additional payment to anyone who claims he has suffered financial hardship as a result of the change in the compensation code brought about by section 25 on the second appointed day. The financial hardship must, however, have been caused by an alteration in the amount of compensation payable to him " or for his benefit ". This latter phrase would include, for example, beneficiaries under trusts. Applications will be subject to the provisions of procedural regulations made by virtue of subsections (1) and (8)(*a*).

The right does not arise until the basis of the compensation code changes on the second appointed day. Therefore hardship cannot be claimed during the transitional period. However, the distinction in terms of hardship between compensation at market price nett of development land tax at 80% to 100% and compensation at current use value is difficult to see. The section has been drafted in terms that make it clear that hardship awards are special payments and not of statutory compensation.

Subsection (5) requires the tribunal to make an order specifying the amount of the additional payment which it considers should be made if it is satisfied that the claim is justified and that an additional payment should be made.   In reaching its decision the tribunal will have to refer to the criteria prescribed by the Secretary of State under subsection (8)(*d*).

This reduces the odds in favour of the individual since not only must he demonstrate to the satisfaction of a tribunal that he has suffered financial hardship but also that the hardship was severe enough to justify an additional payment and was not self-inflicted.

Subsection (6) provides that the person who is responsible for paying the compensation must also pay the additional amount specified in any order made under subsection (5).   By virtue of the Interpretation Act the term person includes an authority.

As the payment ordered by the tribunal will be an addition to the compensation payable for acquisition the same authority should be responsible for making both payments, and to the same person.

Subsection (7) provides that the payment shall be due three months after service of a copy of the tribunal's order on the authority.   If for any reason there should be any delay in making the payment interest will be incurred.   The rate of interest will be that laid down in regulations made under section 32 of the Land Compensation Act 1961 (section 40 of the Land Compensation (Scotland) Act 1963) which apply where entry has been made on land before the payment of compensation.   The current rate of interest is $12\frac{1}{2}\%$.

Three months is a standard period for such purposes (*cf.* sections 32(2) and 52(4) of the Land Compensation Act 1973— home loss payments and advance payments of compensation respectively—sections 29(2) and 48(2) of the Land Compensation (Scotland) Act 1973.

Subsection (8) provides that regulations made under this section can cover:—

    (*a*) the procedure of the tribunals.   The procedural regulations would need to cover the manner in which applications were made and considered, rights of applicants to be heard, what evidence could be adduced, etc.

(b) the method by which applicants will be able to obtain certificates of appropriate alternative development in support of their applications notwithstanding the change in the compensation code effected by section 25. By virtue of section 25(9), the Land Compensation Act 1961, Part III (Land Compensation (Scotland) Act 1963, Part IV), which deal with certificates of appropriate alternative development, cease to have effect in so far as they include the value attributable to the prospect of development being permitted in the assessment of compensation. However, in putting his case before a tribunal an applicant is enabled by this subsection (26(8)(b)) to draw upon the certificate procedure with appropriate modifications in order to establish what level of compensation he might have received if the compensation code had remained unaltered. If such a provision were not made it would be difficult to determine the precise effect which the change in the compensation code had produced on the compensation payable to him.

(c) the claim to be made by the personal representatives of a deceased person.

(d) the criteria by which a tribunal will determine applications. The tribunal will need clear guide lines so as to determine for example what type of individual circumstances might be held to constitute hardship. The Secretary of State is therefore given the power to prescribe criteria in the regulations. It is difficult to forecast what type of circumstances might constitute financial hardship and so the power is widely drawn to permit a flexible approach to the problem. By virtue of subsection (10) the regulations will be subject to affirmative resolution.

Subsection (9) sets a limit of £50,000 to the amount a tribunal can award in respect of any one claim. There is power to increase the limit by regulations made with the approval of the Treasury.

The limits are set to the amount that can be awarded to prevent the possibility of financial hardship tribunals becoming a means of preserving substantial tranches of development value for the benefit of individuals.   The power to increase the limits will probably be used to take account of inflation.

Subsection (10) provides that regulations establishing a hardship tribunal, or conferring its functions on another body or prescribing the criteria by which applications are to be determined shall require affirmative resolution.

Subsection (11) provides that any other regulations made under this section will be the subject of negative resolution.

Subsection (12) provides that the tribunals will also be able to deal with claims in respect of acquisitions by government departments and that any amounts awarded should be provided for out of the appropriate departmental votes.

Subsection (13) provides that the Secretary of State shall be responsible for the expenses of a financial hardship tribunal out of his departmental vote.

Subsection (14) provides for the insertion of a Financial Hardship Tribunal in Part II of Schedule I to the House of Commons Disqualification Act 1975.   It applies to Northern Ireland as does the Disqualification Act.

PART IV—UNOCCUPIED OFFICE PREMISES

Office premises left standing empty for many years since they were completed, thus increasing in capital value, at least on paper, as the rents that could be obtained on a new letting spiralled upwards, gave rise to a great deal of public comment and concern.   They were regarded as an extravagant waste of national resources whilst homelessness was growing through insufficient provision.

Centre Point became a focal point and symbol for all that was considered wrong in property speculation.

The political parties were not insensitive to the growing media comment.

The previous Conservative Government proposed in their Housing and Planning Bill, lost on the dissolution of Parliament in February 1974, that the Secretary of State should have compulsory powers to take over the management of such premises and to let them.   This proposal followed the enactment of section 16 of the Local Government Act 1974 which provides for a progressive surcharge (double, treble, quadruple (and so on) the normal rates) over and above the half rating provisions for unoccupied property in the General Rate Act 1967, in respect of unused commercial buildings.

Part IV of the Community Land Act goes far beyond powers of management and, letting.   It gives the Secretary of State general **powers to acquire** such premises by compulsory purchase where they contain more than 5,000 sq. metres of floor space and have never been more than 25% occupied for at least two years from the date of construction.   The compensation payable on compulsory purchase to be related to the value of the building at the time when it was completed, if that is less than the value at the time of acquisition.

The problem of unoccupied offices has always been seen as primarily a Central London problem but the provisions of Part IV are framed in general terms and can thus be applied throughout Great Britain.

The main provisions are contained in section 28 (power for the Secretary of State to acquire unoccupied office premises) and section 29 (special basis of compensation on compulsory acquisition).   Section 30 enables the Secretary of State to acquire additional land to help in disposing of premises acquired under section 28.   Section 31 applies the Acquisition of Land Acts.   The remaining sections, 32-36, are supplementary and largely formal.

SECTION 28—POWER TO ACQUIRE UNOCCUPIED OFFICE PREMISES

This section contains powers for the Secretary of State to acquire by agreement, or in certain circumstances compulsorily, any building comprising more than 5,000 square metres (approximately 50,000 square feet) of office accommodation where 75 per cent. of that accommodation has been unoccupied for two years or more since the building was erected.

Subsection (1) defines " office building " as a building which consists of office accommodation occupying more than 5,000 square metres of floor space.   It then provides that the section applies to land on which such an office building has been erected, whether before or after the passing of the Act, and to any other land used or intended for use for the purposes of the building (*e.g.* residential accommodation for a caretaker, access land, courtyards, car parks).

The figure of 5,000 square metres is arbitrary.   The long-term unoccupation of smaller premises, can be dealt with by rating surcharge under section 16, Local Government Act 1974.

Subsection (2) enables the Secretary of State to acquire any land to which the section applies if he is satisfied that at least 75 per cent. of the office accommodation calculated by reference to floor space has remained unoccupied for the whole of the period mentioned in subsection (3) and that period is not less than two years.

Subsection (3) defines the period (not less than two years) during the whole of which 75 per cent. of the office accommodation must have been unoccupied (but occupation for less than six months can be ignored—*see* section 32(2)).   The period (*a*) begins with the " completion date " as defined in subsection (7) of section 28 (*see* section 33 for determination of that date) and (*b*) ends with the date of a binding contract to purchase the land or with the first formal step in the compulsory purchase procedure, *i.e.* the first publication of notice that a compulsory purchase order has been prepared in draft.

Subsection (4) excludes from the power of. compulsory acquisition (except in the particular circumstances mentioned in section 30—Additional powers of acquisition), but not from acquisition by agreement, (*a*) the interest of any person who is occupying and effectively using any part of the office building in accordance with planning permission and (*b*) any interest in the land if the Secretary of State is satisfied that the person entitled to possession of the office accommodation has tried his best to let it (*see* subsection (5)).

Paragraph (*a*) covers the case where the premises may comprise some accommodation which is subleased and which is occupied and effectively used but which forms less than 25% of the whole premises. The effect of the subsection is that while in these circumstances compulsory acquisition may include the head lease it may not include the interest of the actual occupier—so long as he is effectively using the accommodation for the purpose for which planning permission was given.

Subsection (5). In determining under the preceding subsection whether a person entitled to possession of unoccupied office accommodation has done his best to let it, the Secretary of State must have regard to the following factors, *inter alia,*

(*a*) the rent sought compared with general levels of rent;

(*b*) the covenants in the lease being insisted upon;

(*c*) whether there have been indications to prospective lessees that there may be lettings of the accommodation in parts;

(*d*) the number and resources of the estate agents retained for letting;

(*e*) the nature and extent of advertising the accommodation.

The intention behind this subsection is to ensure that the premises are not kept empty by the lessor asking unduly harsh or onerous terms which no one could be expected to accept, or by not taking all reasonable steps to try to find a lessee or lessees. It does seem to be objectionable, however, that the Secretary of State shall exercise judgment on the competence of the lessor's professional agents in determining whether the lessor is genuinely trying to let.

The factors set out above are taken from section 17A(5) inserted in the General Rate Act 1967 by section 16, Local Government Act 1974, where the same question is determined in relation to the liability for rating surcharge on unused commercial buildings.

Subsection (6) defines " floor space " (*i.e.* for the purpose of calculating the 5,000 square metres as gross floor space by external measurement walls, if any.

Subsection (7) makes it clear that " erection " of an office building includes conversion of a building into an office building by extension, alteration or re-erection.

Subsection (8) defines " completion date " as used in sub-section (3)(*a*) and in section 29.   It covers the two situations (*a*) where the office building consists only of office accommodation, (*b*) where the office building comprises also other accommodation, *e.g.* flats, shops.   In case (*a*) the completion date is when the building was completed;   in case (*b*) it is when the part of the building which consists of office accommodation was completed.

Subsection (9) precludes the initiation of compulsory purchase proceedings until one month after the passing of the Act. This is standard for provisions of this kind.

SECTION 29.—AMOUNT OF COMPENSATION PAYABLE ON COMPULSORY ACQUISITION UNDER SECTION 28

As the purpose is to deter the keeping of large new office premises deliberately unoccupied, the threat of compulsory acquisition, is coupled with a penal level of compensation.

Under the Land Compensation Acts the basis for compensation for the acquisition of land is the market value current at the date of assessment of the compensation, or of taking possession if earlier.   This section departs from this principle and bases the compensation on the value of the building at the date of construction taking into account any subsequent alterations.

Subsection (1) states that where the interest acquired is an unincumbered freehold interest in the whole of the land, the compensation will be the market value at the date of completion of the building. If it should so happen that the value of the interest at the time of acquisition had fallen below the value at the completion date the compensation would be at the lower value (*see* subsection (5)). (For determination of date of completion, *see* section 33.)

Subsection (2) states that where the land has been leased, sublet or mortgaged, the amount of the compensation for each interest acquired is to be determined by the formula set out in the subsection. This is designed to divide the unincumbered freehold value as above between the various interests, in the proportion which the current value of each interest bears to the aggregate current value of all the interests. The formula takes into account any enhancement by way of alteration since the building was completed but the additional value is also scaled down.

The stages in the process of determination of compensation will run in the following way (using the letters in the formula)—

(i) Ascertain market value, under the normal compensation code, at the " material date " (*see* subsection (4)), of each interest (I) and the aggregate of all interests (A) actually existing in the land which are capable of being acquired under section 28 or otherwise. (The interest of a tenant in possession of land comprised in the order would still have to be valued even though it was not being acquired—*see* section 28, subsection (4)(*a*).)

(ii) Ascertain the value of the freehold interest (F) subject to any easements and restrictive covenants binding the freehold at the material date but free from any other incumbrances (*e.g.* mortgages, leases and tenancies), but this value to be assessed by reference to prices current at the completion date, and not those current at the material date.

(iii) To determine the compensation (C) for a particular interest divide I by A and multiply by F.

Example:

Current market value of a particular leasehold interest	£100,000	I
Current market value of all interests	£10,000,000	A
Value of unincumbered freehold interest in whole of land at completion date	£6,000,000	F

Applying the formula, the amount of compensation (C) payable for an interest with a current market value

$$I = \frac{I}{A} \times F$$

$$= £\frac{100,000}{10,000,000} \times £6,000,000 = £60,000.$$

Subsection (3) deals with the compulsory acquisition of the interest of a mortgagee. The general effect of the normal provisions for compulsory purchase of a mortgaged interest under the Compulsory Purchase Act 1965 is that where the principal, interest and costs do not exceed the value of the mortgaged land those sums shall be paid to the mortgagee. If the value of the land is less than the principal, interest and costs secured on it the sum agreed between the parties (mortgagor, mortgagee and authority) or assessed by the Lands Tribunal is paid to the mortgagee in part satisfaction of the mortgage debt. This leaves the mortgagee his contractual remedies against the mortgagor. The money is paid direct to the mortgagee, to ensure the mortgage is discharged.

The effect of subsection (3) is to retain this rule for the payment of the value of principal, interest and costs to the mortgagee, but to ensure, where the formula reduces the value of the mortgagor's interest below the sums secured, that no more money is paid to the mortgagee than the total payable to the mortgagor. Even though the compensation payable to the mortgagor is reduced by the formula the Secretary of State will pay to the mortgagee compensation up to the value of the mortgagee's interest (not reduced by the formula) so long as it does not exceed the value of the mortgagor's interest as reduced.

Example:

Value of building in 1965	£50,000
Value of building in 1975	£100,000
Value of mortgage in 1975	£60,000

The sum paid to the mortgagee is £50,000. His interest is **not** reduced by the formula.

The intention is that the mortgagor should not be able to take advantage of a collusive mortgage.

Subsection (4) contains definitions of various terms used in section 29. They are self-explanatory.

Subsection (5) provides if, apart from section 29, the compensation payable would be less than it is under section 29, then that lower figure is the amount of compensation. (This circumstance might arise if the current market value is **lower** at the material date than at the date of completion.)

Subsection (6) clarifies that the assessment of compensation for disturbance, severance, injurious affection or any other matter not directly based on the value of an interest in land compulsorily acquired is not subject to diminution under the special compensation provisions.

SECTION 30.—ADDITIONAL POWERS OF ACQUISITION

This section enables the Secretary of State to acquire the interests of persons otherwise excluded from acquisition under section 28(4)(*a*) where inability to acquire such an interest would frustrate the disposal of the remainder of the office building to be acquired (*e.g.* if the owner of the office block had so arranged things that the only access to the empty office accommodation was through the occupied part and the owner had deliberately or inadvertently failed to reserve a right of way).

Subsection (1) accordingly provides that the Secretary of State may acquire by agreement or compulsorily any other land if he is satisfied that it is necessary to do so in order to facilitate the disposal of land he has acquired or proposes to acquire under section 28.

Neither the special compensation provisions in section 29 nor the exclusion in section 31(2) from the normal obligation to specify the purpose for which the land is required, applies to the acquisition of land under this power.

Subsection (2) follows section 28(8) in providing that compulsory purchase procedures cannot commence until one month after the Act is passed.

SECTION 31.—APPLICATION OF ACQUISITION OF LAND ACTS, ETC.

This section ensures that the normal compulsory purchase code under the Acquisition of Land Acts (not the modified code contained in Schedule 4 of this Act) applies to unoccupied office buildings except to the extent of removing any obligation to specify the purpose for which the land is required. It follows that there will be invariably a public enquiry into the exercise of powers under this part of the Act.

Subsection (1) applies the Acquisition of Land Acts and so obliges the Secretary of State to serve on owners, lessees and certain occupiers of the land proposed to be acquired a notice stating that a compulsory purchase order has been prepared in draft and affording such persons an opportunity to make objections. If there is an objection the Secretary of State will be obliged to hold a public local inquiry or offer the objector an opportunity of being heard before deciding whether to make the order or not.

Subsection (2) excludes the need to state the purpose for which the land is required. This prevents the order being frustrated by occupation of the building as offices after publication of the draft order and before acquisition.

Subsection (3) applies all the provisions of Part I of the Compulsory Purchase Act 1965 to purchases by agreement in the same way as if the land were being acquired compulsorily. The most important effect is that the Secretary of State will be enabled to override restrictive covenants affecting the land, on due payment of compensation, without having to resort to compulsory purchase or apply to the Lands Tribunal to suspend the covenants.

Subsection (4) has the same effect in relation to land in Scotland acquired by agreement under section 28 by applying the relevant Scottish enactments.

SECTION 32.—ASSUMPTIONS AS TO OCCUPATION

This section lays down assumptions by which the Secretary of State may satisfy himself that the requisite accommodation has in fact been unoccupied for the whole of the necessary period.   To do this it makes use of the rating provisions under which similar considerations apply in the case of the rating of unoccupied property under the General Rate Act 1967 (the Local Government (Scotland) Act 1966).   However, all without prejudice to the establishment of unoccupancy by any other means.

Subsection (1) entitles the Secretary of State to assume that where the person entitled to possession of an office building or part of it has been rated under Schedule 1 to the General Rate Act 1967 (section 24, Local Government (Scotland) Act 1966) (rating of unoccupied property) for any period, the building remained unoccupied for the whole of that period, or (as the case may be) from the beginning of it until notice was given to the rating authority that the building had become occupied.

Subsection (2) is designed to prevent the frustration of an acquisition by short-term occupancy.   It provides that occupation for a period of less than six months, followed by unoccupation, counts as if the building had not been occupied during that period and does not therefore save the building from liability to compulsory purchase.   (This follows the precedent of paragraph 1(3) of Schedule 1 to the General Rate Act 1967.)

SECTION 33.—DETERMINATION OF DATE OF COMPLETION

This section establishes the date when the erection of the building is to be treated as completed for purposes of section

28 (period of unoccupation) and section 29 (date for compensation).

Subsection (1) provides that where the erection of an office building has been treated as completed on any date for the purposes of Schedule 1 to the General Rate Act 1967 (Schedule 3, Local Government (Scotland) Act 1966) relating to the rating of unoccupied property, the building shall also be deemed to have been completed on that date for this Act subject to the subsequent subsections which may provide an earlier date.

Subsection (2) provides that the Secretary of State may serve on every person entitled to possession of any part of an office building a " completion notice " specifying the date on which the erection of the building is to be deemed to have been completed for this Act.

Subsection (3) makes a notice served under subsection (2) above override the completion date deemed under subsection (1).

The reason for this is that the rating provisions provide that the completion date stated in a completion notice under those provisions may be either the date of service of the notice or such later date as may be specified by the notice, *i.e.* the date cannot be retrospective.   However, office premises may in fact have been completed some time before service of a completion notice under the rating provisions.   Subsection (3) therefore provides that the completion date specified in a completion notice under subsection (2) may only be earlier than the date established for the purposes of the rating provisions.

Subsection (4) provides that if the Secretary of State and every person entitled to possession of any part of the office building agree a date in writing, that date becomes the completion date for the purpose of this Part, and the completion notice is withdrawn.   This subsection, and paragraph (*b*) of subsection (5), enable the appeal procedure in subsection (6) to be avoided if all concerned agree on a completion date.

Subsection (5) enables the Secretary of State to withdraw a completion date notice so as to alter the date.   He may serve a substitute notice at any time before an appeal against the original notice is brought to the county court under subsection (6) (such an appeal must be made within 21 days after the service of the completion notice) or with the agreement of all parties at any time thereafter before any such appeal is determined.

Subsection (6) provides that any person on whom a completion notice is served may appeal to the county court within 21 days on the ground that the erection of the building was not completed by the date specified in the notice.

Subsection (7) provides that if a completion notice is not withdrawn then—

(a) if there is no appeal under subsection (6), or if an appeal is made but abandoned or dismissed, the erection of the building is deemed to have been completed on the date specified in the notice;

(b) if an appeal is made but not abandoned or dismissed the erection of the building will be deemed to have been completed on a date determined by the court.

Subsection (8) makes provision for the case where an office building the subject of a completion notice is not entirely completed in the sense that before it can be effectively used as office accommodation certain relatively minor work needs to be carried out, *e.g.* to adapt it to the specific requirements of any firm which may take a lease. By virtue of this subsection the determination of the date on which the erection of the building was completed is to include such period, after erection would otherwise be deemed to have been completed, as was " reasonably required " for carrying out that kind of work.

It is a frequent practice in speculative office building without particular tenants in mind to construct the building leaving internal walls to be fitted to meet the needs of tenants as and when they are found. This work still to be done will not prevent the building from being treated as completed for the purposes of acquisition under the Act.

Subsection (9) provides that unless the context otherwise requires references in section 33 to an office building include references to part of such a building.

It relates the ascertainment of a completion date (whether by notice or otherwise) to the combined effect of section 28(3) and (7). These enable the Secretary of State to acquire an office building where the erection of the part of it which consists of office accommodation has been completed but the erection of the part consisting of other accommodation has not. Otherwise a developer could escape Part IV by leaving the " non-office " part of the building half built.

SECTION 34.—POWER TO OBTAIN INFORMATION

This section is designed to enable the Secretary of State to obtain the information needed to ensure he may properly acquire office accommodation. The powers are similar to those in section 284 of the Town and Country Planning Act 1971, under which the occupier or any person who directly or indirectly receives rent in respect of any premises may be required to state the nature of his interest and particulars of any other person known to him as having an interest. This section (section 34) goes further and includes powers to demand information other than information about the ownership of interests and to demand the production of documents as evidence of leases, dispositions, and interests in the building.

Subsection (1) sets out the categories of person on whom notice may be served requiring them to give information.

Subsection (2) states the kinds of information which may be specified or described in such a notice. Paragraphs (*a*) and (*b*) relate to the nature of the interests held by the person to whom the notice is addressed and the identity of other interest holders. Paragraph (*c*) provides for such other information as the Secretary of State may reasonably require. What is " reasonable " is in the last resort a matter for the Courts.

Subsection (3) provides that a notice under subsection (1) must give at least 14 days for compliance and may specify the manner of compliance.

Subsection (4) enables a notice to require the addressee to state whether he has any document in his possession or under his control which is itself, or is evidence of, any lease or other disposition in the building, and to produce such document to a duly authorised officer of the Secretary of State. The notice may also require facilities to be afforded for making extracts from or taking copies of a document.

Subsection (5) preserves the confidentiality between solicitor and client in relation to any privileged communication made to the solicitor.

Subsection (6) provides for penalties for refusal or (without reasonable excuse) failure to comply with a notice under this section, and for knowingly or recklessly making any false statement or producing any false document with intent to deceive. The penalties are £400 fine on summary conviction or an unlimited fine or imprisonment of up to two years or both on indictment.

SECTION 35.—POWERS OF ENTRY

This section is complementary to section 34 and gives powers of entry for inspection where the information provided in response to notices may not be sufficient to establish for example whether or not the building is 75 per cent. unoccupied. It may also be necessary to examine a building to ascertain whether it constitutes an " office building " and whether it has been completed within the meaning of Part IV or what works remain to be done if its erection has been substantially completed. More generally the Secretary of State may need first-hand information and advice on the economic and practical aspects of acquisition and disposal which can be obtained only on the basis of a detailed examination and survey. Similar powers are given by section 280(1) and (8), and section 281(1) and (2) of the Town and Country Planning Act 1971.

Subsection (1) enables any person authorised in writing by the Secretary of State to enter any office building, or any building which the Secretary of State reasonably believes to be an office building, at any reasonable time for the purpose of examining and surveying it.

Subsection (2) provides that evidence of authorisation to enter a building must be produced if required, and that at least seven days' notice must be given before admission can be demanded as of right.

Subsection (3) prescribes a maximum fine of £100 on summary conviction where a duly authorised person is wilfully obstructed in the execution of his powers to enter and examine or survey an office building.

SECTION 36.—SERVICE OF NOTICES

This section sets out the methods by which proper service of notices authorised to be served under Part IV may be effected, *i.e.* notices under sections 33(2) and (5) (completion notices), 34(1) (information) and 35(2) (entry for examination and survey). It is based on the provisions in section 283 of the Town and Country Planning Act 1971 (section 269 of the Town and Country Planning (Scotland) Act 1972).

The service upon owners, lessees and certain occupiers of notice that a compulsory purchase order has been prepared in draft is governed by Schedule 1 to the Acquisition of Land Acts applied by section 31.

Subsection (1) provides that a notice may be served by delivering it to the person upon whom it is to be served, by leaving it at his usual or last known place of abode, or by sending it to him at that address by registered or recorded delivery letter. In the case of an incorporated company or other body service may be effected by personal delivery or registered or recorded delivery letter addressed to the secretary or clerk of the company at their registered or principal office.

Subsection (2) covers the case where a notice is required to be served on any person as having an interest in (*e.g.* section 34(1)(*a*)) or being entitled to possession of the whole or any part of an office building (*e.g.* section 33(2)) but reasonable attempts to ascertain his name and address have failed. In that event the notice may be either (*a*) addressed to the person by name or simply to " the owner " or " the person entitled to possession " as the case may be and delivered or sent by the methods in subsection (1), or (*b*) having been addressed in that way and plainly marked as a communication of importance it may be sent by registered or recorded delivery letter, or handed to anyone in the building or affixed to the building in some conspicuous position.

PART V.—MISCELLANEOUS

This part of the Act deals with miscellaneous matters, and in particular contains provisions concerning the land transactions of authorities.

SECTION 37.—ACQUISITION AND DISPOSAL OF LAND BY THE CROWN

This section extends the powers of the Secretary of State to acquire land " for the public service "—in practice normally for Government offices. Additional powers are also given to facilitate disposals.

The basic power to acquire land by agreement for this purpose is section 2 of the Commissioners of Works Act 1852; powers of compulsory acquisition are given by section 113 of the Town and Country Planning Act 1971 (section 103, Scotland Act 1972). Now the definition of " public service " used in these statutes is widened in order to strengthen the powers of the Secretary of State to acquire land. The power of the Secretary of State to dispose of land is also extended so as to enable him to secure that the development of land for the public service (as extended) can be carried out by a purchaser or lessor.

The effect of the section, taken together with the legislation that it amends, will be that the Secretary of State will have the following additional powers:—

(a) Power to acquire (by agreement or compulsorily) land—

(i) which is not itself required " for the public service " (the crucial words of the parent legislation) but which ought to be included in the scheme of development for environmental reasons or to ensure the most economic form of development.

    (ii) with a view to mixed public and private develop-
ment, if that is best for environmental reasons or
to ensure the most economic form of development.

    (iii) which is to replace public open space and
similar land required for public service use.

    (iv) required for use by international organisations
of which this country is, or is to become, a
member.

(*b*) Power to acquire (by agreement)—

    (i) land not itself required for the public service
but needed to facilitate the disposal of land
already owned by the Secretary of State.

    (ii) public service land in advance of requirements.

(*c*) Power to dispose of land to a private developer who
will carry out the development required, *e.g.* under a
lease and lease-back arrangement.

Subsection (1) provides that where the Secretary of State is
acquiring or has acquired, by agreement or compulsorily, land
necessary for the public service, additional land (*i.e.* land not
itself necessary for the public service) may also be acquired in
the following instances:—

(*a*) in the interests of the proper planning of the area
where the public service land is situated, *e.g.* so as to
include in an office development scheme additional land
needed for environmental reasons.

(*b*) to ensure that the public service land can be used or
developed and used in the best or most economic way.

(*c*) to replace land acquired for the public service which
forms part of a common, open space or fuel or field
garden allotment.

Subsection (2) extends the definition in the parent legislation
of land necessary for the public service to include land which it
is proposed to develop for mixed public and private use where

the private element of the development is justified by planning considerations or would secure the best or most economic development or use of the land, *e.g.* land for building of shops on the ground floor and Government offices on the other floors.   Subsection (2) therefore deals with the case where the land being acquired for the public service is **itself** to be used or developed also for non-public service use.   Subsection (1) deals with the case where the land wanted for the non-public service use is **additional** to that wanted for the public service use.

Subsection (3) includes within the scope of the Secretary of State's power to acquire land necessary for the public service the acquisition of land for the service: (*a*) of any international organisation or institution of which the United Kingdom is either already a member, or is proposing to become a member; and (*b*) of any subordinate office or agency established by such an international organisation or institution or established by a treaty to which the United Kingdom is or is to become a party.

The provision will, for example, enable the Secretary of State to provide land for an international organisation that wishes (with Government support) to establish its headquarters in the United Kingdom.   Power of compulsory acquisition is given by this subsection, but it is envisaged that land would normally be acquired by agreement.

Subsection (4) extends the power of the Secretary of State to acquire land by agreement so as to include the acquisition of land adjoining public service land in order to facilitate disposal of the land he already owns.   This is merely to facilitate good estate management.

Subsection (5) allows for the acquisition of land by agreement in advance of requirements.   Any land acquired in this way may then be used as the Secretary of State decides until required for the public service.   This again is for good estate management.

Subsection (6) enables the Secretary of State to dispose of land acquired under the parent legislation (as extended by this section) to a private developer who is to carry out the development required.   It also gives the Secretary of State power to dispose of office buildings acquired by him under Part IV (Unoccupied Office Premises).

Subsection (7) provides for the coming into force of the clause one month after the passing of the Act.

Subsection (8) provides that any expenditure incurred in the exercise of these powers shall be met from money provided by Parliament.

SECTION 38.—ACQUISITION OF LAND BY CROWN IN NORTHERN IRELAND

This section amends the law of Northern Ireland so that the power to acquire land for the public service is extended to the acquisition of land for the service of international organisations in Northern Ireland.   It is analogous to section 37(3).

Subsection (1) extends the relevant provisions in the way indicated above.

Subsection (2) lists the relevant provisions of Northern Ireland legislation.   These are:—

  (*a*) section 5 of the Stormont Regulation and Government Property Act (Northern Ireland) 1933;

  (*b*) Article 65 of the Land Acquisition and Compensation (Northern Ireland) Order 1973.

Subsection (3) provides for the application of the section to Northern Ireland.   (The Act does not generally extend to Northern Ireland.)

Subsection (4) provides for the coming into force of the clause one month after the passing of the Act.

SECTION 39.—APPLICATION OF ACT TO CROWN LAND

This section sets out the circumstances in which the provisions of the Act may apply to Crown or Duchy Land.   Normally it is exempt but this section applies the Act where there are private interests owned in such Land.

Subsection (1) provides that irrespective of the fact that land may be owned by the Crown or the Duchy of Lancaster or Cornwall a private interest in that land shall be subject to:—

(i) the powers of compulsory purchase under section 15 subject to the written consent of the appropriate authority responsible for the land;

(ii) the disposal notification area procedures under section 23 in the same way as if the land were not Crown land;

(iii) the direction of the Secretary of State as to disposal under section 45 in the same way as if the land were not Crown Land.

Subsection (2) defines Crown land, Crown interest, Duchy interest, private interest, and appropriate authority.

SECTION 40.—GRANTS TO AUTHORITIES WHO BUY OR RENT CROWN LAND

This section applies to cases where Crown Land is acquired by a public authority after the first appointed day. The Crown will not be liable for Development Land Tax so that a public authority will not be able to acquire Crown Land at market price less that tax. Also the Crown will not be liable to the current use value compensation but will be at all times entitled to receive current market price for its land. Therefore, provision is made to enable grants to be paid to public authorities to place them in the position they would be in if they were buying from a private source.

Subsection (1) provides that section 39 applies where a body acquires land or any interest in land from the Crown on or after the first appointed day. A body is defined as a local or new town authority, the Land Authority for Wales, the Peak or Lake District Boards, or a joint board under section 2. It also includes a body specified in an order made by the Secretary of State with the consent of the Treasury, subject to approval by the House of Commons.

Subsection (2) authorises the Secretary of State, with Treasury approval, to make a grant to the authority of such amount as may be approved by the Treasury, taking into account the price, rent or other payments made by the authority.

Subsection (3) enables the grant to be paid out of moneys provided by Parliament.   Of course, if there is a surplus on an authority's land account 40% of the grant will go back into the Consolidated Fund under the arrangements for sharing surpluses under the scheme.

SECTION 41.—EXCLUSION OF SPECIAL PARLIA-MENTARY PROCEDURE

This section removes the requirement for a compulsory purchase order on land owned by statutory undertakers or a local authority to be subject to special Parliamentary procedure if they object.   This change does not affect land held inalienably by the National Trust or common land or open space.

Statutory undertakers have other statutory safeguards for their operational land.   These other safeguards are contained in paragraph 10 of Schedule 1 to the Acquisition of Land Acts which provide that an order authorising the compulsory purchase of land used or held by statutory undertakers for the purposes of the carrying on of their undertaking may not be confirmed, if the undertakers make a representation to the appropriate Minister, unless that Minister certifies that the land can be purchased and not replaced, or that it can be replaced by other land belonging to or available for acquisition by the undertakers, without serious harm to the carrying on of the undertaking.

Additionally to this paragraph 5 of Schedule 4 of the present Act now provides that a compulsory purchase order under Part III may be confirmed without a certificate of the appropriate Minister, but in that event the order must be confirmed jointly by the appropriate Minister and the Minister who would otherwise have power to confirm it, *i.e.* the Secretary of State.

Through these provisions the Minister having sponsorship responsibility for the statutory undertakers is involved in the decision processes on the compulsory purchase order, if the undertakers made representations against the order, and he can thus ensure that the effect the acquisition would have on the operational interests of the undertakers is fully considered. On the other hand the exclusion of special parliamentary procedure in these cases will remove inhibitions against the exercise of compulsory purchase powers caused by the knowledge that even if the sponsoring Minister and the confirming Minister are both satisfied that the case for acquisition outweighs the interest of the statutory undertaker theirs is not the final decision which can only be obtained after long and costly procedures.

It should be noted that Parliament agreed, in passing section 70(3)(e) of the Town and Country Planning Act 1968 and the equivalent provision in the Scottish Act of 1969, that the requirement for special parliamentary procedure in respect of compulsory purchase orders under planning powers in relation to land acquired by statutory undertakers should cease to have effect. This repeal was ineffective since it did not affect the general provisions in the Acquisition of Land Acts. Section 40 by modifying paragraph 9 of Schedule 1 to those Acts, completes the repeal in relation to the Planning Acts and extends the exclusion of the procedure to the exercise of compulsory purchase powers, under any enactment, by a Minister, an authority as defined in the Act, a local authority in Wales, a joint board established under section 2 or any statutory undertakers in respect of land owned by statutory undertakers.

The section also excludes from special parliamentary procedure orders[1] made by these bodies in relation to land belonging to local authorities. Compulsory purchase orders by one local authority in respect of land owned by another are rare, but there may be conflicts between the needs of authorities, e.g. where one may wish to acquire for public housing a site

---

[1] Note.—Only two have been made since the 1963/4 Parliamentary Session. Both concerned Manchester buying land in Bury and were laid before Parliament in 1966 by petitions under the special procedure. The hearings took 5 days and the orders confirmed.

owned by another authority which the latter was intending to make available for private development.   Exclusion of special parliamentary procedure in respect of any compulsory purchase order resulting from a situation of this kind will make Ministers the final arbiters.   The incidence of inter-authority compulsory purchase orders could well increase as a result of the removal of the considerable deterrent of the special procedure.

Subsection (1) provides that the modification to the Acquisition of Land Acts effected by subsection (2) is to apply where notice of the making, or preparation in draft (*i.e.* where acquisition is by a Minister) of a compulsory purchase order is first published under the requirements of those Acts on or after the first appointed day.   The modification applies where the land is proposed to be acquired by a local or new town authority, the Land Authority for Wales, the Peak Park or Lake District Special Planning Board, a joint board established under section 2 of the Act, any statutory undertakers, or a Minister.

Subsection (2) provides that in such cases paragraph 9 of Schedule 1 to the Acquisition of Land Acts (under which compulsory purchase orders in respect of land of local authorities and statutory undertakers and inalienable land of the National Trust become subject to special parliamentary procedure if the owners make and maintain objection to the order) does not apply except where the interest belongs to the National Trust or the National Trust for Scotland.

SECTION 42.—CONSENT FOR DISPOSALS

This section provides that local authorities shall not dispose of a material interest in any land without consent of the Secretary of State.   The relative freedom of disposal under section 123 of the Local Government Act 1972 is taken away from the local authorities.

It has been stated[1] that the new overall control of disposals will be effected by general consents setting out the basic

---

[1] *See* General Commentary page 30 above.

framework within which local authorities will operate. The disposal of land for industrial or commercial development will be on a leasehold basis.[1] Land for residential purposes will be made available freehold. Local authorities will be encouraged to enter into building agreements with developers whereby plots can be conveyed direct to house purchasers. Cases which fall outside the scope of the general consents will need to be considered individually. The general duties of authorities in making land available and the rights of former owners and of persons who have identified the land by applying for planning permission are set out in Schedule 6.

The provisions apply to any land owned by a local authority regardless of when it was acquired or under what powers, whether before or after the passing of this Act.

The provisions also apply to the Peak Park Joint and Lake District Special Planning Boards by virtue of Schedule 10, paragraph 8(1). The Secretary of State already has full powers to control disposals by new town authorities by virtue of section 18 and section 4(2) of the New Towns Act 1965. Disposals by the Land Authority for Wales are subject to the consent of the Secretary of State by virtue of section 14(2).

Subsection (1) inserts a new section 123A in Part VII of the Local Government Act 1972.

Part VII of the 1972 Act contains the basic statutory provisions governing land transactions by local authorities. The effect of inserting the new section is to incorporate it fully in the 1972 Act.

Provisions of section 123A

Subsection (1) *of 123A* provides that a principal council shall not dispose of a material interest in any land without the consent of the Secretary of State.

[1] It has been announced in a DOE Press Notice No. 1176 dated 1 December 1975 that local authorities will be given a general consent to grant such leases up to a 99 year term. Longer terms will require special consent. (*See now also* D.O.E. Circular 121/75 para. 39 (*b*).)

The powers of the Secretary of State in giving consents are set out in section 128(1) of the 1972 Act which provides that consent may be given—

" (*a*) in relation to any particular transaction or transactions or in relation to a particular class of transactions; and

(*b*) in relation to local authorities generally, or local authorities of a particular class, or any particular local authority or authorities; and

(*c*) either unconditionally or subject to such conditions as the Minister concerned may specify (either generally or in relation to any particular transaction or transactions or class of transactions)."

Subsection (2) *of section* 123*A* provides that the section has effect notwithstanding the provisions of section 123 of the 1972 Act or of any other statute whenever passed. This means that existing statutory controls, for example over the disposal of public open space, will still remain in force, but in any case where a local authority is at present empowered (whether by section 123 or by any other provision) to dispose of a material interest in land without consent the authority will in future need the consent of the Secretary of State under this provision.

Although the new provision overrides section 123 to the extent that section 123 provides for authorities to dispose of land without consent that section is not repealed because it contains a number of important provisions in respect to controls over open space and public trust land, which therefore continue to operate.

Subsection (3) *of section* 123*A* provides that where a local authority have already entered into a contract before the section comes into force on the first appointed day the disposal can go ahead without the need for consent under these provisions.

Subsection (4) *of section* 123*A* defines " material interest " as a freehold or a lease with at least seven years still to run.

Seven years is the standard period for these purposes (*cf.* section 164 of the Local Government Act 1933 and section 123(7) of the Local Government Act 1972).

Subsection (2) of the section makes the corresponding changes to the Local Government (Scotland) Act 1973 by the insertion of a new section 74A.

Subsection (3) of the section provides for the new sections to come into force on the first appointed day.

SECTION 43.—ACCOUNTS AND RECORDS

This section requires all authorities to keep such accounts and records and prepare and submit such statements of account of their land dealings as the Secretary of State may direct.

The main aims of the section are to enable the Secretary of State to require the preparation and submission of proper financial statements of accounts and other records which will together indicate how authorities are operating the scheme. Financial accounts will be especially important for the purpose of identifying surpluses for redistribution under section 44.

The aim of the provision is to enable the Secretary of State to control the form of the accounts relating to **land for private development acquired after the first appointed day for the Act.** Land acquired by an authority before the first appointed day will normally be specifically excluded from passing through the land accounts. The section does not contain any provision to this effect because, in response to pressure from the local authorities concerned the Government agreed that land acquired by authorities under the previous Government's £80 million scheme should technically be brought within the Land accounts. Land needed for authorities' own use (*e.g.* school sites) will not normally need to pass through the accounts.

The following notes on the section have been written on the basis of each authority keeping a separate land account. But following discussions with local authority associations, Ministers have decided that, besides providing for separate

H

land accounts, there should be the possibility of some form of joint accounting and local equalisation of surpluses. It will be for authorities themselves to decide whether they wish to seek approval for joint accounting arrangements, and the provisions in sections 43 and 44 of the Act are capable of allowing land accounts to be kept by a number of authorities jointly.

The key principle in considering whether joint accounts (whether or not on a county basis) can be used is that accounts should accurately reflect the arrangements for the management of the scheme. Circumstances in which joint accounts would be acceptable are:—

(a) a Joint Board established under section 2 of the Act will be an authority in its own right and will therefore have its own land account. Here, therefore, the keeping of a joint account is acceptable because it reflects the fact that the authorities concerned have decided that the scheme should be managed on a wide basis.

(b) Co-operative arrangements between authorities which fall short of a joint board may also justify the use of a joint account. For instance, authorities might form a joint committee for the operation of the land scheme which could qualify for a joint account provided:—

(i) it produces joint rolling programmes;

(ii) the programmes are operated through shared staff arrangements;

(iii) it defines the policies within which the land scheme will operate within the county, or part county, concerned.

The keeping of joint accounts will require the approval of the Secretary of State who, after the first appointed day, will need to issue the necessary directions under section 43 in approved cases.

The arrangements are described primarily as they will apply to local authorities. The different financial position of new town development corporations may require special arrangements there; the Land Authority for Wales, will be required to submit statements of account under this section but the sharing arrangements in section 44 may differ. The Land Authority may keep other accounts under section 12.

The form of all accounts kept will naturally have to reflect the financial arrangements discussed under General Commentary (pages 32 to 33, above).

Subsection (1) requires every authority to keep such accounts and records and prepare and submit to the Secretary of State such statements of account, as the Secretary of State may with the approval of the Treasury direct.

Authorities are to be required to prepare a number of statements of account for the Secretary of State dealing with various aspects of their operations. It follows that they must keep such accounts and records as will enable them to prepare these statements. The accounts will be subject to audit by the District Auditor or an approved auditor under the Local Government Act 1972. Accounts may be kept by individual authorities, or under certain circumstances on a joint basis.

Subsection (2) enables the Secretary of State with the approval of the Treasury to give directions on certain contents of the accounts, and relating to the form, manner and submission of statements of account.

Generally, in keeping the accounts required by subsection (1) above, the authorities will be allowed to follow their existing accounting practices. However, because of the provisions for the sharing of surpluses with the Exchequer, wide powers are retained by H.M.G. to give directions on the contents of accounts. Also there is a desire that there be a uniformity over the country so as to make it easier to obtain a national picture of the operation of the scheme.

With regard to the contents of the accounts, the general intention concerning infrastructure and servicing is that only costs directly related to the development of the land concerned (*e.g.* costs of estate roads and on-site services where provided by the local authority) should be so debited, and that wider associated costs (*e.g.* schools, highways and trunk sewers) which are included in other public expenditure programmes and which are properly a charge on local authority rates or presently funded from other sources should be excluded.

The accounts will cover all land for disposal, whether this is acquired under the Act or under existing powers to buy land for private development—*e.g.* under the Housing and Planning Acts. As noted above the accounts which the Secretary of State will require will relate only to the land made available for private development, though records of purchases of land for authorities' own use may also be required. Only land acquired after the first appointed day will normally have to pass through the land accounts.

Subsection (3) provides that money credited to a land account may not be used for any purpose without the consent of the Secretary of State.

This is to ensure that the Secretary of State can control the use of any sums credited to a land account, *i.e.* disposal receipts, payments received under the provisions of a land acquisition and management scheme, or redistribution surpluses received under section 44(5). Initially receipts will be used for repaying borrowings to reduce deficits in each land account. Receipts will be available also for financing new land purchases within approved programmes. This provision will operate even when an authority's land account is in surplus so that the Secretary of State's control over the authority's programme may continue. Once a land account is in surplus it will be possible for an authority to use their share of surplus for any purpose for which capital monies may be properly applied. This would comprise:—

(*a*) the repayment of other debt;

(*b*) financing expenditure on a key sector project which is within an agreed programme;

(*c*) financing expenditure within the locally determined sector, on the basis that the agreed level of borrowing for this sector is reduced by an equivalent amount.

Subsection (4) relieves local authorities from their obligation in respect of land acquisitions on the community land account to make annual provision to meet the eventual repayment of debt.

This relieves them of their obligations under, for instance, paragraph 7 of Schedule 13 to the Local Government Act 1972 which requires them to make annual provision to meet the eventual repayment of the debt. The relief is consequential upon the concept that all money required to operate the land scheme, including interest on borrowings and administrative costs, will be raised by borrowing so as not to make any charge on the Rates. (*See* General Commentary, page 32.)

Subsection (5) enables the Secretary of State to obtain information about accounts and records.

This provision enables the Secretary of State to obtain access to the information contained in an authority's accounts and records. Thus an authority could be required to provide an abstract of an account together with a certificate (under paragraph (*b*)) that this was a true reflection of the state of the account.

Subsection (6) empowers the Secretary of State to publish statements of account or information obtained under subsection (5) as he wishes.

The land accounts and records will contain information which it may be desirable to publish to provide an overall picture of the working of the scheme, and this subsection provides the powers to enable this to be done. A similar arrangement exists for the publication of statistical accounts; although the information is actually published by the Chartered Institute of Public Finance and Accountancy, it is compiled with the help and financial support of the Department.

Subsection (7) provides that this section and section 44 shall extend to local authorities in Wales.

Land acquisition in Wales under the Act will generally be carried out by the Land Authority for Wales and new town development corporations. However, local authorities in Wales will be able to acquire land for private development

under existing powers as they do now.   Each local authority
in Wales will therefore need to keep a land account.   Transactions in which Welsh local authorities act solely as agents of
the Land Authority for Wales will, however, be reflected in the
land accounts of the Land Authority which will meet all the
local authority costs.

SECTION 44.—COMMUNITY LAND SURPLUS ACCOUNTS

This section enables the Secretary of State to direct that
some or all of any surplus in an authority's community land
surplus account is to be paid to him; and to make payments
to authorities out of the sums so collected.   The use of any
surplus in an account which accrues to an authority is made
subject to the Secretary of State's control.

Surplus is defined basically in cash terms—*i.e.* when disposal
receipts are sufficient not only to pay off outstanding debt and
to finance further purchases within the year but also to leave
a credit in the account at the end of the year.   Land accounts
could be in accounting surplus (*i.e.* assets in terms of land held
will exceed liabilities in terms of outstanding borrowing); but
it is only when an authority reach a position of cash surplus
that redistribution of surpluses will apply.

We have seen in the General Commentary (page 33) that for
local authorities in England and Scotland, it is proposed to
redistribute the cash surplus in the following way.   When an
individual local authority's land surplus account comes into
overall cash surplus, the amount of the surplus at the end of
the financial year will be divided into two parts:—

    (*a*) 30% will be left with the authority concerned (subject
           to any arrangements for sharing between authorities
           which might be agreed through LAMS under the
           provisions of paragraph 3(1)(*c*) of Schedule 5).

    (*b*) 70% will be payable to the Secretary of State who
           will:—

           (i) pay 40% into the Consolidated Fund; and

           (ii) distribute 30% to other authorities.

Initially the 30% share for redistribution to other authorities would be distributed among authorities whose land accounts showed a cash deficit *pro rata* their deficits. The Government hopes that in time the pool of the distributable shares will be greater than the total of the deficits of those authorities whose land accounts are still in deficit. Should this occur a scheme will be drawn up for distributing the excess among authorities generally.

The same 60:40 split between local authorities and the Exchequer will apply in Wales. A surplus in the accounts of the Land Authority for Wales would (subject to leaving a working balance) be paid to the Secretary of State who would pay 40% into the Consolidated Fund and distribute the balance of 60% to local authorities on the basis of a formula to be determined. Differing arrangements may be needed in new towns in the light of the different basis of financing there.

The percentage figures are not written into the section to maintain a degree of flexibility. For example, when the land surplus account of an authority which has received payments from the redistribution pool itself comes into surplus it will be necessary to protect this redistributed payment from being subject to a further sharing with the Exchequer, but at the same time to return it all to the redistribution " pool ". Achieving this will require a different percentage of surplus from that authority than under the general arrangements.

Land account surpluses accruing to local authorities will be available for the purposes indicated in the note on section 43(3) above.

Subsection (1) enables the Secretary of State, with the approval of the Treasury, and after consulting the local authority associations, to direct which statement of account shall be the community land surplus account.

Subsection (2) requires each authority in surplus to pay to the Secretary of State so much of the surplus as he may with the approval of the Treasury direct.

This payment to the Secretary of State will be set at a proportion that covers not only the Exchequer share, but also any
redistribution payments to be made to authorities.   The latter
will then be paid out again on the agreed basis under the
provisions of subsection (5).

Subsection (3) provides for the application of the remainder
of the surplus (if any) left with an authority.

Local authorities will be able to use this locally retained share
of a surplus in two ways.   First, it may be used for any purpose
for which capital monies may be applied as set out in the
note to section 43(3).   Second, the "local" share of a surplus
may be used for meeting any liability under a land acquisition
and management scheme.   This needs to be read in conjunction with paragraph 3(1)(c) of Schedule 5, which provides that
a land acquisition and management scheme may contain, where
appropriate, provisions for the transfer of sums between
authorities.   The reason for this is that when a county and a
district agree on the exercise of functions they may at the same
time want to agree on the sharing of surpluses.   For instance
authority A might be prepared to agree that authority B should
handle all land for private development provided that authority
A received a percentage of the " local " share of the surplus in
authority B's land account.

The need for the words ' if any ' arises from the way in which
the 30% share to be redistributed between authorities will work.
It has been agreed with the local authority associations that in
the early years, this will be distributed between authorities *pro
rata* to their deficits, as a recirculating pool.   Thus the first
claim on any authority's surplus will be to repay to the redistribution pool any payments which they have received from it.
The repayments are thus a prior charge on surpluses, and until
they have been repaid, they may eliminate an authority's
retained share of surplus.

Subsection (4) provides that any application of surplus under
subsection (3)(a) shall be subject to the consent of the Secretary
of State, except in relation to the Land Authority for Wales
and new town development corporations, where the Secretary

of State has or will have adequate powers of direction, and subject to section 27 of the Town and Country Planning Act 1959 (which allows for the application of a sum not exceeding £1,000 without consent).

This control will be exercised generally through the issue of general, rather than specific, consents.   Although land account surpluses will not represent a net addition to local authority resources, there will be some benefit to local authorities in that anything financed by surpluses will not need to be financed by borrowing, so that the rates will be relieved of the interest charges which would otherwise have had to be met on the borrowing.

It should be noted that this subsection deals only with the control of the locally retained share of a surplus under subsection (3)(*a*).   Surpluses received under subsection (3)(*b*) or as a result of redistribution under subsection (5) will be controlled by a direction by the Secretary of State under section 43(2) that they should be credited to the accounts kept by the authority under that section.

Subsection (5) empowers the Secretary of State with the approval of the Treasury and after consulting the associations concerned, to redistribute some of the surplus received under subsection (2) to other authorities.

The intention is that this percentage of the surplus (at present set at 30%) should initially be distributed to authorities whose land accounts are still in deficit.

Subsection (6) requires the Secretary of State to prepare accounts of sums that he receives from land accounts under subsection (2) and of those that he pays to authorities under subsection (5) in a form and manner approved by the Treasury.

Subsection (7) requires the Secretary of State to send a copy of the account to the Comptroller and Auditor General by the end of each November.

Subsection (8) requires the Comptroller and Auditor General to examine, certify and report on the account, and lay copies of it and his own report before Parliament. These are normal provisions for the types of transaction in question. The Comptroller and Auditor General invariably audits accounts of transactions involving a government department.

SECTION 45.—DISPOSAL OF LAND AT DIRECTION OF SECRETARY OF STATE

The Government wishes to remain in a position to exercise complete control over the public acquisition and disposal of land. This the Secretary of State will be able to do in large measure through his consent powers under section 41, by his appraisal of local authority programmes of acquisition and disposal, and by general guidance on disposals policy and procedure.

In addition to all this where an authority are not prepared to make land available or to develop it themselves this section will give the Secretary of State the necessary overriding power of direction.

The Secretary of State will also have power under section 48(3)(*a*) to make an order transferring the function of management and disposal of land in an account kept by the authority under section 43 to another body, but the use of that power might not be an appropriate means of dealing with particular problems; hence the power of direction provided by this section.

The section applies only to local authorities and the two Park Planning Boards. It does not apply to new town authorities or the Land Authority for Wales because there are adequate powers of direction under the New Towns Act 1965, and under section 8(3) of this Act respectively.

Subsection (1) gives the Secretary of State power to direct a local authority or the two Park Planning Boards to dispose of any land entered in an account kept by them under section 43. It also gives him discretion to decide whether the disposal should be freehold or leasehold, how the disposal should be achieved (for example by means of a building agreement) and what terms and conditions should apply.

The power of direction is restricted to land which is for the time being entered in an account kept by the authority under section 43 because it would not be appropriate for the Secretary of State to have powers of direction over land which authorities have already acquired under existing powers and are not holding under the scheme. The power of the Secretary of State to direct (under section 43) what items are or are not to be included in the accounts will ensure that the provisions of this section cannot be evaded by simply appropriating land out of the section 43 accounts.

Subsection (2) provides that where a direction is given under this section a planning permission which is specified in the direction shall not be suspended under section 21, and that planning permission subsequently granted by the Secretary of State shall not be suspended by virtue of sections 20 or 21.

As the intention of the direction power is to ensure that land is made available for development it must follow that the planning permission which permits that development should not be suspended by sections 20 or 21. (A planning permission obtained before the disposal will not still be suspended under section 20 because such a suspension ends when the land is acquired by an authority.)

Subsection (3) provides that the Secretary of State must consult the authority before issuing a direction.

The issue of a direction will be a drastic measure and clearly every attempt should be made beforehand to reach agreement with the authority concerned.

Subsection (4) provides that the power of direction shall not be used until the scheme is brought into operation on the first appointed day.

SECTION 46.—REGISTER OF LAND HOLDINGS

This section gives the Secretary of State powers to make regulations providing for the setting up of registers of land holdings by authorities including details of their acquisitions, holdings, and disposals of land.

The regulation-making power applies regardless of whether the land is acquired under the new powers in this Act or under existing statutory powers. Furthermore the power is not restricted to land acquired after the commencement of the Act.

The requirement is analogous to that upon local planning authorities to keep a register with details of planning applications and decisions open to the public under section 34, Town and Country Planning Act 1971 (section 31, Scotland Act 1972).

Subsection (1) provides that the Secretary of State can make regulations requiring authorities to keep registers recording their acquisitions, holdings and disposal of land.

Subsection (2) provides that the regulations may set out—

  (*a*) what type of land and what type of transaction is to be included in the registers;

  (*b*) what form they are to take and what details they should contain;

  (*c*) the circumstances and conditions under which they are to be open to public inspection.

Subsection (3) provides that regulations may be made requiring local authorities in Wales to keep registers. (The Land Authority for Wales and new town authorities in Wales are already covered by subsection (1).)

It is necessary to provide specifically for the section to apply to local authorities in Wales because section 1(1)(*b*) defines " authority " in relation to Wales as the Land Authority for Wales or a new town authority, but not a local authority; and local authorities in Wales will still be able to acquire " Community Land " under their existing powers.

SECTION 47—CERTIFICATION OF APPROPRIATE
ALTERNATIVE DEVELOPMENT

SECTION 47.—CERTIFICATION OF APPROPRIATE ALTERNATIVE DEVELOPMENT

This section amends the provisions governing certificates of appropriate alternative development, which are used in certain cases as a guide to the assessment of compensation. The certificate procedure covers situations where the current development plan fails to provide an adequate basis for assessing the value of the land to be acquired, *e.g.* where land is being acquired for a generally unremunerative use, for example a road scheme or open space, and is either allocated for that use in the development plan or not allocated for any use at all.

Under such circumstances the claimant or the acquiring authority can ask the local planning authority to give its opinion of what class or classes of development " might reasonably have been expected to be " permitted if the land were not being acquired. This is done through the issue of a certificate of appropriate alternative development the terms of which must be taken into account in assessing the compensation due to the claimant.

During the transitional period of the scheme, compensation for compulsory purchase will continue to be assessed on the basis of the present statutory provisions concerning the planning assumptions which may be made in arriving at the market value. Even after the change to current use value has been made on the second appointed day, it will still be permissible in assessing compensation to take account of the prospect of obtaining permission for development of a class which is within current use value by virtue of section 25. There will therefore continue to be a need for the certificate procedure.

Nevertheless the Government consider that there has in practice been a tendency for authorities to specify in the certificate alternative developments for which there would in reality be little prospect of obtaining planning permission even if the land were not to be acquired. The result has been that some acquiring authorities are paying more for land for public works than the Government considers justified. The provisions of the section are therefore intended to ensure that the certificate system operates more in favour of the public sector in the future.

Subsection (1) provides for section 17 of the Land Compensation Act 1961 and section 25 of the Land Compensation (Scotland) Act 1963, both of which deal with certification of appropriate alternative development, to be amended as set out in subsections (2) to (5) of this section. It also provides that the sections as amended shall have effect as set out in Schedule 9.

(**Note:** *Scottish references:* Section 25 of the Scottish Act of 1963 has already been amended by virtue of section 49(3) of the same Act to substitute references to the Lands Tribunal for Scotland for references to the official arbiter. It has also been amended by virtue of section 172(2) of the Local Government (Scotland) Act 1973 so that references to a local planning authority read simply as references to a planning authority, which by virtue of section 172(3) of the 1973 Act falls to be construed as a reference to a general planning authority and to a district planning authority. Both sets of amendments are incorporated in the new version of the section which appears in Part II of Schedule 9.)

Subsection (2) provides that section 17 of the 1961 Act and section 25 of the Scottish Act of 1963 shall both be amended by substituting a new subsection (3) for that of the existing provision. The new subsection provides that—

(*a*) an applicant for a certificate shall state whether or not he considers that there are any classes of development which either immediately or at a future time would be appropriate for the land if it were not being acquired by an authority possessing compulsory purchase powers. If the applicant considers that there are such classes of development he must say what they are and when they would be appropriate.

The intention here is two-fold. First, by use of the words " shall state whether or **not** " it is made clear that applicants can apply for a " nil " certificate indicating that no development would have been permitted. Acquiring authorities are required at present to specify a class of development in their applications even when they do not believe that any development would in fact be appropriate other than that proposed by the acquiring authority. Secondly the onus is put on the applicant to state what classes of development (if any) would be appropriate and when. The timing can be particularly important from the valuation point of view. The assumption that planning permission would be forthcoming for a particular class of development in say 10 years' time may be of considerably less value when the compensation is assessed than an assumption that permission would be available immediately.

  (b) an applicant must give his grounds for the opinions expressed in his application;

  (c) the application must be accompanied by a statement which gives the date when a copy of the application was served on the other party involved in the negotiations for the acquisition, or if it has not yet been served, the date when it will be served.

Subsection (3) provides for the reference in section 17(4) to paragraph 3(b) to read " 3(c) ". This is a purely consequential amendment. More importantly the subsection provides that the certificate when issued must state that the local planning authority considers either that planning permission **would have been given** for development of one or more classes specified in the certificate or that planning permission **would not have been given** for any development other than that which is proposed to be carried out by the acquiring authority.

By substituting a more positive wording for that which appears in the existing provision (" might reasonably have been expected to be granted ") the intention is to ensure that local planning authorities only specify classes of development which would actually have obtained planning permission.

Subsection (4) makes the corresponding amendments to section 25 of the Scottish Act of 1963.

Subsection (5) makes consequential amendments to subsections (5) and (7) respectively of the two Acts where the same wording appears.

Subsection (6) provides that the clause shall come into effect one month after Royal Assent.

PART VI—SUPPLEMENTAL

Part VI contains supplemental provisions, most of which are in common form and deal with such matters as powers to obtain information, service of documents, and regulations and orders.   Schedules 10 and 11, dealing with minor and consequential amendments and repeals also go with this part of the Act.

The main substantive provisions in this Part are to be found in sections 48-50.   These deal with the reserve powers of the Secretary of State, and enable him to take away from a local authority the function of operating the scheme and transfer it either to himself, or to another authority, or to a new body set up under the enabling power in section 50.

SECTION 48.—POWERS OF SECRETARY OF STATE

This section provides reserve powers for the Secretary of State to transfer the functions of any authority (other than the Land Authority for Wales or a new town authority) to himself, to another authority, or to a new body set up under section 50. The powers are not needed in relation to the Land Authority or to new town development corporations as these bodies are appointed by the Secretary of State and he has adequate powers of direction over them.

In England and Scotland the operation of the land scheme will depend on the ability and willingness of local authorities to press ahead with public acquisition within available resources.

Therefore the Reserve Powers are retained by the Government to deal with cases where an individual authority would be unable or unwilling to acquire land for private development and to provide a means of dealing with any case of default once the duty under section 18 of the Act has been imposed in an area.

Just as there are a variety of possible reasons for transferring functions, there are also a variety of financial effects which the Secretary of State might wish to achieve in respect of land account surpluses—they might go to the transferor authority, to the authority to which the functions are transferred, to the Secretary of State, or to any combination of these in any proportions. The provisions of the Act allow any of these objectives to be achieved.

Subsection (1) provides that the Secretary of State may act where it appears to him expedient that an authority should cease to be responsible for exercising functions under the Act, or land disposal and management functions under any other Act. The wording is wide enough for the Secretary of State to be able to act in a case where the authority concerned have not even begun to exercise the powers—*e.g.* where, before the first appointed day, an authority have publicly declared that it is not their intention to exercise them.

This subsection covers not only land acquisition powers under this Act, but also the exercise of powers to dispose of and manage land under the Local Government Act 1972. This is necessary because local authorities will generally carry out these functions under these existing powers and not under new powers conferred by the Act. Without this provision a body set up under section 50 could not be given effective powers to manage or dispose of land.

Subsection (2) enables the Secretary of State to transfer these functions to himself, to another authority or to a special authority appointed under section 50.

The form of arrangements used will inevitably depend upon the circumstances of each case—hence the wide range of alternative provision. Where only one authority was involved, it might be sufficient to transfer the functions to another authority acting within the same land acquisition and management scheme. In other cases the choice might lie between transfer to the Secretary of State or to a new body set up under section 50.

Subsection (3) enables the order to transfer the functions of management and disposal of land in any account kept by the authority under section 43, and in so far as seems expedient, any other functions under the Act, and any functions under other Acts relating to the disposal and management of land. It may also transfer such property, rights, liabilities and obligations as seem appropriate.

This provision gives wide enough powers to transfer functions under the order to ensure that the Secretary of State or body to whom the functions are transferred will be able to operate the community land scheme and related functions in place of the authority from whom the following are transferred. This subsection, in conjunction with subsections (2) and (5) of section 44, makes it possible to achieve a variety of financial effects. At one extreme, the administration of land in an authority's land accounts might be transferred to another authority, but the land accounts themselves and any surpluses accruing to them could remain with the authority from whom functions are transferred. At the other extreme, the whole account could be transferred. By virtue of section 44(2) and (5), any surpluses accruing could be left with the authority to which the functions were transferred, taken by the Secretary of State, redistributed to the transferor authority, or any combination of these. In between the two extremes, there could be a partial transfer of the land in the land accounts in the way the Secretary of State thought best. The order-making power is sufficiently flexible to achieve the desired policy result in each case, and decisions on which approach to adopt will need to be taken in the light of the circumstances of each case.

Subsection (4) provides that the Secretary of State shall not make the order without a public enquiry unless the authority concerned have consented to the making of the order. The order will also be subject to negative procedure before either House of Parliament.

Subsection (5) provides that any sums which the Secretary of State certifies were incurred by the authority to which functions were transferred in performing those functions shall be met by the authority from which the functions were transferred.

Subsection (6) provides that any expenses to be met by the transferor authority under subsection (5) shall be dealt with in the way that they would have been if the functions had not been transferred.

Subsection (7) provides that the transferor authority shall have powers to raise money to meet any expenses incurred under subsection (6) as if their functions had not been transferred.

The majority of expenses, if not all expenses, of an authority to which functions are transferred will be met through the land accounts, and these expenses are in no way affected by the provisions of subsections (5) to (7). But section 43(2)(*a*) gives the Secretary of State power to direct which items are or are not to be included in land accounts and it is certainly possible to envisage a situation where an authority to which functions were transferred would incur expenses in connection with its functions which they were unable to debit by virtue of the Secretary of State's directions under section 43(2)(*a*). Provision therefore is made for the authority to which functions are transferred to be reimbursed for these expenses by the transferor authority. If it were considered right, once the land account concerned was in surplus, for the transferring authority to be partly or wholly reimbursed for these expenses from the surplus, the powers under the Act are sufficiently flexible to achieve this (*see* comment on subsection (3) above).

Subsection (8) prohibits functions of a new town authority from being transferred under this section. This does not apply to any functions transferred to a new town authority under this section, and subsequently re-transferred under section 49.

Section 4(2) of the New Towns Act 1965 and the corresponding provision for Scotland give the Secretary of State power to give directions to a new town development corporation. This will be sufficient to ensure that a corporation exercise their functions under the Act in the way intended.

Subsection (9) excludes Wales from the application of this section.

This provision is made for similar reasons to subsection (8) above. Except for agency arrangements under section 14(4), which are at the discretion of the Land Authority for Wales, functions under the Act in Wales will be exercised solely by the Land Authority and new town development corporations. The Secretary of State can give directions to both of these under section 8(3) of the Act and section 4(2) of the New Towns Act 1965 respectively. So there is no need for the provisions of this section to apply to Wales.

Subsection (10) provides that any payment made by the Secretary of State for the purpose of this section shall be paid out of money provided by Parliament.

Payments by the Secretary of State under this section can be of two kinds. First, there are any expenses involved in the holding of a public inquiry under subsection (5). Second, there are the payments which will need to be made where the functions of an authority are transferred under this section to the Secretary of State. These could either be expenses which would be debited to the land account concerned, or expenses which could not be so debited, and which would therefore be reimbursed under subsections (5) to (7) of this section. In either case there would be no permanent charge falling on the Secretary of State.

Subsection (11) provides that no order shall be made before the first appointed day.

Under Part I of Schedule 2 to the Act, the first appointed day will bring into operation, amongst other things, the provisions of section 17 (which gives authorities the general duty to have regard to the desirability of bringing land into public ownership) and section 15 (which gives authorities the necessary powers of acquisition). Until these provisions are in force, there will be no functions of the Act in operation which might need to be transferred under the provisions of this section.

SECTION 49.—RE-TRANSFER OF FUNCTIONS

This section enables the Secretary of State to reverse the effect of any order made under section 48 above by re-transferring the functions to the orginal authority.

Subsection (1) empowers the Secretary of State to make an order re-transferring functions.   A re-transfer order must cover **all** the functions originally transferred.

Subsection (2) enables the order to make such provision as the Secretary of State considers appropriate, regarding property, rights, liabilities and obligations held in respect of transferred functions.

This is the counterpart of section 48(3).   The precise provision to be made under the re-transfer order will depend amongst other things on how the original transfer was carried out.

Subsection (3) provides for the treatment under the re-transfer order of expenses incurred by the authority to which functions were originally transferred and which were not admissible in the land account concerned.

This provision achieves the same effect as subsections (5) to (7) of section 48 for transfers in the reverse direction.

SECTION 50.—BODIES TO EXERCISE RESERVE POWERS

This section enables the Secretary of State to set up new bodies specifically to exercise functions to be transferred to them by order under section 48 of the Act.

The nature of the bodies to be set up under this section would depend very largely on the extent to which there was a need for such bodies to take over local authority functions. There is a possibility that such bodies might operate on a regional basis in England, with a separate body for Scotland. But this might not be appropriate if a section 50 body were needed to deal with a few isolated cases of default.   Whatever form such a body took it could operate only on the basis of the functions transferred to it.

Subsection (1) provides that the Secretary of State may establish by order one or more bodies corporate to exercise, or to be available to exercise, functions transferred by order under section 48.

These bodies need not all be set up at the same time— different bodies could be set up at different times. The provision also makes it clear that bodies could be set up in advance of any order under section 48 giving them functions to exercise. As with the joint boards which may be set up under section 2 of the Act, such bodies are invariably made bodies corporate, with perpetual succession and a common seal.

Subsection (2) allows any order under this section to provide for the membership and conduct of any body set up, and the payment of members and staff.

Subsection (3) requires that all appointments are to be made by the Secretary of State, and the rates of any payments to members or staff are to be determined by him, subject to the approval of the Minister for the Civil Service.

These provisions are normal when setting up such *ad hoc* authorities.

Subsection (4) makes any order under this section subject to affirmative resolution procedure.

Subsection (5) provides that payments made pursuant to an order under this section shall be met from money provided by Parliament. Such payments will need to be made where a body is set up in advance of the transfer of functions by order under section 48, but incurs expenses in making necessary preparatory arrangements.

SECTION 51.—POWER TO OBTAIN INFORMATION

This section empowers the Secretary of State or an authority to demand information concerning the ownership of interests in land. If any person obliged by the section fails to give such information or knowingly makes a misstatement, he is made liable to a fine.

Subsection (1) empowers the Secretary of State or an authority to require the information. The information must be sought for the purpose of enabling the Secretary of State or an authority to make an order, or serve a notice or other document, which he or they are authorised or required to serve by any provisions of the Act. The Secretary of State or the authority may require both the occupier and any person who, either directly or indirectly, receives rent in respect of any premises to state the nature of his own interest and to give the name and address of any other person known to him to have an interest in the land, whether as a freeholder, mortgagee, lessee or otherwise.

Subsection (2) imposes a penalty of a fine not exceeding £100 on summary conviction on any person who fails to give the information required by subsection (1).

Subsection (3) provides that any person required by the section to give information, who knowingly makes a misstatement is to be guilty of an offence and liable on summary conviction to a fine not exceeding £400 or on conviction on indictment to imprisonment for a period not exceeding 2 years or to a fine, or to both.

These provisions are based on the precedent of section 284 of the Town and Country Planning Act 1971.

SECTION 52.—SERVICE OF DOCUMENTS

Subsection (1) applies the general provisions concerning service of documents by and on local authorities, as laid down in sections 231 and 233 of the Local Government Act 1972, to the Land Authority for Wales and new town authorities in accordance with the following subsections of the section.

Section 231 of the Local Government Act 1972 states that any notices or documents required or authorised by any instrument or enactment to be served on a local authority (or the chairman or officer of a local authority), should be addressed to the local authority and left at, or posted to, the authority's principal office, or any of their other offices specified by them. Similarly notices authorised or required to be served on parish meetings, should be given to, left at, or posted to the address of the chairman of parish meetings.   However, these provisions do not apply to documents which are to be given or served on any proceedings in Court.

Section 233 of the Local Government Act 1972 makes similar provisions for bodies corporate and partnerships, etc.

Subsection (2) provides that sections 231 and 233 of the Local Government Act 1972 shall apply to the Land Authority for Wales as though it were a local authority.   The Land Authority have no functions other than those under the Act so it is not necessary to refer specifically, as it is in subsection (3) for new town authorities, to the particular documents to which the sections are to apply.

Subsection (3) states that the same sections of the Local Government Act 1972 shall apply to a new town authority, as though it were a local authority, both in respect of documents required or authorised under the Act to be served **on** a new town authority, and of documents required or authorised to be served under the Act on any person **by** a new town authority.

Subsection (4) provides that as regards the service of documents by and on a local authority or new town authority in Scotland, the provisions of sections 190 and 192 of the Local Government (Scotland) Act 1973, shall apply as if the local authority or new town authority were a local authority within the meaning of that Act.   This applies in relation to documents required or authorised by the Act to be served on a local authority or new town authority in Scotland, and to such documents served under the Act on any person by a local authority or new town authority in Scotland.

Section 190 of the Local Government (Scotland) Act 1973 provides for the service of legal proceedings on a local authority and section 192 provides for the service of notices, etc., by a local authority.

SECTION 53.—REGULATIONS AND ORDERS

This section provides for the making of regulations and orders under the Act.

Subsection (1) provides for the Secretary of State to make regulations prescribing the form of any documents required or authorised by the Act to be served by or on any authority (as defined in section 1 of the Act).

Subsection (2) provides that the power to make orders and regulations under any provision in the Act, except paragraphs 17(4) and 19(5) of Schedule 4, shall be exercisable by statutory instrument.

Paragraph 17(4) and 19(5) of Schedule 4 are exempted because the orders for which they provide are following the precedent of the Planning Acts not statutory instruments. The orders under paragraph 17 of Schedule 4, which concern the extinguishment of rights of way, and rights as to apparatus of statutory undertakers, are precedented by section 230 of the Town and Country Planning Act 1971, where the power to make orders was similarly not exercisable by statutory instrument. Paragraph 19(5) is similar to paragraph 17(4) but provides for statutory undertakers to take the initiative in serving a notice on authorities claiming rights to enter land, to remove or to resite apparatus. It is based on the provisions of section 232 of the 1971 Act. These two exceptions of Schedule 4 therefore ensure that section 53 is consistent with previous planning legislation.

Subsection (3)(a) enables the Secretary of State in making regulations or orders under the Act to have different provisions for different areas, different authorities or other different cases.

This provision enables the Secretary of State to bring the land scheme into operation area by area and by reference to particular types of development as the capacity of authorities to implement it dictates. In the case of Joint Boards (section 2) and bodies exercising reserve powers (section 50) there might be different circumstances within the areas for which they are responsible and here again subsection (3)(a) provides the flexibility needed to deal with the situation.

Subsection (3)(b) provides for the inclusion of transitional and other supplemental and incidental provisions in regulations and orders which the Secretary of State may make under the Act.

This subsection is in standard form and is designed for example to accommodate provisions which might need to be made for planning applications made, but not decided, before the relevant date.   Thus the Secretary of State would be able to exempt some applications from the procedures laid down in regulations and orders, where those applications were made prior to, but were still undecided by, the date.

Subsection (3)(c) provides for regulations and orders varying the kinds of development which are relevant development to include transitional provisions which modify the Act itself in ways which the Secretary of State deems expedient.

Similarly to (3)(*b*) this subsection provides for flexibility.   It provides for transitional provisions to vary the provisions of the Act (*e.g.* relating to the handling of planning applications) and at the discretion of the Secretary of State, where the definition of relevant development is altered.   It is a very far-reaching power enabling a Minister to alter a Statute by regulation rather than requiring him to submit a new Bill to Parliament.

Subsection (4) provides for the variation of revocation of any order or provision made under the Act, except for the first and second appointed day orders under section 7.

The appointed day orders will bring into effect major provisions of the Act.   To allow such an order to be revoked or modified would create uncertainty and the possibility of upsetting retrospectively arrangements entered into by private individuals.

SECTION 54.—DIRECTIONS AND CONSENTS

This section provides that a direction or a consent given by the Secretary of State under the Act may be:—

   (*a*) either of general application or limited to a particular case or class of case;

(b) addressed to a particular authority or class of authority;

(c) either unconditional or subject to such conditions as the Secretary of State may wish to impose.

This provision is relevant to:—

(i) Section 8(3)—directions to the Land Authority for Wales;

(ii) Section 13(2)(b)—contents of the annual report of the Land Authorities for Wales;

(iii) Section 43—directions to authorities to keep accounts and records of their land transactions;

(iv) Section 44—direction as to which statement of account is a " community land surplus account " and to the sharing of surpluses in it;

(v) Section 45—directions to local authorities to dispose of land entered in an account kept by the authority under section 43;

(vi) Schedule 5—directions that additional matters be taken into account by authorities in preparing a land acquisition and management scheme and additional matters to be included in a scheme;

(vii) Schedule 6, paragraph 1—directions that additional matters be taken into account by an authority in discharging their functions under section 17(1) (general duties of authorities).

The provision is designed to give the Secretary of State the widest power to give directions and consents. It would, for example, enable the power of direction in Schedule 6 to be used to ensure that an individual authority took account of particular circumstances existing within their area. (The subsection does **not** apply to section 42. That section introduces a new section into the Local Government Act 1972 and section 128 of that Act contains a provision similar to this subsection.)

SECTION 55.—LOCAL ENQUIRIES

This section applies section 250 of the Local Government Act 1972 (section 210, Scotland Act 1973) to any public local enquiry held and the Act.

SECTION 56.—OFFENCES BY CORPORATIONS

Subsection (1) provides that where an offence has been committed under the Act by a body corporate, and it is proved that the offence was committed with the consent or connivance of, or was attributable to the neglect of an officer of that body, the officer concerned, as well as the body corporate should be considered to be guilty of an offence, and be liable to be proceeded against accordingly.

Subsection (2) provides that where the affairs of a corporation are managed by its members, the provisions of the section apply to an individual member's acts and defaults as if he were a director of the body corporate.

This section is common form in Acts which provide for offences of the type which can be committed under this Act; for example it appears in the Land Commission Act 1967, section 97, the 1971 Planning Act, section 285, and in the Water Resources Act 1963, section 118(iii) and (iv).

SECTION 57.—FINANCIAL PROVISIONS

This section contains the usual provisions for expenses incurred by the Secretary of State to be paid out of money provided by Parliament, and for any sums received by the Secretary of State under the Act to be paid into the Consolidated Fund.

Subsection (1) requires that any expenses incurred by the Secretary of State under the Act, and any increase attributable to the provisions of the Act in sums payable by Parliament under any other Act, shall be paid out of money provided by Parliament.

Expenses of the Secretary of State arising directly under this Act will be principally administration costs, related to the level of local authority activity. It has been estimated that when the scheme is in full operation, central government expenditure on administration will be about £8 million a year. (This figure is based on a calculated increase in central Government staff of 1,400, including Valuation Office and Inland Revenue staff.) Provision for the payment of such costs will be incorporated into the Consolidated Fund Acts passed from time to time by Parliament, which will authorise such payments from the Consolidated Fund.

Further costs may arise from the setting up of Financial Hardship Tribunals (section 27), or of bodies to exercise powers transferred from local authorities (section 48) or from expenditure on dealing with unoccupied office premises under Part IV.

Subsection (2) provides that any sums paid to the Secretary of State under the Act shall be paid into the Consolidated Fund, except where otherwise expressly provided.

Sums will be paid to the Secretary of State by authorities which have moved into surplus in their community land accounts. 70% of any surplus in the community land account of an authority will be paid to the Secretary of State (section 44(2)). He will then pay 40% into the Consolidated Fund and redistribute the serving 30% amongst local authorities. The express provision in section 44(4) means that this 30% does not have to be paid into the Consolidated Fund. The Secretary of State may also receive payments on the disposal of office premises acquired by him under Part IV.

SECTION 58.—SHORT TITLE, ETC.

Subsection (1) states that the Act may be cited as the Community Land Act 1975.

Subsection (2) provides for the implementation of the consequential and minor amendments made in Schedule 10, including amendments to the Commissioners of Works Act 1894, The Lands Tribunal Act 1949, The Land Compensation Act 1961, The Land Compensation (Scotland) Act 1963, The Town and Country Planning Act 1971, The Town and Country Planning (Scotland) Act 1972, The Local Government Act 1972, the Local Government Act 1974 and the Local Government (Scotland) Act 1975.

Subsection (3) provides for the repeal of the enactments mentioned in Schedule 11 to the extent specified by the Schedule: that is in section 194(2) of the Town and Country Planning Act 1971, the words " (in the case of land falling within paragraph (*a*) or (*c*) but not (*d*), (*e*) or (*f*) of section 192(1) of this Act) "; and in section 183(2) of the Town and Country Planning (Scotland) Act 1972, the words " (in the case of land falling within paragraph (*a*) or (*c*) but not (*e*), (*f*) or (*h*) of section 181(1) of this Act) ".

Subsection (4) states that the Act shall not extend to Northern Ireland, except where otherwise expressly provided. Such express provision is made in section 38, and in paragraph 3 of Schedule 3 of the Act.

SCHEDULE 1
EXEMPT DEVELOPMENT

This Schedule sets out classes of " exempt development ". The provisions of the Act where the Schedule is mentioned are:—

(*a*) section 3(2)(*a*) (which takes exempt development outside the definition of relevant development);

(*b*) section 15(2) (which takes exempt development outside the scope of the acquisition power);

(*c*) section 25(3)(*b*) (which provides that value due to the prospect of carrying out exempt development is to be included in current use value.

The notes on those sections and the general commentary explain more fully the significance of exempt development in each of these three contexts. A wider range of development is to be put outside the normal range of the acquisition scheme by virtue of the **excepted** development regulations to be made under section 3; but for the purposes of defining the scope of the acquisition power and the basis for assessing current use value only very minor development is **exempted.**

Paragraph 1 classes as Exempt Development any development which (*a*) is permitted by a General Development Order currently in force OR (*b*) would have been permitted but for a direction given under the Order (in both cases provided that it is carried out in accordance with any conditions or limitations imposed in the G.D.O.).

The General Development Order 1973 (which is currently in force) grants permission for a wide range of minor development, such as certain enlargements or alterations of buildings, some recreational development, and certain development by statutory undertakers. Under Article 4 of the Order, a Direction can be given to exercise tighter control over development than is normally used; for example in national parks or areas of outstanding beauty. Such a direction will not prevent the development being Exempt Development for the purposes of the Act. This is the effect of sub-paragraph (*b*) of this paragraph (" would be so granted but for a direction given under the order ").

So far as the assessment of current use value is concerned provision is made, in section 25(4)(*b*) to " freeze " the form of the G.D.O. as it exists at the second appointed day (when the change to current use value takes place).

Paragraphs 2 and 3 class as exempt development a wide range of development for the purposes of agriculture and forestry. The categories are:—

(*a*) building or other operations for the purposes of agriculture or forestry, other than the erection of dwellings (paragraph 2);

(*b*) the working of minerals in conjunction with agriculture and for agricultural use, together with ancillary buildings and works (paragraph 3).

These paragraphs follow the wording of paragraphs 4 and 5 of Schedule 8 of the 1971 Act (and the equivalent Scottish provisions), save that the references to buildings for market gardens, nursery grounds and timber yards as being outside the class are not repeated. This is to ensure that buildings or operations for horticulture and timber yards (other than dwellings) are included in Exempt Development as well as for agriculture and forestry.

SCHEDULE 2
COMMENCEMENT DATES, ETC.

Section 7 provides for three dates which bring in the provisions of the scheme by stages.

Part I of the Schedule sets out in tabular form a useful guide for the reader to the main provisions of the Act to which the dates apply, *i.e.*—

1st appointed day	...	Sections 15, 17, 19, 20, 23, 24, 48.
2nd ,, ,,	...	Section 25.
Relevant dates	...	Sections 18 and 21.

Part II of the Schedule provides for registers to be kept of all the " relevant date " orders made.

Paragraph 1(1) requires the Secretary of State to maintain and keep up to date a register showing all the " relevant date " orders made under section 18 in such a way as to enable members of the public to inform themselves of the dates when they came into force and the areas and categories of designated relevant development to which they apply.

As explained in the note on section 7, orders under section 18 (bringing in the full duty and the section 21 prohibition of development) will be made in stages as individual authorities build up their resources. There are therefore likely to be a considerable number of such orders as the full duty and prohibition are extended to more and more areas and the scope of designated relevant development in those areas is widened. Registers showing precisely the extent of these orders throughout Great Britain are needed so that members of the public can ascertain how they stand with regard to their land. This is not necessary, however, for the first and second appointed day orders which will be of general effect in all areas.

Paragraph 1(2) provides that separate registers shall be kept for England, Scotland and Wales at the principal offices of the respective Secretaries of State having responsibility for planning matters in those countries. The registers will therefore be kept in London, Edinburgh and Cardiff.

Paragraph 1(3) requires that the registers must be available for public inspection at reasonable hours.

In addition it is proposed to make available in the regional offices of DOE copies of that part of the register which relates to the particular region concerned.

Paragraph 2 provides that as soon as practicable after the making of a section 18 order each of the authorities affected must publish notices in newspapers one of which, if possible, must be a local paper and must also deposit for public inspection without fee a copy of the order at their principal offices.

SCHEDULE 3
THE LAND AUTHORITY FOR WALES

This Schedule sets out the constitution and regulates the proceedings of the Authority.

Many of the provisions are common form and much of the Schedule is drawn from recent enactments.

Paragraph 1 provides that the Authority shall be a body corporate who shall be no less than 6 and no more than 9 in number, the number of members being decided by the Secretary of State.

A body corporate is a legal entity with an existence separate from that of its constituent members.   It has perpetual succession and a common seal and is capable of holding land and of using and being sued in the Courts.

It is usual to allow the Minister discretion within the prescribed limits in the number of members appointed.

Paragraph 2 provides for all appointments as members of the Authority to be made by the Secretary of State who may appoint one to be a chairman and another a deputy chairman of the Authority.   It also provides for the appointment of four members after consulting organisations representing local authorities in Wales.

The requirement to consult organisations representative of local authorities in Wales about the appointment of four members does not of itself require the Secretary of State to appoint four local authority members to the Land Authority, nor to accept nominees from the authority organisations.   Two members are appointed, however, from the Welsh County Councils and two from the district councils.

Paragraph 3 provides that a member of the Authority shall be disqualified for membership of the House of Commons, even in the unlikely event of his coming from Northern Ireland.

Paragraph 4 provides for the holding and vacation of office by the Chairman, Deputy Chairman and Members of the Authority; for their resignation and removal by the Secretary of State in certain circumstances and eligibility for re-appointment.

Sub-paragraph (1) provides for the holding and vacation of office by the Chairman, Deputy Chairman and members to be in accordance with the terms of their appointments. This leaves the widest possible discretion to the Secretary of State.

The appointments will normally be made for a term of years and they could be made subject to conditions which provide for the vacation of office if they are not complied with. A condition in relation to a local authority member might, for example, require the member to cease to be a member should he cease to be a member of a local authority.

Sub-paragraph (2) provides that notice of resignations from the Authority shall be given in writing.

Sub-paragraph (3) provides for the removal of persons from membership of the Authority in certain specified circumstances, *i.e.* bankruptcy or making an arrangement with creditors, incapacity through illness, absence for more than six consecutive meetings of the Authority otherwise than for a reason approved by the Secretary of State. There is also power to remove a person from membership if he is " otherwise unable or unfit to discharge the functions of a member, or is unsuitable to continue as a member ", *i.e.* he is unfit for some other reason due to his personal circumstances.

Sub-paragraph (4) provides that a person who ceases to be a member, Chairman or Deputy Chairman of the Authority may be re-appointed.

Sub-paragraph (5) provides that a member who is also Chairman or Deputy Chairman of the Authority shall be required to give up that post if he ceases to be a member of the Authority.

This is linked with sub-paragraph (3).   Any person removed by the Secretary of State from membership would automatically have to give up any appointment as Chairman or Deputy Chairman.

Sub-paragraph (6) allows the same person to be an Officer, Secretary, Member, Chairman or Deputy Chairman of the Authority all at the same time except that one person cannot be both Chairman and Secretary or Deputy Chairman.

In the initial stages there might be advantages in one person filling two posts where the work load is not sufficiently heavy to justify separate appointments.   In the event of a sudden death it may also be useful to be able to appoint someone already on the Authority to fill the vacancy for a while without requiring him to give up his other position.   The prohibition on one person being both Chairman and Secretary was introduced in the House of Commons to meet opposition criticism that it would be undesirable even for a short time that a single individual should hold the two most important appointments of Chairman and Secretary.

Paragraph 5 enables the Authority to appoint:—

   (i) a Secretary with the approval of the Secretary of State;

  (ii) other officers and servants in consultation with the Secretary of State and with the consent of the Minister for the Civil Service.

The Authority has a Chief Officer acceptable to the Secretary of State since it is the Secretary of State who is responsible to Parliament and who will initially be making loans to the Authority and who in the last resort determines the policy they must execute.   For statutory purposes the Chief Officer can be known as the Secretary but this does not necessarily determine the title by which his appointment will be publicly known.   The Chief Officer of the Land Commission was known as the Director although he also held the statutory position of Secretary. In the case of other officers and servants, control is kept of the overall complement and staffing structure of the Authority so as to ensure that they do not seek to poach local authority staff or to inflate their requirements for people with scarce professional skills.

Paragraph 6 provides for payment of remuneration and, in special circumstances, of compensation to members of the Authority and also for payment of pensions on the vacation of office as Chairman, Deputy Chairman or member.

Sub-paragraph (1) provides for the Secretary of State to determine, with the consent of the Minister for the Civil Service, the amount of the remuneration and allowances to be paid to members of the Authority.

It is normal for the Government to exercise control in this way over the remuneration and allowances of members of statutory authorities.

Sub-paragraph (2) provides that the Secretary of State may with the consent of the Minister for the Civil Service require the Land Authority to pay to any of their members or their dependents any pension, allowance or gratuity, or to make payments towards such pension, allowance or gratuity.

The principle that part-time members of public boards could be eligible for a pension was agreed between Ministers of the Treasury and Civil Service Department in the Spring of 1973.

The decision to award any pension or similar payment rests with the Secretary of State and the Minister for the Civil Service. It is not envisaged that pensions would be agreed for every member. Such an award might be justified where someone had given a period of long and distinguished service to the Land Authority. Each case will be taken on its merits. Payments could be made in a variety of ways, depending on the circumstances of a particular case. A pension might be paid following the retirement or death of a member and it could take the form of a pension directly paid by the Authority or the Authority could be directed to make payments to initiate or continue the member's membership of some other pension scheme.

Sub-paragraph (3) provides that the Secretary of State, with the consent of the Minister for the Civil Service, may in special circumstances, require the Authority to pay a specified sum as compensation to a person when he ceases to be a member of the Authority.

This provision is included primarily to make it easier to remove a member before the expiry of his term of office, but it is not limited to that.

Sub-paragraph (4) provides for a statement of the making of any determination under sub-paragraph (2) or (3) to be laid before each House of Parliament.

Paragraph 7 provides for payment by the Authority to their officers and servants of such remuneration and allowances as they may determine after consultation with the Secretary of State and with the consent of the Minister.

It may be necessary to guard against the Land Authority seeking to attract scarce staff (particularly from local authorities) by offering particularly favourable terms of employment.

Paragraph 8 provides for the payment of pensions, allowances or gratuities to employees of the Authority or their dependents.

Sub-paragraph (1) provides arrangements for the payment of staff pensions, allowances or gratuities and for payments to dependents of employees and for the funding of pensions schemes.

Sub-paragraph (2) relates to the case of an officer who later becomes a member of the Authority. The sub-paragraph provides for the whole of his service to be regarded for pension purposes as service as an employee.

Paragraph 9.

Sub-paragraph (1) gives the Authority complete power to regulate their own procedure subject only to the following provisions of the Schedule.

Sub-paragraph (2) provides that the quorum at meetings of the Authority shall be four, *i.e.* just under a half of the maximum membership of nine.

Sub-paragraph (3) applies the provisions of the Public Bodies (Admission to Meetings) Act 1960 to the Land Authority for Wales. The 1960 Act provides (with safeguards for confidentiality) for the admission of the press and public to meetings of the bodies to which it applies.

This paragraph puts the Land Authority so far as possible in the same position as a local authority in relation to the admission of the press and public to their meetings. Welsh local authorities acting as agents of the Land Authority will be subject to the provisions of the 1960 Act when discussing their agency functions.

Paragraph 10 provides for the disclosure by any member of any interest that he may have in matters concerning the Authority.

This is a normal provision which is particularly necessary in the case of the Land Authority because of the great power they will have over the development of land. Many aspects of the Authority's operations will impinge directly on what have hitherto been regarded by the public as individual rights resulting from the ownership of property. In deciding to whom land is to be made available and on what terms, the Authority will have tremendous powers of patronage.

Sub-paragraph (1) provides that any member of the Authority who is, in any way, directly or indirectly interested in any land which is the subject of a transaction shall disclose the nature of his interest at the meeting where the matter is being discussed and shall not take part in any deliberation or decision of the Authority with respect to the transaction.

Sub-paragraph (2) provides that a member can declare his interest by a general notice rather than by the method set out in sub-paragraph (1). He can give notice at a meeting that he is a member of a specified company or firm and is to be regarded as interested in any transaction which may be entered into in relation to that company or firm.

In the circumstances referred to, the member would be disqualified from taking part in any deliberation or decision touching any transaction to which the general notice is directed, but he would not be required to repeat his notice at every meeting.

Sub-paragraph (3) provides that a member need not attend a meeting of the Authority in order to make a disclosure under this paragraph, if he take steps to secure that the disclosure is made by notice brought up and read at the meeting.

Paragraph 11 provides a safeguard for persons who have been involved in transactions with the Land Authority (*e.g.* purchasing land from them) should it be found that there was some technical defect in the appointment of members, etc., or should some member have failed (as required by paragraph 12) to declare an interest in land which is the subject of a transaction involving the Authority.

This provision is commonly included in legislation dealing with the proceedings of public bodies. While there is no reason to expect the situation to arise, the balance of public advantage should it happen would almost invariably be served by letting the transaction stand.

Where there is fraudulence or corruption in a transaction, quite apart from any criminal proceedings which might ensue, the provision would not override section 173(1) of the Law of Property Act 1925 (conveyances made with intent to defraud purchasers) and it is considered that the Courts would have jurisdiction under that section.

Paragraph 12 provides for the authentication of the seal of the Authority by the signature of the Secretary or of any person whom the Authority have authorised to sign.

Paragraph 13 provides that a certificate signed by the Secretary that any instrument has been issued or made by the Authority shall be conclusive evidence of such issuing or making.

Paragraph 14 provides that every document purporting to be an instrument made or issued on behalf of the Authority and either sealed and authenticated as provided in paragraph 11, or signed or executed by the Secretary or authorised person, is to be received in evidence and deemed without further proof to be so made or issued unless the contrary is shown. A certificate signed by the Secretary and to the effect mentioned in paragraph 12 is also presumed to be such a certificate as therein mentioned.

Such documents could therefore be put in evidence and it would lie with the person seeking to question the fact, to prove the invalidity of the making or issue of the certificate as the case may be. On challenge to any of these matters, a certificate could be given under paragraph 12 which would dispose of the point although it would be open to the person making the challenge to show that the certificate itself was not properly made. Until that proof was given, the certificate would be evidence of its own validity.

Paragraph 15 provides, broadly, that any person dealing with the Authority or with someone claiming under the Authority, need not be concerned with whether the Authority have acted in accordance with directions given to them or have obtained any of the directions, consents or approvals of the Secretary of State or the Minister that they are required to obtain under the Act.

Paragraph 15 is for the protection of the subject. If, for example, someone bought land from the Authority and his title was being challenged on the grounds that the Authority themselves were not empowered to acquire the land because they had not obtained the necessary consent from a Minister or had breached a direction given to them, the challenge would fail.

Paragraph 16 provides that " the Minister " referred to in the Second Schedule shall be the Minister for the Civil Service.

SCHEDULE 4
ACQUISITION AND APPROPRIATION OF LAND

This Schedule falls into four parts.

Part I—is the most important and makes a number of serious modifications to the existing code of compulsory purchase.

Part II—deals with the acquisition of land by agreement.

Part III—contains such supplemental matters as the extinguishment of rights of way, etc., over land.

Part IV—is concerned with the appropriation of land by local authorities.

PART I.—MODIFICATIONS OF ACQUISITION OF LAND ACTS

All the modifications made are for the purpose of facilitating the public acquisition of land and in so doing diminish much of the protection hitherto afforded by the law to the private citizen against authoritarian action. In particular his grounds for objections are severely curtailed and his right to a public enquiry greatly eroded.

Paragraph 1.

Sub-paragraph (1) applies the procedural code in the Acquisition of Land Acts to the compulsory acquisition of land under the section 15 power and introduces the modifications to that code contained in paragraphs 2-6 below.

Sub-paragraph (2) provides that these modifications will not apply unless the compulsory purchase order contains a certificate that there are no material interests in the land other than outstanding material interests in development land.

This means the certificate must deal with two matters:—

(i) whether the land is needed for relevant development within ten years, and

(ii) whether there are any private interests in that land.

If there are no private interests then the modifications to the Acquisition of Land Acts will not apply.

Similarly if the land is not needed for relevant development *e.g.* only in respect of excepted development again the modifications will not apply.

This provision is of particular interest to parish councils, community councils, and charities. If they object to a compulsory purchase they will be entitled automatically to a public enquiry since what they own are not " outstanding " material interests in land (*see* notes on section 4, pages 52-54).

Sub-paragraph (3) provides that a certificate given under (2) above may not be questioned in any legal proceedings whatsoever.

This in effect means that the certificate will be conclusive and binding as between the authority giving it and the private citizen affected but not necessarily as between the authority and the Secretary of State.

Paragraph 2(1) provides for a new paragraph 4 to be substituted for the existing paragraph 4 of Schedule 1 to the Acquisition of Land Acts.   In the substituted paragraph 4:—

Sub-paragraph (1) enables the Secretary of State, if he thinks fit, to confirm a C.P.O. with or without modifications (or by inference reject it), if he is satisfied that the proper notices have been served (on owners, lessees and certain occupiers) and published (in two successive weeks in one or more local newspapers) and if no objections have been duly made by such persons or they have withdrawn their objections.   [This sub-paragraph is the same as in the existing Acts.]

Sub-paragraph (2) provides that if any owner, lessee or occupier objects the Secretary of State **may** (*i.e.* not **shall** as in the existing Acts) hold a public local inquiry or offer a hearing, but if sub-paragraph (3) below applies then an inquiry or hearing **must** be held.

Sub-paragraph (3) provides that an inquiry or hearing **must** be held **unless** the Secretary of State is satisfied that:—

> (*a*) planning permission for relevant development is in force in respect of the land, and the planning permission was granted by the Secretary of State after an inquiry, or

> (*b*) there is an adopted or approved local plan for the district and the grant of planning permission for relevant development of the land would be in accordance with the provisions of that plan, or

(c) where there is no adopted or approved local plan the grant of planning permission for relevant development would be in accordance with the provisions of the development plan (*i.e.* an old-style development plan, " overlaid " by an approved structure plan if one exists).

Where one of these conditions is satisfied then the Secretary of State may hold an inquiry or hearing into the C.P.O. " if he considers it expedient " but he will be under no obligation to do so.

The greatest reservations have been expressed by Justice, and the Council of Tribunals is uneasy that an inquiry may only be held where the Secretary of State considers it expedient. Previous planning enquiries are not necessarily of interest to an ordinary citizen who will be only concerned to enquire or attend one when his property is directly threatened.

Sub-paragraph (4) empowers the Secretary of State to confirm a C.P.O., with or without modifications (and by inference to reject it) after considering any objections and, if an inquiry or hearing has been held, the report of the person appointed to hold it. [The substance of this sub-paragraph is the same as in the existing Acts.]

Sub-paragraph (5) provides that, if any objector is given and accepts an opportunity of being heard, the acquiring authority and any other persons (not necessarily owners, lessees or occupiers of the land) as the Secretary of State may consider expedient are to be afforded the opportunity of being heard on the same occasion. [This sub-paragraph is the same as in the existing Acts.]

Sub-paragraph (6) empowers the Secretary of State to require objectors to state in writing the grounds of their objections, and provides that he may disregard objections which relate solely to compensation (as in the existing Acts) or are made on the ground that the acquisition is unnecessary or inexpedient.

This removes one of the major grounds under the existing law for objection to a Compulsory Purchase Order. Effectively it leaves an objector only with the grounds that either the purchase is premature—something which it is very difficult for him to establish as against the authority—or that it will cause him hardship. However, as the Secretary of State may disregard under the existing law any objection that the objection relates exclusively to matters of compensation, the hardship ground is of limited application.

The justification given for the removal of the ground that the acquisition is " unnecessary or inexpedient " is that the passing of the Act constituted the acceptance by Parliament that development land is to pass into public ownership and ultimately development will only take place on publicly owned land. This being so the need or expediency for the acquisition is not open to question.

However, it is to be noted that the modification does not enable the Secretary of State to disregard objections that the *development* for which the land is required is unnecessary or inexpedient.

Sub-paragraph (7) provides that an objection may be disregarded if an objector does not respond within the time allowed (which must not be less than 28 days) to a requirement under subsection (6) to state the grounds of his objection in writing.

Sub-paragraph (8) provides for owners, lessees and occupiers (whether they have objected or not) to be notified of the Secretary of State's decision to confirm or not to confirm the order where there has been no inquiry or hearing, if they have expressed a wish to be notified. (There is no requirement in the Acquisition of Land Acts for objectors to be informed where the order is not confirmed; and the notification requirements of the Compulsory Purchase by Local Authorities (Inquiries Procedure) Rules 1962 and the Scottish Rules of 1964 apply only where a public local inquiry or hearing has been held.

It will be of particular importance to owners to know of the Secretary of State's decision where the order is not confirmed since any planning permission which has been suspended will be activated when the Secretary of State serves notice of a decision not to confirm.)

Sub-paragraph (9) defines new terms introduced.

Paragraph 2(2) of the Schedule makes Scottish adaptations in the substituted paragraph 4 to be inserted in Schedule 1 to the Acquisition of Land Acts with consequential references to Scottish Acts.

Paragraph 3 provides reserve power for the bringing in of a procedure under which the Secretary of State would be able to dispense with an inquiry or hearing if the grant of planning permission would be in accordance with either a draft local plan which has been the subject of adequate public participation or a non-statutory plan which has been subject to public participation which would have been adequate for the purposes of the 1971 Act. It may be brought in only by an order subject to affirmative resolution and for a period (at any one time) of up to five years only; and the Secretary of State can make such an order only where he considers it necessary to do so in the public interest.

Where the Secretary of State is relying on a draft local plan or a non-statutory plan under this procedure, he cannot dispense with an inquiry or hearing in relation to an objection made by a residential occupier. If the order comprises land other than a dwelling-house but the occupier of the dwelling-house objects then the Secretary of State must either hold an inquiry or hearing or, if he does not but decides to confirm the order, the dwelling-house must be excluded.

Paragraph 4 provides, in the manner of, *e.g.* section 132(2) and (3) of the Town and Country Planning Act 1971, that the Secretary of State may confirm a C.P.O. insofar as it relates to part of the land and postpone consideration of the order in relation to other land. The purpose of this provision is to enable the acquisition to go ahead of such part of the order land as the Secretary of State is satisfied should be brought into public ownership and defer his decision in relation to the remainder, for example because the decision is dependent upon the determination of other issues which do not affect the first part.   Such a case may arise where part of the order land is clearly suitable for the provision of housing and urgently needed for that purpose and can be developed independently of the remainder, while the suitability of the remainder for development of any kind may depend on planning considerations still to be resolved.

Postponement, for a specified period, is effected by direction of the Secretary of State; and the notices required to be published and served under paragraph 6 of Schedule 1 to the Acquisition of Land Acts stating that the order has been confirmed must contain a statement of the effect of any directions.

Paragraph 5 makes provision, in relation to the compulsory purchase of the operational land of statutory undertakers, dispensing with the need for a certificate under paragraph 10 of Schedule 1 to the Acquisition of Land Acts.   Normally, such a C.P.O. may not be confirmed, where a representation has been made to the Minister with direct responsibility for the undertaking within the objection period, unless that Minister certifies that the nature and situation of the land are such:—

    (i) that it can be purchased and not replaced without serious detriment to the carrying on of the undertaking, or

    (ii) that if purchased it can be replaced by other land belonging to, or available for acquisition by, the undertakers without serious detriment to the carrying on of the undertaking.

Paragraph 5 follows section 229 of the Town and Country Planning Act 1971 (section 218 of the Scottish Act) in providing in *sub-paragraphs* (1) *and* (2) that a C.P.O. of this kind may be confirmed without such a certificate, but in that event it must be confirmed jointly by the appropriate Minister and the Minister who would otherwise have sole power to confirm it, *i.e.* the Secretary of State.

This provision does not supplant paragraph 10, which remains available. Under either procedure the Minister responsible for the undertakers must take a view about the effects of the acquisition and an order cannot be confirmed unless he agrees. However, the ability to confirm an order without the pre-condition of a certificate in response to representations by the undertakers allows the case for acquisition and the interests of the undertakers, to be considered together.

Sub-paragraph (3) of paragraph 5 provides that the sections of the 1971 and 1972 Acts referred to (which provide for " equivalent reinstatement " compensation and which are designed for the particular situation where statutory undertakers are displaced from their land by compulsory purchase and are forced to acquire other land or provide new buildings, etc.) apply where by virtue of the paragraph the order is confirmed without a paragraph 10 certificate being given. These special compensation provisions do not apply to acquisitions under the Act if the order was confirmed without a certificate in other circumstances, *i.e.* because the statutory undertakers did not make representations to the appropriate Minister under paragraph 10.

Paragraph 6 enables local authorities in Wales to object to compulsory purchase orders promoted by the Land Authority for Wales.

PART II.—ACQUISITION OF LAND BY AGREEMENT

Part I of the Compulsory Purchase Act 1965 applies automatically whenever land is acquired compulsorily under an enactment to which the provisions of Schedule 1 to the Acquisition of Land (Authorisation Procedure) Act 1946 applies. This governs the procedure for taking land when compulsory purchase has been authorised, and contains certain provisions about compensation.

It does not apply automatically, however, where power is given to acquire land by agreement. This Part of the Schedule applies Part I of the 1965 Act to acquisitions by agreement under section 15 in so far as it is applicable to such acquisition.

Paragraph 7(1) puts all authorities under the Act in England and Wales in the same position as regards the application of Part I of the 1965 Act to the acquisition of land by agreement under section 15 of the Act as are principal councils in relation to acquisition by agreement under their existing powers.

Paragraph 7(2) makes similar provision in relation to the relevant Scottish enactments.

PART III.—SUPPLEMENTARY PROVISIONS

This Part makes available in respect of land acquired under the Act various supplemental powers and provisions available in respect of land acquired for planning purposes under the Town and Country Planning Acts with necessary modifications and adaptations.

Extinguishment of rights over land compulsorily acquired

Paragraph 8 makes provision corresponding with section 118 of the Town and Country Planning Act 1971 (section 108 of the Scottish Act).

The effect of *sub-paragraphs* (1) *and* (2) is that upon the completion of a compulsory acquisition all private rights of way and rights as to apparatus (except apparatus of statutory undertakers—*see* paragraph 17 of the Schedule) are extinguished; and any apparatus on the land vests in the acquiring authority.

Under *sub-paragraph* (3) any right or apparatus may be retained after completion of the acquisition if the acquiring authority direct to that effect before the completion or if at any time the authority and the person in whom the right or apparatus is vested so agree.

Sub-paragraphs (4) *and* (5) provide entitlement to compensation, determined in accordance with the Land Compensation Acts, for any person who suffers loss by the extinguishment of a right or the vesting of apparatus.

Development of land acquired under Part III of Act

Paragraph 9 (corresponding with section 124 of the Town and Country Planning Act 1971 (section 114 of the Scottish Act)) confers on authorities a general power to carry out development on land acquired under the Land Scheme, subject to the consent of the Secretary of State; and not confined to development for the purposes of specific functions.

Sub-paragraph (1) confers powers to erect, construct, or carry out, on land acquired under Part III, any buildings or works where no power exists or could be conferred under an " alternative enactment " (as defined in sub-paragraph 8).

The words " (notwithstanding any limitation imposed by law on the authority by virtue of their constitution) " mean that although an authority's constitution might not allow them to carry out some of the works covered by the paragraph any such restriction is overridden by the power conferred by this paragraph. For example a local authority may not have power to erect offices except for their own use; but for the purposes of securing satisfactory development it may be necessary for the authority to construct offices for commercial use. Paragraph 9 gives the required power.

Sub-paragraph (2) obliges an authority to obtain the Secretary of State's consent to the exercise of the powers of sub-paragraph (1). Such consent may be given either in respect of a particular operation or a class of operation, and may be subject to conditions or limitations. This consent does not constitute planning permission, which must be obtained under the relevant planning control procedures.

Sub-paragraph (3) requires an authority to give notice to the Secretary of State of any proposal to carry out an operation under the power in sub-paragraph (1); and the Secretary of State may direct the authority to advertise the proposal.

Sub-paragraph (4) enables an authority, notwithstanding any limitations which may otherwise be imposed on them (*see* note to sub-paragraph (1)), to repair, maintain and insure any buildings or works carried out under sub-paragraph (1), and generally to deal with such buildings or works in a proper course of management.

Sub-paragraph (5) enables an authority, with the consent of the Secretary of State, instead of carrying out development themselves under the powers of sub-paragraph (1), to arrange for the carrying out of such development by an authorised association as defined in sub-paragraph (9).

Sub-paragraph (6) makes it clear that sub-paragraph (5) does not confer power on an authorised association to carry out development if that association does not itself possess the powers to do so.

Sub-paragraph (7).   An individual may not take action against an authority on the ground that anything done by that authority (provided it is in pursuance of or within the powers of sub-paragraph (1)) is *ultra vires* the authority.   Subject to this limitation, sub-paragraph (7) preserves to an individual the right to take action against an authority on any other grounds that may be open to him.   For example, an authority may be liable to an action for damages if in the exercise of their powers under this paragraph, they are guilty of negligence.   In other words, sub-paragraph (7) merely protects against an action for lack of powers but expressly preserves any other right of action.   This is a common form provision to achieve this objective.

Sub-paragraph (8) defines " alternative enactment " (*see* sub-paragraph (1)) as any enactment not contained in the Community Land Act, the Town and Country Planning Acts, and certain provisions of the Local Authorities (Land) Act 1963 and the Local Employment Act 1972, all of which authorise the carrying out of development for specified purposes.

Sub-paragraph (9) defines " authorised association " (with whom an authority may make arrangements for the carrying out of development on land acquired under Part III of the Act—*see* sub-paragraph (5)) as any society, company or body of persons approved by the Secretary of State whose objects are concerned with garden cities, garden suburbs or garden villages or with buildings for the working classes and others and without profit motive.

Power to override easements and other rights

Paragraph 10 (corresponding with section 127, Town and Country Planning Act 1971 (section 117 of the Scottish Act)) authorises an authority or a person deriving title from them to interfere with easements and contractual restrictions affecting land acquired by the authority under Part III of the Act, provided always that the development giving rise to the interference is done in accordance with planning permission and that compensation is paid under the Compulsory Purchase Act 1965 or, in Scotland, the Lands Clauses Consolidation (Scotland) Act 1845 and the Railways Clauses (Consolidation) (Scotland) Act 1945.

Sub-paragraph (1) constitutes the power to override easements and rights.

Sub-paragraph (2) excludes rights belonging to statutory undertakers from the power of paragraph 10.   These rights are dealt with in paragraphs 17, 18 and 19 of the Schedule.

Sub-paragraph (3) specifies the nature of the rights and interests to which the paragraph applies, chiefly easements and restrictive covenants.

Sub-paragraph (4) provides for the assessment and payment of compensation for injurious affection arising from the exercise of the power.

Sub-paragraph (5) provides that any liability of a person deriving title from the authority to pay compensation under sub-paragraph (4) is enforceable against the authority if that person fails to discharge the liability.

Sub-paragraph (6) provides that if there is an agreement between the authority and any other person for indemnifying the authority against any liability for compensation under sub-paragraph (4) that agreement is not affected by the provisions of sub-paragraph (5).

Sub-paragraph (7) makes it clear that paragraph 11 does not affect any rights to take proceedings against the authority in respect of any interference or breach except as mentioned in sub-paragraph (1).

Sub-paragraph (8) derives from section 290(7) of the 1971 Act and makes it clear that any successor in title to a person deriving title is himself a person deriving title for the purposes of paragraph 9, and that any reference to deriving title is a reference to deriving title directly or indirectly.

Use and development of consecrated land and burial grounds

Paragraph 11 (corresponding with section 128 of the 1971 Act) authorises the use and development of consecrated land and burial grounds, acquired under Part III of the Act notwithstanding the special provisions normally relating to them under ecclesiastical law or otherwise.

Sub-paragraph (1) contains the basic power to use consecrated land or buildings for development in accordance with planning permission; and *sub-paragraph* (2) excludes from sub-paragraph (1) any consecrated land which consists of or forms part of a burial ground (*see* sub-paragraph (6)).

Sub-paragraphs (3) *to* (5) provide for the making of regulations prescribing the requirements and conditions governing the use of land, consecrated or otherwise, acquired under Part III of the Act, which is or was formerly occupied as a church or a place of religious worship.   The matters to be covered by the regulations include the removal and reinterment of human remains, disposal of monuments, etc., requirements as to consent to the use of consecrated land, the disposal of land and any other incidental and consequential provisions as may be necessary.

Sub-paragraph (6) is a power similar to sub-paragraph (1) but in relation to burial grounds (both consecrated and unconsecrated), acquired under Part III.

Sub-paragraphs (7) *to* (10) provide for regulations governing the removal and reinterment of human remains from land which has been used for the burial of the dead.   Section 25 of the Burial Act 1857 is disapplied in relation to a removal carried out under the regulations, which will be subject to annulment by resolution of either House of Parliament.

It is expected that the regulations will follow closely the Town and Country Planning (Churches, Places of Religious Worship and Burial Grounds) Regulations 1950 (S.I. 1950 No. 792) which are the current regulations for the purposes of the similar provisions in section 128 of the Town and Country Planning Act 1971.

Sub-paragraph (11) provides that paragraph 12 does not affect any rights to take action against an authority or any person in respect of any contraventions except as is mentioned in sub-paragraph (1) or (6).

Sub-paragraph (12) defines " burial grounds " as including any churchyard, cemetery or other ground, whether consecrated or not, which has at any time been set aside for interment, and " monument " as including a tombstone or other memorial.

Sub-paragraph (13) provides that paragraph 11 does not apply in Scotland (*see* paragraphs 12 and 13).

Use and development of churches and burial grounds in Scotland

Paragraph 12 applies to land in Scotland which is acquired under Part III by a local authority, section 118 of the Town and Country Planning (Scotland) Act 1972 (Provisions as to churches and burial grounds).   **Paragraph 13** applies to land in Scotland which is acquired under Part III by a new town authority, the provisions of section 20 of the New Towns (Scotland) Act 1968 (Use and development of churches and burial grounds).

Use and development of land for open spaces

Paragraph 14: The purposes for which common land, open space or fuel or field garden allotments can be utilised are generally regulated by statutory enactments of a severely restricted nature.   Restrictions may be overridden by acquisition under a compulsory purchase order, which in the case of land of these categories is subject to special Parliamentary procedure except where the Secretary of State gives a certificate under paragraph 11, Schedule 1, Acquisition of Land Acts (that the area does not exceed 250 square yards, or is required for the widening or drainage of a highway, or that equally advantageous land is to be given in exchange).   In other cases, where the land is acquired by agreement, it would be doubtful, in the absence of the provisions of paragraph 14, whether such land could in fact be used for development purposes. **This paragraph removes the doubt.** It corresponds with section 129 of the Town and Country Planning Act 1971 (section 119 of the Scottish Act).

Sub-paragraph (1) provides that land being or forming part of a common or open space or fuel or field garden allotment which has been acquired by an authority under Part III of the Act may be used by any person in accordance with planning permission notwithstanding any restrictions in any other enactment.

Sub-paragraph (2) makes it clear that paragraph 14 does not affect any right to take action against an authority or any person in respect of any contravention of any regulating enactment except as is mentioned in sub-paragraph (1).

Note: " common ", " fuel or field garden allotment " and " open space ", are defined in section 6.

Saving for paragraphs 11 *to* 14

Paragraph 15 (corresponding with section 133(2) and (3) of the Town and Country Planning Act 1971 (section 122(2) and (3) of the Scottish Act)), applies to paragraphs 11-14.

Sub-paragraph (2) makes it clear that the exercise by any authority or body corporate of the powers conferred by paragraphs 11 to 14 (use and development of churches, burial grounds and open spaces) is subject to any limitations imposed by law on an authority by virtue of their constitution.

Sub-paragraph (3) makes it clear that the powers to use land (in accordance with planning permission) conferred by paragraphs 11 to 14 cover any use whether or not it involves the erection, construction, carrying out or maintenance of any building work.

This is necessary because in planning law " use " does not usually include the carrying out of building or other operations.

Construction of the Compulsory Purchase Acts in relation to this Act

Paragraph 16: Since the Acquisition of Land Acts are applied to compulsory purchase under Part III of the Act, Part I of the Compulsory Purchase Act 1965 is automatically incorporated in relation to acquisitions in England and Wales (in Scotland the Lands Clauses Acts and section 6 of the Railway Clauses Consolidation (Scotland) Act 1845). **The effect of paragraph 16** is to provide that a claim for compensation for injurious affection under enactments is not defeated either by the fact that the works carried out and giving rise to the claim do not fall within the meaning of the works in those enactments, or by the fact that they may not be carried out by the acquiring authority within the meaning of those enactments. For example, without sub-paragraph (1)(*b*) no claim for compensation could be made under paragraph 10(4) of Schedule 4 in respect of injurious affection caused by the erection of a building, by a person deriving title under an authority of land acquired by that authority under Part III of the Act, in a manner which involves interference with a right of way enjoyed by the claimant.

Sub-paragraph (1) provides that where the Compulsory Purchase Act 1965 applies under the Act references to the execution of works include references to works authorised by paragraph 10 of Schedule 4 (notwithstanding interference with an interest or right or any breach of restriction as to user); and that references in section 10 of the 1965 Act to the acquiring authority are to mean references to the persons by whom the buildings or works are erected, constructed or carried out.

Sub-paragraph (2) makes similar provision to sub-paragraph (1) in relation to the relevant Scottish enactments. [The provisions of paragraph 17 correspond with section 132(4)(*a*) and (*b*) of the Town and Country Planning Act 1971 and section 121(4)(*a*) and (*b*) of the Scottish Act.]

Extinguishment of rights of way, and rights as to apparatus, of statutory undertakers

[Paragraph 8 of Schedule 4, dealing with the extinguishment of private rights of way and rights as to apparatus over land required compulsorily under the Act has no application to rights vested in or apparatus belonging to statutory undertakers. **Paragraphs 17, 18 and 19** (corresponding to sections 230, 231 and 232 of the 1971 Act (sections 219, 220 and 221, of the Scottish Act)) provide special treatment for interference with such rights and apparatus.]

Paragraph 17.   *Sub-paragraph* (1) provides that if statutory undertakers have any right of way, or any right connected with apparatus, on, under or over land acquired by an authority under Part III of the Act, or if there is any apparatus belonging to statutory undertakers, the authority may serve on the undertakers a notice stating that the rights will be extinguished after the period specified in the notice (not less than 28 days) or requiring the removal of any apparatus before the end of that period.   The authority must first be satisfied that the action is necessary for the purpose of carrying out any development.

Under *sub-paragraph* (2) the undertakers may serve a counter-notice specifying their grounds of objection, within 28 days.

Sub-paragraph (3) provides that if the undertakers do not serve a counter-notice all rights of way and all rights as to apparatus are extinguished at the end of the period mentioned in the notice and any apparatus may be removed and disposed of by the authority.

Sub-paragraph (4) provides that in the event of a counter-notice the authority may either withdraw their notice or apply to the Secretary of State and the " appropriate Minister ", *e.g.* in the case of land acquired from an electricity undertaking the Secretary of State for Energy, for an order embodying the terms of the notice.   The procedure for making an order is set out in paragraph 18.

Sub-paragraph (5) (corresponding with section 237(2), 1971 Act (section 226(2) of the Scottish Act)) makes provision for compensation for the extinguishment of any right or any requirement to remove apparatus.

Sub-paragraph (6) applies the relevant provisions of the Town and Country Planning Acts to the calculation of compensation payable under sub-paragraph (5). Under these provisions, based on the principle of equivalent reinstatement, the assessment takes account of the reasonable cost of acquiring alternative land or rights of providing apparatus, etc., and the estimated cost of any decrease in net receipts of the undertaking. In default of agreement compensation falls to be settled by the Lands Tribunal.

Orders under paragraph 17

Paragraph 18 (corresponding to section 231, 1971 Act, and section 220, Scottish Act) prescribes the procedure for making orders under paragraph 17(4) extinguishing rights of statutory undertakers in land acquired under Part III of the Act where the undertakers have objected to a notice served on them under paragraph 18(1).

Sub-paragraph (1) provides that the Minister and the " appropriate Minister " must give the statutory undertakers an opportunity of objecting to the application made by the authority under paragraph 17(4) and that the Ministers must consider the objection and afford both parties, *i.e.* the statutory undertakers and the authority, an opportunity of being heard by a person appointed jointly by the Secretary of State and the appropriate Minister. The " Ministers " may then if they think fit, make the order as applied for, either with or without modification.

Sub-paragraph (2) provides that the effect of an order made under paragraph 17(4) is to extinguish the rights in question at the end of the period specified in the order and to enable the authority to remove and dispose of any apparatus which the order has required the undertakers to remove but they have not done so.

Notice for same purposes as paragraph 17 *but given by statutory undertakers to authority*

Paragraph 19 confers on statutory undertakers the right to remove their apparatus from land which has been acquired by an authority under Part III of the Act, or to re-site their apparatus, if the proposed development necessitates this on technical or other grounds connected with the carrying on of the undertaking.

Sub-paragraph (1) provides that the undertakers may serve on the authority a notice claiming right to enter on the land and remove or re-site the apparatus.

Sub-paragraph (2) provides that a notice of claim must be served not later than 21 days after the beginning of the development of the land.

Sub-paragraphs (3) *to* (5) provide for a counter-notice procedure. If no counter-notice is served within 28 days the statutory undertakers have the rights they have claimed. If the authority serve a counter-notice the statutory undertakers may either withdraw their notice of claim or apply to the Secretary of State and the appropriate Minister for an order conferring the rights claimed or such modified rights as the Ministers may decide.

Under *sub-paragraph* (6) where the undertakers are given rights they may arrange for the authority to carry out the removal or re-siting under their superintendence or may do the works themselves.

Under *sub-paragraph* (7) the statutory undertakers are entitled to compensation in respect of the removal or re-siting works, and *sub-paragraph* (8) applies the relevant compensation provisions of the Planning Acts.

Rights of Entry

Paragraphs 20 and 21 contain powers for officers of the Valuation Office of the Inland Revenue and other duly authorised persons to enter land for the purpose of surveying it, or estimating its value in connection with any proposal to acquire it under Part III of the Act or any consequential claim for compensation. In relation to the Land Authority for Wales an additional power of entry is provided to enable the Authority to decide whether to make an application for planning permission to carry out relevant development of the land in question. The power to survey includes a power to bore into the subsoil or search for minerals.

Consequential matters covered by paragraph 21 include

(1) notice of intended entry and production of authority to enter;

(2) penalties for wilful obstruction of lawful entry;

(3) penalties for disclosure of trade secrets by person authorised to enter;

(4) compensation for damage to land in exercise of right of entry;

(5) determination by Lands Tribunal or, as the case may be by the Lands Tribunal for Scotland of disputed compensation for damage of land;

(6) notice of intention to carry out works to ascertain nature of subsoil or presence of minerals in the course of survey.   If the land in question is held by statutory undertakers who object on grounds of serious detriment to their undertaking the works may not be carried out except with the authority of the appropriate Minister.

Paragraphs 20 and 21 (except 20(2)) correspond with provisions in sections 179(1) and (2), 280(7) and 281 of the 1971 Act (sections 168(1) and (2), 265(7) and 266 of the Scottish Act).

Displacement of Rent Acts

Paragraph 22 (corresponding with section 130(3), 1971 Act (section 120(3) of the Scottish Act)) enables an authority to obtain possession of a house they have acquired under Part III of the Act, notwithstanding the fact that the house is occupied and the tenancy is a protected tenancy under the Rent Act 1968 (or the Rent (Scotland) Act 1971 or Part III of the Housing (Scotland) Act 1974 as the case may be).   This only applies where the Secretary of State certifies that possession of the house is immediately required to enable the authority to utilise the house or the land on which it stands for the purpose for which the land was acquired by the authority.   The Land Compensation Act 1973 and the Scotland Act apply so as to provide for such matters as rehousing, home loss payments and disturbance payments, where possession is obtained under this paragraph.

PART IV—APPROPRIATION OF LAND

Paragraph 23: The powers of local authorities to appropriate land, contained in section 122 of the Local Government Act 1972 (section 73, Scotland Act 1973), are restricted to land which is no longer required for the purpose for which it was held immediately before the appropriation. Paragraph 23 modifies these Local Government Act provisions by removing the restriction, with the effect that, in the case of *sub-paragraph* (1)(*a*) a local authority may appropriate land in order to take advantage of provisions which apply to land acquired under Part III of the Act, *i.e.* the powers in Part III of Schedule 4 other than paragraph 8. [The provisions of the Town and Country Planning Acts corresponding with Part III of Schedule 4 cover both land acquired **or appropriated** for planning purposes.] In the circumstances of *sub-paragraph* (1)(*b*) the effect is to enable land which was held for the purposes of Part III, and which can be said to be still required for those wide purposes, to be appropriated for the purposes of specific functions, *e.g.* housing, education.

Sub-paragraph (2) applies Part III of this Schedule (other than para. 8) to land appropriated under Part III of the Act as if it were land acquired under that Part.

[**Note:** Section 122 of the Local Government Act 1972 is applied to the two Boards by the Lake District Special Planning Board Order 1973 and the Peak Park Joint Planning Board Order 1973.]

SCHEDULE 5
LAND ACQUISITION AND MANAGEMENT SCHEMES

This Schedule deals with the preparation, revision and contents of the land acquisition and management schemes (LAMS) which authorities in England and Scotland are required to prepare under section 16 of the Act. The Schedule lays down only the major factors to which authorities must have regard, and the essential ingredients which must appear in each scheme. It also contains default powers for the Secretary of State to prepare a scheme if the authorities concerned do not do so, and to revise a scheme where necessary.

The role of the Secretary of State is limited. He is not required to approve LAMS so he need not intervene where authorities can agree on a LAMS within the time-limit set by section 16. But he is given power to direct authorities to revise a scheme, and a power to make or revise a LAMS himself in cases of default.

Paragraph 1 lists certain matters that are to be considered by authorities in preparing or revising a scheme. These are:—

(*a*) available resources, including qualified staff;

(*b*) previous experience in dealing with land for private development;

(*c*) statutory provisions governing the discharge of planning and local government functions;

(*d*) existing arrangements for the division of planning functions between authorities;

(*e*) any authority functions, particularly housing functions;

(*f*) any other matters that the Secretary of State may direct.

The object of this paragraph is to list only the items which it is essential for authorities to take into account in preparing or revising a scheme. They remain free to take account of other items which they consider to be important. The paragraph contains a power for the Secretary of State to add other matters; this is because experience and changing circumstances may throw up other matters which authorities should be required to take into account.

The specific requirements in the paragraph relate to three broad fields. The first, which is likely to be critical in the early years of operation of the community land scheme, is available resources—in particular manpower. This provision is not restricted in scope to manpower directly employed by the authorities—it extends to the total manpower situation involved in the implementation of the community land scheme in the area of each county authority and of each regional and general planning authority in Scotland, and includes, for instance, the availability to authorities of the services of the District Valuer. The second field is the experience of individual authorities in exercising the kind of functions they will now be required to exercise under the community land scheme. In practice this criterion seems likely to run with that concerning resources. Finally, account must be taken of the existing allocation of functions between authorities, whether on a statutory basis or by agreement; this applies in particular to housing and planning functions.

Contents of Schemes

Paragraph 2 provides that each scheme shall contain arrangements for authorities' functions in connection with land for private development. Particular reference is made to arrangements for the service of notices under Part II of Schedule 7 to the Act in connection with the suspension of planning permission; it will be important to the avoidance of delay that there shall be clear and well-understood arrangements in this field.

Paragraph 3 provides that each scheme shall contain arrangements for co-ordination of action between authorities; for common staffing (where appropriate); for transfer of funds between authorities (where appropriate); for resolving disputes; for periodic reviews of the scheme; and for any other matters that the Secretary of State may direct. Each scheme may also contain such transitional, supplemental and incidental provisions as appear expedient to the authorities concerned. The provisions relating to arrangements for co-ordination, transfers between land accounts, and determination of disputes are not to apply to any scheme made by a general planning authority in Scotland.

These provisions are generally self-explanatory, given the nature of the schemes. The provision for transfer of funds between authorities is intended to cover payments for joint use of staff. It will also enable part of the 30% " local " share of surplus occurring in an authority's community land surplus account (*see* section 44) to be transferred to another authority, and thus assist in ensuring that the distribution of functions is settled on a pragmatic basis and is not distorted by financial considerations.

In general, planning authority areas in Scotland only the general planning authority themselves have functions under the Act and theirs will be the only community land accounts for that area. It follows that general planning authorities will not be required to co-ordinate action under the Act with their district authorities and their schemes can be simplified accordingly. But there will still be matters among those listed under paragraph 3 above justifying the making of schemes by general planning authorities, and the Act provides accordingly.

Supervision by Secretary of State

Paragraph 4. *Sub-paragraph* (1) provides for each county authority (or regional or general planning authority in Scotland) to send a copy of each scheme or revision to the Secretary of State as soon as it has been made or revised.

Sub-paragraph (2) gives the Secretary of State power to require a scheme to be revised, after proper consultations, and to set a date by which this is to be done. This will enable the Secretary of State to act where he considers that circumstances require an existing scheme to be revised earlier than the scheme itself provides (under the requirement of paragraph 3(*e*) above), or where he considers that the scheme (or revision) prepared by the authorities is inadequate (possibly because of representations made to him by one of the authorities). It will also, in Scotland, provide a means whereby the Secretary of State can require further weight to be given to the view of a district planning authority where he feels this has not been adequately taken into account in the scheme.

Sub-paragraph (3) gives the Secretary of State powers to make or revise a scheme himself in the event of default by the authorities involved. Default may arise either from failure to prepare an initial scheme within the time allowed or from failure to comply with a direction under the previous sub-paragraph.

Public Inspection

Paragraph 5 requires that each authority within the area of a county authority shall deposit a copy of the scheme (or the scheme as revised) at their principal office and keep it available for public inspection at reasonable hours. It also requires each of the authorities concerned to furnish copies of the current scheme to any person who so applies on payment of a reasonable sum for each copy and further to send copies to every parish council concerned. (*Sub-paragraphs* (1) *and* (2))

General Planning Authorities in Scotland send not to parish councils but to district councils. (*Sub-paragraph* (3))

Although LAMS are concerned with the distribution of functions between authorities operating the scheme, it is important for the public—individuals as well as builders and developers—to be able to find out which authority will be exercising particular functions in a given area. Also it is helpful to keep local authorities which are not authorities for the purposes of the land scheme informed of the arrangements made in their area.

Paragraph 6 applies the provisions of paragraph 5 to any direction made under section 16(7) which would make a LAMS legally enforceable.

SCHEDULE 6
GENERAL DUTIES OF AUTHORITIES

Paragraph 1 sets out the criteria whereby authorities interpret the general duties imposed on them by section 17. In particular the criteria are to be applied in deciding whether development land should be developed by them, or made available for development by others, and what use should be made of the land until it is developed.

Under the scheme authorities will have a basic responsibility to ensure that an adequate supply of land for development is maintained. As they move towards a monopoly position over development land objective guidance will become more and more necessary. Hence the duty to have regard to the various matters enumerated in paragraph 1.

Sub-paragraph (1) sets out under seven headings the matters to which authorities are required to have regard:—

(1) the needs of people living in their area, or wishing to do so; also the needs of commerce and industry.

(2) the needs of builders and developers (particularly the small builder) in the area.   One major danger of the scheme especially as the authorities expand their direct labour departments under the recent urgings of ministers is that work will disappear for the private sector builder.

(3) the needs of agriculture and foresty.   This is to ensure that regard is had to the conservation of the country-side and there is not a headlong rush to turn land to profit.

(4) the needs and obligations of other authorities, *e.g.* a county authority should take account of the require-ments of a district authority and *vice versa*.   This will inevitably lead to pressures from metropolitan autho-rities in need of housing land upon authorities near the major cities.   Authorities should also have regard for the needs of parish councils and, in Wales, community councils, who have limited land acquisition powers and may look to authorities to help them meet their land needs.

(5) the needs and obligations of charities to ensure there is sufficient land to enable them to pursue their socially beneficial activities.

(6) Although statutory undertakers (by virtue of sections 18(3)(*d*) and 22(8)(*b*)) will be able to acquire and develop land they need for operational purposes with-out local authority intervention, authorities are required to conduct their planning and allocation of land in a way which takes into account statutory undertakers' own needs.

(7) This gives the Secretary of State power to prescribe additional matters which authorities will have to take into account.

K

Sub-paragraph (2) states that in Scotland a general planning authority shall also have regard to the needs and obligations of district councils within their area.

In Scotland district councils are not planning authorities but have important functions involving acquisition and development of land.   These functions need to be recognised by the general planning authority.

Paragraph 2 is concerned with applications to develop land from former owners and from developers with the former owner's consent who have identified a site for development by applying for planning pemission.

It contains the prior right provisions (*see* general commentary pages 30 to 32).

Sub-paragraphs (1) *and* (2) provide that where an authority decide that neither they nor any other authority will develop land acquired by them as development land they shall not dispose of it to anyone else nor enter into a binding contract to do so until they have first had regard to an application made under sub-paragraph (3).

Sub-paragraph (3) defines the relevant applications as those made, before all outstanding material interests in the land have been acquired by the authority, by:—

(*a*) the immediate former owner of the land;

(*b*) a person applying for planning permission for development of the kind for which the land is being made available (subject to the provisions of sub-paragraph (4) below requiring the owner's consent),

and as applications for an opportunity to negotiate either—

(i) the purchase of a material interest in the land to carry out the development for which the land is being made available, or

(ii) to carry out that development (*e.g.* under a building agreement).

In either case the terms must be acceptable to the authority.

Sub-paragraph (4) states that sub-paragraph (3)(*b*) only applies where the application is accompanied by the written consent of the immediate former owner.

Ministers have already made it clear that although prior right cannot be absolute they would expect a very strong presumption to operate that land would be made available to a prior right applicant. Authorities will be advised in disposing of land that, where there are prior right applicants, only in exceptional circumstances should authorities dispose of interests in land to other than such applicants, provided always that acceptable terms can be agreed.

It will have been noted that a third party (*i.e.* a developer) may not be given a prior right in respect of land for which he has made a planning application unless it is accompanied with the written consent of the owner. This provision was introduced to meet objections that otherwise seemingly unconscionable arrangements might be entered into between local authorities and developers. However, the denial of a prior right will not prevent a developer having identified land for an authority tendering with other developers with possibility of " rings " growing up in different areas.

SCHEDULE 7
PLANNING PERMISSION FOR RELEVANT DEVELOPMENT

This Schedule complements the provisions of sections 19 and 20. It sets out the procedural arrangements in relation to planning permissions for relevant development granted before[1] the relevant date in respect of:—

(*a*) applications made **before** the first appointed day where permission granted after 12 September 1974[2] (section 19); and

(*b*) applications made **on or after** the first appointed day (section 20).

In some cases the provisions are common to both sections: in others separate provisions are needed to deal with the different circumstances.

It may be helpful to set out here the manner in which the arrangements for handling applications for relevant development will operate under this Schedule.

---

[1] Permissions after relevant date are automatically suspended, section 21.
[2] Permissions before 12 September 1974 will be excepted development under regulations.

PLANNING APPLICATIONS ON OR AFTER FIRST APPOINTED DAY

(1) Section 20 and Schedule 7 provide that any planning permission for relevant development granted on an application made on or after the first appointed day will be " suspended " until either the land is acquired by an authority (whether by agreement or compulsorily) or all the authorities concerned abandon their powers of compulsory purchase under the Act. (This procedure would not apply to land in which no material interests are outstanding or to the operational land of statutory undertakers.)

(2) Where, therefore, an application for planning permission for relevant development is made after the first appointed day each authority within whose area the land lies will be required to serve, within the time laid down for giving a planning decision (including any extension of time) a notice stating whether or not, in the event that planning permission is granted, they intend to acquire any or all of the land in question. Where no notice is served within the prescribed period this will be treated as a deemed notice of no intention to acquire. Paragraph 9 of the Schedule provides that a notice may apply to part only of the land in question. For simplicity, this note is written in terms of one notice covering all of the land, but it should be borne in mind that there could be different notices for different parts. This does not however affect the general principles.

(3) Although the Act provides that all authorities will have concurrent powers of acquisition for land in their areas, the intention is that Land Acquisition and Management Schemes should provide for one of the authorities only to exercise these powers in any particular case. In practice, therefore, the multiple approach implicit in the procedure is unlikely to arise, save in exceptional cases. In the following paragraphs it is assumed, for the sake of simplicity, that we are concerned with the attitude of one authority only—*i.e.* that all the other authorities concerned have either issued notices of no intention to acquire or else are deemed to have done so as a result of failing to issue any notice at all within the required period (with consequent loss of compulsory powers under the Act—*see* next paragraph).

SITUATION WHERE ACQUISITION NOT PROPOSED

(4) Where the authority concerned serve a notice of no
intention to acquire (whether or not this is conditional, *see*
next paragraph), or fail to serve any notice within the required
period, the suspension imposed by the Act will be lifted from
the planning permission. The authority concerned will then
lose their power to acquire the land compulsorily under the
Act for a period of 5 years; and the owner will know that he
is free to go ahead with his development.

CONDITIONAL NOTICES

(5) Paragraphs 7 and 8 of Schedule 7 provide that notices of
no intention to acquire may be made subject to certain conditions, in particular:—

> (*a*) that the land is developed in accordance with the
> planning permission for which application is being
> made (or in accordance with a previous—specified—
> permission);

> (*b*) that the development is begun—and/or completed—
> within a reasonable time (specified in the notice).

If a condition is included in a notice of an intention to acquire,
and is not complied with, then the authority concerned will
regain their powers of compulsory acquisition under the Act.

SITUATION WHERE ACQUISITION IS PROPOSED

(6) Where an authority serve notice of intention to acquire
the land, and planning permission is granted (either by the
local planning authority or on appeal), the permission will
remain suspended until one or other of the following events
occurs:—

> (i) the authority withdraw their notice of intention to
> acquire;

> (ii) the authority fail to acquire, or to publish notice of
> the making of a C.P.O., within the requisite time[1];

---

[1] In the case of a planning application granted by the planning authority the
time limit for acquisition by agreement, or publication of the C.P.O., is 12 months
from the date of the notice of intention to acquire. Where permission is granted
on appeal the time limit is 12 months from the date on which the copy of the
notice of appeal is served on the Secretary of State.

  (iii) a C.P.O. having been made and confirmed, the
authority fail to serve a notice to treat the date on
which the C.P.O. becomes operative;

  (iv) The Secretary of State says that he does not intend to
confirm the C.P.O.;

  (v) the C.P.O., having been confirmed, is quashed by a
Court;

  (vi) the land is acquired by an authority (either compulsorily or by agreement).

(7) Where any of the events set out in paragraphs (6)(i)-(iii)
occurs, the authority will lose their powers to make a compulsory purchase order **under the Act** for any of the land in
question for a period of 5 years. The date from which the
5 years runs is as follows:—

In the case of

(6)(i)	...	the date of the notice of withdrawal;
(6)(ii)	...	the end of the period for acquiring the land or making the C.P.O.;
(6)(iii)	...	the end of the period for serving the notice to treat.

An authority will not lose their powers of compulsory acquisition when events at (6)(iv) or (v) occur, as in these cases failure
to pursue acquisition will not arise of the authority's own
volition.

ENFORCEMENT

(8) The start of development while a planning permission is
still suspended will be regarded as development carried out
without planning permission and the existing enforcement
provisions of section 87 of the Town and Country Planning
Act 1971 (section 84 of the Scottish Act of 1972) will apply
(section 22(1)). Moreover, if an authority then decide to
acquire the land the value of any relevant development covered
by the planning permission actually carried out while it was
suspended would be disregarded for the purpose of assessing
the compensation payable.

PLANNING APPLICATIONS MADE BEFORE FIRST APPOINTED DAY

(9) A modified procedure is provided in section 19 and Schedule 7 to enable persons who applied for planning permission before the first appointed day to serve a notice on the authorities with powers under the Act asking them whether or not they propose to acquire their land. On receipt of the notice the planning permission concerned will be suspended and the authorities will have 3 months in which to decide whether or not to acquire. If they decide not to acquire the land the suspension of the planning permission will be lifted and they will be debarred from acquiring the land (using their compulsory powers under the Act) for 5 years from the date of their decision. If they decide to acquire, the procedures in paragraph (6) would apply.

PLANNING PERMISSION GRANTED WHEN " PROHIBITION "
    IMPOSED

(10) These provisions will not apply to development which is the subject of a " relevant date " under section 18. From the time such an order is made all planning permissions for " designated " relevant development by virtue of section 21 will be automatically suspended until such time as either:—

(i) the development is carried out by an authority, or

(ii) the land has passed through public ownership and has been made available for a particular development by the authority concerned.

The arrangements outlined above for handling the planning applications for Relevant Development are set out in the three parts of this Schedule:—

Part I of the Schedule deals with the abandonment of the power to purchase (which arises in sections 19(4) and 20(2)), and the manner in which the suspension of planning permission (mentioned in sections 19(5) and 20(3)) may be lifted.

Part II deals with the notices which authorities are required to serve under the new arrangements, including the conditions which may be imposed in such notices.

Part III concerns the transmission of copies of planning applications to other interested authorities.

PART I—

Abandonment of power to purchase

Paragraph 1 deals with both section 19 and section 20. It explains in what circumstances and at what time an authority are regarded as abandoning their powers of compulsory purchase under section 15. The concept of abandonment of powers of compulsory purchase is important not only because it effectively deprives an authority of the opportunity to buy the land in question compulsorily under the powers contained in the Act for a period of 5 years, but also because it ends the suspension of planning permission referred to in those sections (and paragraph 2 of the Schedule) and thus allows the owner to go ahead and develop his land.

Sub-paragraph (1) defines, by reference to the table which follows, when—and in what circumstances—authorities are regarded as abandoning their powers of compulsory purchase.

Sub-paragraphs (2) *and* (3) provide that the period for which the powers are lost is 5 years from the time indicated in the table unless the authority served a conditional notice that they did not intend to purchase the land and some or all of the conditions have not been complied with. In the latter event the period would end on the first failure to comply with the conditions (*i.e.* the authority would regain their powers at that point in time).

The Table sets out the various circumstances in which authorities lose their powers of compulsory purchase under the Act, and the point in time from which the 5-year loss of powers runs. These are:—

Circumstance	Time of abandonment of powers
1. An authority serve notice of no intention to acquire the land (whether or not subject to conditions—*see* paragraphs 7 and 8).	Date of service of the notice.

Circumstance	Time of abandonment of powers
2. An authority serve notice of intention to acquire the land in cases falling within section 19.	12 months from the date of service of the notice unless the authority have by then taken the steps to acquire laid down in *sub-paragraph* (5) *below*.
3. An authority serve notice of intention to acquire the land in cases falling within section 20.	As 2 above **or,** where there has been an appeal against refusal of planning permission, 12 months from the date when the Secretary of State is notified of the appeal, unless the authority have by then taken the steps to acquire laid down in *sub-paragraph* (5).
4. An authority publish notice of the making of a compulsory purchase order.	12 months from the date the C.P.O. becomes operative, unless the authority have by then served notices to treat in respect of all outstanding material interests in the land.

There are two more circumstances not specifically mentioned in the table where an authority loses its power.   There are:—

5. Where an authority fail to serve any notice (*see* paragraphs 4(3) and 5(4) below).	On the latest date allowed for serving a notice.
6. Where an authority, having served a notice of intention to acquire the land subsequently decide not to go ahead (*see* paragraph 6 below).	Date of service of the notice of their change of mind.

Sub-paragraph (4) defines a notice as meaning one served under Part II of the Schedule on (*a*) a person making an election under section 19, and (*b*) where section 20 applies, an applicant for planning permission.

Sub-paragraph (5) defines, for the purposes of the Schedule, the time when an authority complete the first step towards acquisition as being either the date they enter into a binding contract to purchase the land (by agreement) or when notice of the making of a compulsory purchase order is published.

End of suspension of planning permission

Paragraph 2 is common to both sections. It defines the circumstances in which the suspension of planning permission (imposed by sections 19(6) and 20(3)) is lifted.

Sub-paragraph (1) explains that the suspension ends when all the authorities concerned have abandoned their power to purchase the land or when one of them has purchased it, which-ever first occurs.

The purpose of the suspension is to allow an authority time to acquire the land if it wishes. Once the decision is made there is no reason to prevent development taking place.

Sub-paragraph (2) introduces two further circumstances where, for the purposes of ending the suspension of a planning permission only, an authority are regarded as having aban-doned their power to purchase. These are:—

(*a*) when the Secretary of State gives notice that he does not intend to confirm the compulsory purchase order on the land in question; or

(*b*) when a compulsory purchase order, having been made confirmed by the Secretary of State, is quashed by a court.

In these two circumstances, though the suspension is lifted from the planning permission, the authority concerned do not lose their powers of compulsory purchase as their failure to pursue acquisition does not arise of their own volition. For example, the order may be quashed, or not confirmed, because of some technicality, and the authority may wish to make another order without this defect.

Sub-paragraph (3) makes it clear that " authority " in paragraph 1(1)(*b*) includes a local authority in Wales whose area includes the land. This is because although the powers and duties under the Act in Wales are to be exercised by the Land Authority for Wales and not the local authorities, Welsh local authorities already have powers to buy and dispose of land for private development and must, therefore, be able to " unsuspend " planning permissions.

Interpretation

Paragraph 3 is also common to both sections. It makes it clear that subject to paragraph 9(3)—which provides that paragraphs 1 and 2 may apply differently to different parts of the land covered by the planning permission—references in the Schedule to the purchase or acquisition of land shall cover all outstanding material interests in the land in question—that is to say that all material interests must be in public ownership before references to purchase or acquisition are to be regarded as satisfied.

PART II.—NOTICES BY AUTHORITIES

Planning permission to which section 19 *applies*

Paragraph 4 deals with the section 19 situation and relates to notices by authorities under that section.

Sub-paragraph (1) provides that where a notice of election under section 19 is served each of the authorities concerned must serve a notice on the person making the election stating whether or not they intend to acquire the land to which the planning permission relates. This will enable the owner to establish whether or not he can go ahead with development on the land without public intervention.

Sub-paragraph (2) requires the authorities to serve the notice in the prescribed form within 3 months of the service of the notice of election on them.

Sub-paragraph (3) makes it clear that failure on the part of an authority to serve the notice within the 3 months' period will have the same effect as if they had at the end of the 3 months served a notice of no intention to acquire.

Planning permission to which section 20 *applies*

Paragraph 5 deals with the section 20 situation and concerns notices to be given by authorities receiving applications for planning permission for relevant development after the first appointed day.

Sub-paragraph (1) requires each of the authorities to serve a notice on the applicant, and on all those persons whom the applicant was required to inform when making his planning application, stating whether or not they intend to acquire the land to which the application relates in the event that planning permission is granted.

Although the requirement to serve notices applies to all the authorities in the area the intention is that arrangements should be made in the Land Acquisition and Management Schemes proposed under section 16 for one of the authorities only to exercise the powers of acquisition—and therefore to serve notices—in any particular case (*see* Schedule 5, paragraph 2(2)). The multiple approach implicit in the procedure is therefore unlikely to arise in practice. The category of persons who must be notified of a planning application under section 27 of the 1971 Act (and section 24 of the Scottish Act of 1972) is widened by Schedule 10 paragraphs 6 and 7 to include any person entitled to a material interest in the land.

Sub-paragraph (2) provides that notices under paragraph 5 shall be in the prescribed form and shall be served within the time allowed for giving a planning decision (normally two months but may be extended if the applicant agrees).

Sub-paragraph (3) deals with the situation where the planning application is one deemed to have been made under section 88 of the 1971 Act (or section 85 of the Scottish Act of 1972). Those sections relate to planning permissions granted on appeal against an enforcement notice. In these cases there has been no planning application as such, but one is deemed to have been made at the time of the appeal. Provision is therefore made for the service of notices, under the paragraph, where planning permission is granted in this manner, but in this case the time limit for serving the notices is 3 months from the grant of permission. The notices must be served not only on the applicant but also on any other person on whom the enforcement notice was served.

Sub-paragraph (4) is similar to paragraph 4(3) and provides that failure on the part of an authority to serve a notice on the applicant for the planning permission within the time limit allowed will have the same effect as if they had, at the end of that time, served a notice of no intention to acquire.

Paragraph 5(1) requires the authority to serve notice both on the applicant **and** those persons on whom the applicant has given notice of intention to apply for planning permission. It is only failure to serve the notice on the former which operates in the same way as a notice of intention not to acquire under 5(4).

Duty to Notify Change of Intention

Paragraph 6 is common to both sections.

Sub-paragraph (1) provides that where an authority, having served a notice of intention to acquire, subsequently decide not to proceed with acquisition they must serve a notice to that effect on all persons on whom the original notice was served. In addition, where they have already made a compulsory purchase order on the land they must also serve notice of their change of intention on all those persons on whom the notice of the making of the order was required to be served.

Sub-paragraph (2) states that the notice shall be in the prescribed form and shall be served as soon as practicable after the authority have decided not to proceed.

Notices subject to Conditions

Paragraphs 7-8 are common to both sections, and deal with conditional notices.

Sub-paragraph (1) provides that notices stating that an authority do not intend to acquire the land may be expressed to be subject to conditions. The kinds of conditions which may be imposed are set out in paragraph 8.

An authority may, for example, be quite content for the development proposed in the planning application to go ahead without their intervention provided they can be sure that that development, and no other will take place and that the development will be started or completed within a reasonable time. This provision would enable them to say they do not intend to acquire the land so long as these conditions are satisfied. If any of the conditions are not complied with however, the authority's powers of compulsory acquisition, which are regarded as abandoned on the serving of the notice, would then be restored. It would, however, be for the authority to decide whether to exercise its restored powers; there will be no obligation on the authority to do so.

Sub-paragraph (2) makes it clear that if any of the conditions imposed on a notice falls outside those laid down in paragraph 8 the notice shall be treated as if it were unconditional.

Sub-paragraph (3) permits a person to challenge the validity of a condition within 6 weeks of the date of service of the notice by applying to the High Court (or in Scotland, the Court of Session) to determine the question.

Sub-paragraph (4) states that except where so provided, *i.e.* in paragraph 7(3), conditions shall not be questioned on the grounds that they do not comply with paragraph 8 in any legal proceedings whatsoever.

A situation could arise where, for example, an invalid condition was not challenged at the time under paragraph 7(3) but a developer in subsequently selling land to someone else breaks that condition. The authority might then wish to use their revived compulsory purchase powers, and will not be inhibited from doing so by a claim by the new purchaser that they were acting *ultra vires*. (This provision is similar to that in paragraph 15 of Schedule 1 to the Acquisition of Land (Authorisation Procedure) Act 1946 which gives persons affected by compulsory purchase orders a limited time to question their validity.)

Kinds of Conditions

Paragraph 8 deals with the kind of conditions which may be imposed under paragraph 7.

Sub-paragraph (1) spells out the conditions. These are:—
— that the development shall be carried out in accordance with the originating planning permission (defined in paragraph 8(7)) or in accordance with a previous— specified—permission (conditions 1 and 2);

— that the development shall be begun, or completed, by a specified date (conditions 3 and 5);

— that, in the case of an outline planning permission, application for approval of all reserved matters is made by a specified date (condition 4);

— other conditions specified in regulations made by the Secretary of State (condition 6). The regulations will be subject to negative procedure sub-paragraph 8(6).

These conditions will of necessity be of a general rather than a specific nature since clearly regulations cannot be made to deal with individual cases. A purchaser of land for development will have to satisfy himself that not only have the conditions imposed by the authority been fulfilled but also those in all regulations issued.

Sub-paragraph (2) provides that a condition requiring the carrying out of development permitted by the originating planning permission (*i.e.* the one that is the subject of the procedures under sections 19 or 20—*see* paragraph 8(7)), or by an earlier specified one, implies a requirement that the development be begun within the time laid down in sections 41 and 42 of the 1971 Act and the equivalent sections 32 and 39 of the Scottish Act of 1972 (which prescribe a limit on the duration of planning permissions—normally five years from the date of grant), unless the condition itself provides for a shorter period.

This means that, where an authority tie a conditional notice of no intention to acquire to a specific planning permission (by the use of conditions as at 1 and 2 above) but do not lay down a time limit for commencement of the development (by the use of condition 3) the Planning Act time limit on the permission concerned applies for the purposes of the Act. The authority's powers of compulsory purchase under the Act would then be restored if development was not begun with the Planning Act time limit.

Sub-paragraph (3) requires any period prescribed by a notice to be a reasonable period.

Any question whether or not a period was reasonable would fall to be decided in the courts, by application under paragraph 7(3), within 6 weeks.

Sub-paragraph (4) makes it clear that the reference (in paragraph 7(1)) to a condition may be taken to mean a combination of two or more of those allowed by the paragraph.

Sub-paragraph (5) permits the relaxation of a condition at any time by a subsequent notice (served in the same way as the original one) provided that the condition as relaxed is one allowed by the paragraph. A condition may not however be relaxed after a failure to comply with it.

The effect of a breach of condition is to restore the authority's power of compulsory acquisition. Once a condition has been broken, therefore, it is a question of whether the authority propose to exercise their power, rather than whether they will relax the condition.

Sub-paragraph (6) provides that regulations made under this paragraph (8(1)6), *i.e.* attaching general conditions by the Secretary of State shall be subject to annulment by either House.

Sub-paragraph (7) defines the " originating planning permission " (which appears in paragraphs 8(1) and 8(2)) as meaning the permission referred to in sections 19 and 20 respectively; and " outline planning permission " and " reserved matters " as having the same meaning as in the Planning Acts.

Notices for parts of the land

Paragraph 9 relates to both sections and deals with notices for parts of a site.

Sub-paragraph (1) makes it clear that a notice given under Part II of the Schedule may relate to part only of the land included in the planning permission (in cases where section 19 applies) or the planning application (where section 20 applies).

Sub-paragraph (2) requires a notice given by an authority under Part II of the Schedule to be accompanied by a plan indicating the land to which the notice relates, except where the notice is one which states unconditionally that the authority do not intend to acquire any of the land.

A plan would be needed where, for example, the authority proposed to acquire only part of the land or to apply different conditions to different parts of the land.

Sub-paragraph (3) states that the provisions relating to the loss of compulsory purchase powers (paragraph 1) and the suspension of planning permission (paragraph 2) can apply differently to different parts of the land. This follows from the provisions of paragraph 9(1) that a notice may relate to part only of the land.

Sub-paragraph (4) makes it clear that, although a notice may relate to part only of the land, an authority must nevertheless serve a notice or notices in respect of the other part or parts as well.

Registration of Notices

Paragraph 10 is common to both sections and provides for the registration of notices given under paragraphs 4 and 5 of the Schedule in the Local Land Charges Register.

Sub-paragraph (1) provides that a notice under paragraph 4 or paragraph 5 to the effect that an authority intends to acquire the land shall be a local land charge.

This is more for the protection of a purchaser than the applicant for planning permission or the owner of land because the latter will know whether the authority have served a notice. The purchaser must have a certain means of discovering whether permission is suspended and what the authority's intention may be.   Search of the land charges register will give him this.

The registration does not apply to conditional notices of **no** intention to acquire for these do not suspend planning permissions; nor does the breach of a condition included in such a notice lead to suspension (though it does cause an authority to regain their powers—Schedule 7, paragraph 1(3)).

Sub-paragraph (2) provides that where an authority serve a notice under paragraph 6 stating they have changed their mind and decided after all not to proceed with acquisition they must send a copy of the notice to every authority keeping a register under the Land Charges Act 1925, whose area comprises any part of the land if the authority serving the notice do not themselves keep such a register.

Such a notice of course removes a suspension and is of importance again to intending purchasers.

Paragraph 11 makes similar provisions to that in paragraph 10 above but is worded to cover the requirement in procedure before changes are brought about by the Local Land Charges Act 1975 when it comes into operation.

Sub-paragraph (1) states that prior to the operation of the Local Land Charges Act 1975 paragraph 10 above shall operate with the following modifications.

Sub-paragraph (2) states that as soon as practicable after serving a notice of intention to acquire under paragraphs 4 and 5 the authority shall send a copy in respect of every other authority whose area comprises part of the land to the proper officer who shall register it in the manner prescribed under the Land Charges Act 1925.

Sub-paragraph (3) requires the substitution in 10(2) of the term " proper officer " for " local authority keeping the register ".

Sub-paragraph (4) makes it clear that a " local authority ", mentioned in paragraph 10 does not include a county council

or the G.L.C.   This is because the appropriate registers are
those kept at district rather than county level.

Paragraph 12 makes comparable provisions for Scotland to
those in paragraph 10, but takes account of the different
registration requirements there.   In this case the notice is
registered by the authority in the register kept by them by virtue
of section 31(2) of the Scottish Act of 1972: where they are
not the authority responsible for keeping such a register they
must send a copy of the notice to the responsible authority for
registration.

PART III.—TRANSMISSION OF INFORMATION
Copies of application for planning permission
Paragraph 13 deals with the section 20 situation.   It ensures
that all the authorities required to serve notices under para-
graph 5 receive copies of the relevant planning application.
This is necessary so that they can exercise their duty under the
Schedule to issue notices stating whether or not they intend to
acquire the land which is the subject of the application.

Paragraph 15(3) of Schedule 16 to the Local Government
Act 1972 already requires a district or county council outside
Greater London to send copies of applications made to one of
them to the other.   Paragraph 12 deals with the remaining
cases (including all those in Scotland where there is no provision
similar to the 1972 Act).

It is envisaged that, in practice, authorities will arrange
between themselves who is to operate the procedures under
section 20.   It will not usually be necessary, therefore, for
copies of all planning application to go to other authorities.
There is provision, both in the 1972 Act and in paragraph 13(3)
of this Schedule for an authority to direct that they do not wish
to see certain, or indeed any applications.

Sub-paragraph (1) states that paragraph 13 applies to applications for planning permission for development of any
description made on or after the first appointed day.

Sub-paragraph (2) with the Table provides that where certain authorities (mentioned in column 1 of the Table) receive applications for planning permissions to which the paragraph relates they must, as soon as practicable after receipt, send copies to the authorities specified in the second column of the Table.

Sub-paragraph (3) provides that the requirement of those authorities specified in column 1 of the Table to send copies to those specified in column 2 need not apply if the latter otherwise direct. This will enable the authorities in column 2 to specify, for example, that they only wish to see planning applications for those types of development in which they are likely to have an interest.

There is a similar provision in paragraph 15(3) of Schedule 16 to the 1972 Act.

Planning Permissions in Wales

Paragraph 14 is relevant to both sections 19 and 20.

Sub-paragraph (1) provides that on any grant of planning permission in respect of land in Wales (whether granted by the local planning authority or by the Secretary of State) the authority or the Secretary of State shall send a copy of the notification of the planning permission to the Land Authority for Wales.

The Land Authority will already have had a copy of the planning application and decided whether or not they propose to purchase the land in the event that planning permission is granted. They will therefore need to know when the permission is granted so that they can if necessary take steps to acquire the land in question.

Sub-paragraph (2) enables the Land Authority to direct that it does not wish to see some or any such notifications of planning permission.

This is a similar provision to that in paragraph 13(3).

SCHEDULE 8
DISPOSAL NOTIFICATION AREAS

This Schedule lays down the procedures to be adopted when an authority declare a disposal notification area under section 23, and when all or part of such an area is terminated under section 24.   It deals also with the Secretary of State's functions, including a power of veto, in relation to the declaration of disposal notification areas.

Most of the procedures concerned are based on those in the Housing Act 1974 concerning Housing Action Areas.

Part I of the Schedule deals with the arrangements for publishing notices of resolutions and with the functions of the Secretary of State.

Part II lays down the procedures for notifying an intended disposal.

Part III gives the circumstances when it is permissive not mandatory to give notice of an intended disposal.

Part IV deals with publicity arrangements when all or part of a disposal notification area is terminated.

Part V contains miscellaneous provisions.

PART I
Procedure on passing a resolution

Paragraph 1.   *Sub-paragraph* (1)(*a*) provides for early publication of a resolution declaring a disposal notification area, together with a map defining the area, and naming a place where it may be inspected.   This is necessary so that owners and purchasers of land in that area will know where they stand.   Paragraph 5 defines what is meant by publication.

Sub-paragraph (1)(*b*) requires the authority to send a copy of resolution, and of the map, to every parish or community council affected by the D.N.A.

Sub-paragraph (2) declares the resolution to be a local land charge which requires its registration under the Land Charges Act 1975 (paragraph 8 deals with procedure prior to that Act coming into force).

Functions of the Secretary of State

Paragraph 2 deals with the functions of the Secretary of State in regard to resolutions declaring disposal notification areas.

Sub-paragraph (1) requires an authority passing a resolution to send a copy of the resolution, and of the map, to the Secretary of State, as soon as practicable.

Sub-paragraph (2) enables the Secretary of State, if he thinks fit, at any time, to send the authority a notification that—

(a) the area covered by their resolution is no longer to be a disposal notification area, or

(b) a defined part of that area is to be excluded.

The Secretary of State will be advising authorities[1] of the circumstances in which he would consider the use of the disposal notification area procedure to be acceptable. The power of veto will give force to his guidance.

It is to be noted that the power of revocation is a continuing power and can be used at any time to meet changing circumstances, *e.g.* in the planning strategy for an area which no longer allocates land for relevant development.

Sub-paragraph (3) provides that a notification revoking all or part of a disposal notification area shall take effect on the date it is received by the authority. The paragraph also makes provision (similar to that in paragraph 1(1)) for the authority to publish a notice of the effect of the Secretary of State's decision and, for them to send a copy of the decision to every authority keeping a land charges register and to every parish and community council affected.

PART II

Notification of disposals

Paragraph 3 lays down the procedures for persons notifying intended disposals in disposal notification areas.

Sub-paragraph (1) states that paragraph 3 applies to notices of intended disposals given under section 23(5).

Sub-paragraph (2) requires such notices to be given (in the prescribed form) between 4 weeks and 6 months before the date of the intended disposal. This gives adequate time for the procedure to operate, whilst requiring the vendor to be

[1] *See also* Circular 121/75 para 28.

fairly near the point at which he would sell privately. He need not have a particular purchaser in mind and in effect must give notice as soon as he places his property in the hands of an estate agent provided he genuinely hopes to find a buyer within 6 months. Possibly in a difficult " buyers' market " he might leave notification until his solicitor prepares the draft contract. As a matter of caution a vendor's solicitors should prudently search in the local land charges register before he sends out a draft contract to see if the property falls within a disposal notification area.

Sub-paragraph (3) sets out the information to be contained in notices. This is:—

   (*a*) the name and address of the person furnishing the notice (*i.e.* the vendor);

   (*b*) the address or location of the land in question;

   (*c*) the interest which the vendor has in the land at the time of service of the notice.

Sub-paragraph (4) defines the address of the vendor (in Sub-paragraph 3(3)(*a*)) as that of his residence, his business address or, in the case of a company, its registered office.

Sub-paragraph (5) provides that the land may be identified by reference to a plan.

Sub-paragraph (6) requires the notice to indicate whether the vendor will retain any material interest in the land, or any part of it, after the disposal, and if so to specify the nature and extent of that interest.

PART III
Disposals of which notice may, but need not, be given

Paragraph 4 excludes (by virtue of section 23(6)) land of up to an acre in extent on which is built the owner's main dwelling-house from the obligation to give notice of an intended disposal. The vendor is still permitted to serve a notice if he wishes and will presumably do so where the resolution has so killed the private market that he wishes to take advantage of the blight provisions of section 23(8).

Sub-paragraph (1) states that the whole of the paragraph applies to a disposal by someone of a material interest in land which is the whole or part of his home.

Sub-paragraph (2) states the paragraph also applies where land is vested in trustees and comprises the whole or part of a private residence and the beneficiary is entitled under the trust either to occupy it or receive the whole income or proceeds of sale from the material interest.

Sub-paragraph (3) defines the terms used in the paragraph and in particular that " private residence " means the individual's main residence occupying with its grounds not more than one acre.

PART IV
Termination of all or part of a disposal notification area

Paragraph 5 deals with the publicity requirements where an authority terminate all or part of a disposal notification area. These are the same as those provided in Part I of the Schedule for resolutions declaring disposal notification areas.

Sub-paragraph (1) applies the provisions of the paragraph where an authority pass a resolution declaring that all or part of a disposal notification area shall no longer be such an area.

Sub-paragraph (2)(*a*) is similar to sub-paragraph 1(1)(*a*) and requires an authority to publish a notice of the effect of their resolution under paragraph 5(1) and naming a place where a copy of the resolution and (where the resolution affects a part only of the area) the accompanying map may be inspected.

Sub-paragraph (2)(*b*) is similar to sub-paragraph 2(3)(*b*) and requires the authority to send a copy of the resolution, and of the map, to every authority keeping a local land charges register and to every parish or community council whose area is affected by the resolution.   If the authority is itself one keeping a local land charges register there is no need for it to send copies to others who also do so.

Sub-paragraph (3) is similar to paragraph 2(1) and requires the authority to send a copy of the resolution and of the map to the Secretary of State.

Although in the case of a termination resolution there is no power of veto by the Secretary of State he will wish to be kept informed of the extent of disposal notification areas in a particular authority's area.

PART V

Publication

Paragraph 6 defines what is meant by publication in the foregoing paragraphs of the Schedule. It is in common form and requires the notices under those paragraphs to be published in two or more newspapers circulating in the area, of which one should if practicable be a local newspaper. In addition the notices must be published in the London Gazette (or, in the case of a D.N.A. in Scotland, the Edinburgh Gazette).

Savings

Paragraph 7 provides that the passing of a resolution terminating all or part of a disposal notification area, or action to the same effect by the Secretary of State under paragraph 2(3), shall not affect—

(*a*) the liability for any offence committed under section 23(9) (*i.e.* failure to give notice of a disposal or giving false information in such a notice);

(*b*) the operation of any blight notice served,

before the passing of a resolution or the action by the Secretary of State as the case may be.

Transitory provisions

Paragraph 8 contains transitory provisions pending the coming into force of the Local Land Charges Act 1975.

Scotland

Paragraph 9 deals with the different situation in Scotland where no local land charges registers are kept. It provides that the resolutions or notifications referred to in paragraphs 1(1), 2(3), or 5 shall be registered as soon as practicable in the registers kept by virtue of section 31(2) of the Town and Country Planning (Scotland) Act 1972, where the authority making a resolution is not responsible for keeping such a register they shall send a copy to the responsible authorities who shall register the resolution. It also provides that in the case of a resolution passed by, or notification received by, a general planning authority, that authority shall send a copy to every district council concerned.

These provisions replace, in so far as Scotland is concerned, paragraphs 1(1)(*b*) and (2) and 2(3)(*b*) and 5(2)(*b*) of this Schedule.

The effect is that an intending purchaser's solicitor is given the opportunity to learn of the existence of a disposal notification area when he inspects the planning register, in the same way as, in England, a solicitor learns of this on inspection of the local land charges register.

SCHEDULE 9
LAND COMPENSATION ACTS AS AMENDED

This Schedule merely reproduces for ease of reference the other legislation as amended by section 47.

Part I reproduces section 17 of the Land Compensation Act 1961 as amended.

Part II reproduces section 25 of the Land Compensation (Scotland) Act 1963 as amended.

SCHEDULE 10
MINOR AND CONSEQUENTIAL
AMENDMENTS

This Schedule gives a general power to bodies corporate and makes minor and consequential amendments to certain existing Acts.   These Acts are as follows:—

The Commissioners of Works Act 1894.

The Lands Tribunal Act 1949.

The Land Compensation Act 1961 and the corresponding Scottish Act of 1963.

The Town and Country Planning Act of 1971 and the corresponding Scottish Act of 1972.

The Local Government Act 1972.

The Local Government Act 1974 and the corresponding Scottish Act of 1975.

General

Paragraph 1 gives to a body which has made a " prior-right " application under Schedule 6 power to acquire its former land back from an authority for the purpose of carrying out

the development, even though there might be a limitation on
its power to acquire land for that purpose.

For example, British Railways have power under section 11
of the Transport Act 1962 to " retain any part of their land
which is not required for the purposes of their business and
develop it for use by other persons ", but under that section
they are also precluded from acquiring land for the purposes
of purely non-operational development. It may be that in
operating the land scheme an authority, having acquired land
from British Railways, would be prepared to lease it back to
them to carry out approved development but British Railways
would be unable to take the lease because of the terms of the
Transport Act.

In this example paragraph 1 would give British Railways
the power to acquire a material interest in the land and thus
enable them to pursue the non-operational development, in
effect, as if the local authority acquisition had not intervened.

The paragraph provides powers for all bodies which are in
this position, for example a private company whose powers
to re-acquire land are constrained by their Memorandum and
Articles of Association. The power given is very limited. It
only applies where a " prior-right " application has been made
by the body as previous owner. If the body could not have
carried out the development as owner of the land, it cannot
use this power to acquire the land.

Sub-paragraph (1) provides that where a body corporate
(having owned a material interest in the land prior to its
acquisition by the authority) has applied under Schedule 6 for
an opportunity to negotiate the purchase of a material interest
in order to carry out development for which the land is being
made available, that body shall have power to **acquire** such an
interest despite any legal limitation on their capacity to do so.

Sub-paragraph (2) provides that sub-paragraph (1) does not
apply where there is a legal limitation on the capacity of the
body to carry out the **development** on its own land.

Sub-paragraph (3) is a standard provision where special
powers are being given. Its purpose is to make it clear that

the body is merely being given extra powers and is not protected against actions for negligence or nuisance, but that an action cannot be brought on the grounds that the body had no power to acquire the land.

The Commissioners of Works Act 1894

Paragraph 2. *Sub-paragraph* (1) of this paragraph replaces section 1(1) of the Commissioners of Works Act 1894 (a subsection applying certain of the provisions of the Lands Clauses Consolidation Act 1845 to purchases of land for the public service by agreement under the Commissioners of Works Act 1852) by a somewhat wider provision applying the provisions of the Compulsory Purchase Act 1965 (an Act which has, in practice, largely replaced the Lands Clauses Act 1845). The amended subsection provides that where the Secretary of State is acquiring land by agreement under the Commissioners of Works Act 1852 the provisions of Part I of the Compulsory Purchase Act 1965 (except section 31 dealing with ecclesiastical property) should apply where relevant. The main effect of this provision is to extend the power of the Secretary of State to over-ride restrictive covenants and other third party rights when purchasing land by agreement under the parent legislation and so avoid the necessity of an " agreed " compulsory purchase order. Compensation is payable under section 10 of the Compulsory Purchase Act 1965. The wording of the new provision follows the wording of section 120(3) of the Local Government Act 1972 and puts the Secretary of State in the same position as local authorities so far as regards this power.

Sub-paragraph (2) replaces section 1(1) of the 1894 Act, in relation to Scotland, by a provision which has an equivalent effect as sub-paragraph (1) has in relation to England and Wales.

Sub-paragraph (3) provides that the substituted provisions apply only to agreements entered into later than one month from the passing of the Act.

The Lands Tribunal Act 1949

Paragraph 3. The intention of this paragraph (and of the related provisions in paragraphs 4(1) and 5(1) below) is to make it clear that there is no statutory bar on a simplified procedure being introduced whereby claims before the Lands Tribunal could be dealt with on the basis of written representations without the need for an oral hearing.

The prospect of having to appear " in court ", perhaps at some expense and with professional support, may well deter many claimants from taking their case to the Lands Tribunal, especially in cases where the amount at stake is small.

A number of steps have already been taken administratively to cut down delays in the Tribunal and to simplify procedure but further progress requires amendment of existing references in statutes to the Lands Tribunal holding oral hearings to remove any doubt about the power of the Lord Chancellor (or in Scotland the Lord Advocate) to make rules under section 3(6) of the Lands Tribunal Act 1949 providing for cases to be determined without an oral hearing.

Sub-paragraph (1) provides for the insertion of two new subsections after subsection (6) of section 3 of the Lands Tribunal Act 1949, which contains the basic powers to make rules regulating proceedings before the Lands Tribunal (and the Lands Tribunal for Scotland).

Subsection (6A) makes it clear that section 3 authorises the making of rules allowing the Tribunal to dispense with an oral hearing.

Subsection (6B) adds the proviso that in cases concerning land compensation the rules are to require the consent of the person making the claim before the case can be determined without an oral hearing.

Subsection (6C) provides that where the Tribunal determines a case without an oral hearing, subsection (3) of section 3 (which deals with the procedure where a case is dealt with by two or more members of the Tribunal) can be modified by the rules.

Sub-paragraph (2) provides that in section 3(6)(*b*) of the 1949 Act (which provides for the Tribunal to sit with assessors) the words " sit with " shall be replaced by the words " be assisted by ".

This further minor amendment to the 1949 Act is a consequence of allowing cases to be determined without an oral hearing.

The Land Compensation Act 1961

Paragraph 4 makes a number of minor and consequential amendments to the Land Compensation Act 1961. Sub-paragraph (1) amends section 2(2) of the Act to ensure consistency with the provisions of paragraph 3 of the Schedule which allows cases before the Lands Tribunal to be determined without an oral hearing. Sub-paragraphs (2) and (3) make amendments to sections 15(5) and 19(3) respectively which are consequential on the amendments to section 17 (certificates of appropriate alternative development) made by section 47.

Sub-paragraph (1) provides that a proviso should be added at the end of section 2(2) of the 1961 Act (which provides for the Lands Tribunal to sit in public) to the effect that nothing in that subsection shall prevent a case being determined without an oral hearing.

Sub-paragraph (2) provides that in section 15(5) of the 1961 Act (which deals with assumptions as to planning permission) the words " would have been " are to be substituted for the words " might reasonably have been expected to be " and after the word " thereof " the words " if it were not proposed to be acquired by any authority possessing compulsory purchase powers " are to be inserted.

Sub-paragraph (3) provides that in section 19(3) of the 1961 Act (which deals with extensions of sections 17 and 18 to special cases where the person entitled to the interest in land is absent or cannot be found) the paragraph references should be adjusted so as to refer correctly to the new subsection which is to replace the existing subsection (3) of section 15 by virtue of the provisions of section 47.

Sub-paragraph (4) provides that an acquisition under Part III of the Act should be added to the list of enactments in paragraph 2(1) of Schedule 2 to the 1961 Act. Paragraph 2 of Schedule 2 enables orders to be made, concurrently with compulsory purchase orders to which the paragraph applies, declaring houses to be unfit for human habitation so that they can be acquired at site value. The effect of sub-paragraph (4) therefore is simply to ensure that the same procedure can be followed where an unfit house is to be acquired under Part III of this Act.

Orders made under paragraph 2 of Schedule 2 to the 1961 Act have to be served on the owners of the properties and if there are objections, the Secretary of State has to hold a hearing or public inquiry. These procedures are not affected by the Act.

Sub-paragraph (5) provides that section 47 shall have effect only in relation to applications or certificates issued in pursuance of applications made one month after Royal Assent.

The Land Compensation (Scotland) Act 1963

Paragraph 5. This paragraph makes amendments corresponding to those in the preceding paragraph to sections 9(2), 23(5), 27(5) and paragraph 1(1) to Schedule 2 to the Land Compensation (Scotland) Act 1963.

The Town and Country Planning Act 1971

Paragraph 6. *Sub-paragraph* (1) states that in section 27 of the 1971 Act, which deals with notification of planning applications to owners and agricultural tenants, subsection 1(a) shall cease to have effect, as regards every planning application made on or after the first appointed day. The second part of the sub-paragraph redefines ' owner ' in section 27(7) of the 1971 Act as anyone having a material interest in land as defined in the Community Land Act.

Section 27(1) of the 1971 Act states that a local planning authority shall not entertain a planning application unless it is accompanied by one of four certificates prescribed in the subsection. The first of these (provided in section 27(1)(a)) is a certificate stating that the applicant is either the freeholder

or entitled to a tenancy.   In practice this has meant that a
person entitled to any tenancy, even a weekly one, could make
a planning application without notifying the freeholder of the
land in question.   The effect of repealing section 27(1)(*a*) will
be to ensure that any planning application made on or after
the first appointed day will have to be notified to the owner.
' Owner ' is defined in section 27(7) of the 1971 Act as being
a person who is for the time being the estate owner in respect
of the fee simple of the land, or is entitled to a tenancy with
not less than ten years remaining unexpired.   ' Owner ' is
redefined on the second part of the sub-paragraph as anyone
having a material interest in land as defined in section 6 of the
Community Land Act.

Sub-paragraph (2) states that in section 34 of the 1971 Act
(which concerns registers of planning applications and decisions), after subsection (1) a further subsection 1A should be
inserted to the effect that details of any certificate relating to a
planning permission and given under section 21 of the Act
must be entered in the register of planning applications and
decisions.

A certificate under section 21 of the Act is evidence of the
fact that the suspension of a planning permission applied by
that clause is lifted.   It is clearly essential for such a certificate
to be public knowledge where, for instance, a would-be purchaser is interested in buying the land.   The planning Register
is the appropriate place for this information to be made
available.

Sub-paragraph (3) provides that in section 194(2) of the 1971
Act (which deals with the grounds of objection in counter-
notices served by authorities in response to blight-notices the
provision in paragraph (*d*), which enables authorities to object
on the grounds that they do not intend to acquire within
fifteen years or such longer period as may be specified from the
date of the counter-notice, shall be amended so that the period
referred to is **ten** years, or such longer period as may be specified.
The provision will also be made of general application.   At

present it only applies in cases where there has been an indication in a structure plan that the land may be needed for development, or in a development plan that it may be needed for a highway.

This provision is necessary because section 18(4)(a) provides that authorities shall not be under any duty to acquire land which is not needed for development within ten years. Once the duty begins to be brought in by orders under section 18 it would be inconsistent if authorities were to continue to issue counter-notices simply stating that they do not intend to acquire the land at all if it is required for relevant development. They should therefore be able where appropriate to state in their counter-notices that they do not intend to acquire the land within ten years or such longer period as they are able to specify. This provision has to be made of general application because authorities can use their existing powers as well as the new powers under Part III of the Act to acquire land for relevant development.

During the transitional period authorities will still be able to issue counter-notices to the effect that they do not intend to acquire the land at all. There is, moreover, an important safeguard for the owner-occupier in section 194(3) of the 1971 Act which provides that an objection cannot be made on the grounds that the land is not needed for ten years or longer if the proper response is in fact that there is no intention to acquire it at all. If the owner-occupier does not accept the counter-notice he can appeal to the Lands Tribunal. Guidance will be given to authorities, emphasising the need to give the owner-occupier the maximum degree of certainty in their handling of blight notices.

The Town and Country Planning (Scotland) Act 1972

Paragraph 7. *Sub-paragraph* (1) states that in section 24 of the Scottish Act of 1972, which deals with notification of planning applications to owners and agricultural tenants, subsection (1)(a) shall cease to have effect in respect of every planning application made on or after the first appointed day. The second part of the sub-paragraph redefines ' owner ' in section 24(7) of the Scottish Act of 1972 as anyone having a

L

material interest in land as defined in section 6 of the Community Land Act.

Schedule 24(1) of the 1972 Act states that a planning authority shall not consider a planning application unless it is accompanied by one of 4 certificates prescribed in that subsection. Section 24(1)(*a*) prescribes a certificate that the applicant is the proprietor of the *dominium utile* or is a leaseholder.   This has meant that the holder of even a short-term lease, or a lease about to expire, could apply for planning permission without notifying the owner of the land.   The effect of the repeal will be to ensure that any application made on or after the first appointed day will have to be notified to the owner, owner being defined in section 24(7) as any person able to sell or convey the land or entitled to possession of the land under a lease with not less than 10 years remaining unexpired.   The redefinition of ' owner ' in the second part of the sub-paragraph brings the Scottish definition into line with the English and Welsh as explained in paragraph 6 above.

Sub-paragraph (2) provides for the making of two amendments to section 31 of the 1972 Act (which concerns registers of planning applications and decisions).   The first of these states that there shall be added to section 31(2) the provisions requiring that resolutions and notifications made under Schedule 8 of the Community Land Act (relating to disposal notification areas) be entered in the planning register.   The second amendment states that after subsection 32(2) a further subsection (2A) should be inserted to the effect that details of any certificate relating to a planning permission given under section 21 of the Community Land Act must be entered in the planning register.

The first amendment is consequential on the provisions of Schedule 8, paragraph 7.   Since section 31 makes no provision for the inclusion of additional material in the register an amendment is necessary.

Sub-paragraph (3) makes the corresponding amendment to that described in the note on sub-paragraph (3) at page 256, above.

The Local Government Act 1972

Paragraph 8. *Sub-paragraph* (1) provides that section 123A of the 1972 Act (inserted by section 42 of the Act) shall apply to the Peak Park Joint and Lake District Special Planning Boards as if they were principal councils. This is the provision which requires the consent of the Secretary of State to any disposal of land.

As these two Planning Boards are authorities for the purposes of the Act by virtue of section 1(1)(*a*) it is appropriate that they should be subject to the same controls as local authorities.

Sub-paragraph (2) provides that in paragraph 55 of Schedule 16 of the 1972 Act (which deals with the exercise of functions under section 17 of the Land Compensation Act 1961 other than in Greater London) the words " would have been granted if the land in question were not proposed to be acquired by any authority possessing compulsory purchase powers " should be substituted for the existing wording. This is a purely consequential amendment, to that Act intended to bring the wording of this provision in line with the wording of section 17 of the 1961 Act as amended by section 47.

This sub-paragraph only has effect in respect of applications made after the expiration of one month from Royal Assent.

Local Government Act 1974

Paragraph 9 applies to the Land Authority for Wales and to bodies established under section 50 of the Act to exercise reserve powers in case of default by a local authority, the machinery whereby complaints of maladministration against local authorities and certain other bodies are investigated by a Local Commissioner under the terms of Part III of the Local Government Act 1974. Maladministration is not defined in the 1974 Act and it will be for the Local Commissioner to decide on the facts of each case whether it has occurred.

Sub-paragraph (1) adds the new bodies to the lists of bodies who may be investigated under the 1974 Act.

Sub-paragraph (2) places an obligation on the Local Commissioner, where the complaint relates to the Land Authority for Wales to send a copy of his report or statement on his investigations to the Secretary of State. The Commissioner's reports would, under the existing provision of the Act, have to be sent to the person, if any, who referred the complaint to the Local Commissioner, to the complainant, and to the authority concerned and to any other authority or person who is alleged in the complaint to have taken or authorised the action complained of. The Secretary of State will also need to know the results of investigations in Wales in view of his general oversight responsibility for the Land Authority and his power to give them directions.

Local Government (*Scotland*) Act 1975

Paragraph 10 provides that there be inserted into section 23(1) of the Local Government (Scotland) Act 1975 (authorities subject to investigation) a new paragraph adding to the lists any body set up under the reserve powers contained in section 50 in case of default by an authority in Scotland.

This provision brings the Scottish legislation in line with the English and Welsh as set out in the paragraph above.

SCHEDULE 11
REPEALS

This Schedule is applied by section 58(3) of the Act which repeals the enactments specified in the Schedule to the extent shown in the third column of the table.

The deletion in section 194(2) of the Town and Country Planning Act 1971 (section 183(2) of the Scottish Act of 1972) flow from the amendments to those Acts made by paragraph 6(3) and paragraph 7(3) of Schedule 10 to this Act respectively (pages 256-258 above).

These repeals will have effect from the first Appointed Day.

C:- COMMUNITY LAND ACT 1975
CHAPTER 77

ARRANGEMENT OF SECTIONS

ELIZABETH II

COMMUNITY LAND ACT 1975

1975 Chapter 77

An Act to enable local authorities and certain other authorities to
acquire, manage and deal with land suitable for development,
and to make other provision for and in connection with the
public ownership of land; to amend planning law and the
rules for assessing the value of land for compulsory acquisition
and other cases where compensation is payable; to make
provision concerning unoccupied office premises; and to
establish a Land Authority for Wales.

[12 November 1975]

BE it enacted by the Queen's most Excellent Majesty, by and with
the advice and consent of the Lords Spiritual and Temporal, and
Commons, in this present Parliament assembled, and by the
authority of the same, as follows:—

PART I
PRELIMINARY
Authorities for purposes of the Act

Authorities.

1.—(1) In this Act, unless the context otherwise requires,
" authority "—

> (*a*) in relation to England means a local authority or a new
> town authority, or the Peak Park Joint Planning Board or
> the Lake District Special Planning Board,

> (*b*) in relation to Scotland means a local authority or a new
> town authority,

> (*c*) in relation to Wales means the Land Authority for Wales
> established under Part II of this Act or a new town
> authority.

(2) For the purposes of this Act—

> (*a*) the area of a new town authority is the area for the time
> being designated under section 1 of the New Towns Act
> 1965, or under section 1 of the New Towns (Scotland) Act
> 1968, as the site of the proposed new town;

> (*b*) the area of the Land Authority for Wales is the whole of
> Wales;

> (*c*) the area of the Peak Park Joint Planning Board and the
> area of the Lake District Special Planning Board is, in each

case, the area of the National Park for which the Board is responsible.

(3) In this Act, in relation to any land, "authority" means the authorities whose areas include the land.

Joint boards.

2.—(1) If it appears to the Secretary of State expedient that a joint board should be established as an authority for all or any of the purposes of Part III, Part V or Part VI of this Act in the areas of two or more authorities, or in any parts of those areas, he may after consulting those authorities by order—

(a) constitute those areas or parts as a district for the purposes specified in the order, and

(b) constitute a joint board as the authority to act in that district for those purposes instead of any other authority, or instead of such other authorities as are specified in the order.

(2) The Secretary of State shall not make the order except after holding a public local inquiry unless all the authorities concerned have consented to the making of the order; and an order made after such an inquiry has been held shall be subject to annulment in pursuance of a resolution of either House of Parliament.

(3) The joint board shall be a body corporate consisting of such number of members as may be determined by the order, to be appointed by the constituent authorities.

(4) The order constituting the joint board, and any order amending or revoking an order under this section may, without prejudice to the provisions of section 241 of the Local Government Act 1972 (which authorises the application of the provisions of that Act to joint boards), provide for regulating the appointment, tenure of office and vacation of office of members of the board, for regulating the meetings and proceedings of the board, and for the payment of the expenses of the board by the constituent authorities.

(5) An order under this section may make such incidental, consequential, transitional or supplementary provision as appears to the Secretary of State to be necessary or expedient and, in particular—

(a) may provide for the transfer and compensation of officers, the transfer of property and liabilities, and the adjustment of accounts and apportionment of liabilities,

(b) may adapt or modify any of the provisions of this Act or of any other enactment concerning the acquisition of land.

(6) This section shall not apply in Wales.

(7) An order under this section shall not come into force before the expiration of a period of one month beginning with the passing of this Act.

Interpretation

Development land and relevant development.

3.—(1) In this Act " development land " means land which, in the opinion of the authority concerned, is needed for relevant development within ten years from the time at which they are acting.

(2) In this Act " relevant development " means any development except—

> (*a*) development of any class specified in Schedule 1 to this Act,

> (*b*) development consisting exclusively of the building of a single dwelling-house, and

> (*c*) development of such class or classes as may be prescribed by the Secretary of State by regulations.

(3) The reference in subsection (2) above to the building of a single dwelling-house includes a reference to the construction or laying out of any garage, outhouse, garden, yard, court, forecourt, or other appurtenance for occupation with, and for the purposes of, a single dwelling-house.

(4) Regulations under this section shall not be made unless a draft of the regulations has been approved by a resolution of each House of Parliament.

Outstanding material interests.

4.—(1) A material interest in land shall be treated as outstanding for the purposes of this Act unless—

> (*a*) it is owned by an authority, a local or new town authority, a parish or community council or, in Scotland, the council of a district within the area of a general planning authority, or

> (*b*) during the whole of the period beginning with 12th September 1974 and ending with the relevant time, it has been owned by a charity (but not necessarily the same charity throughout), or

> (*c*) it is of a description specified in an order made under this subsection by the Secretary of State.

(2) For the purposes of subsection (1) above, a material interest in land shall be treated as owned by any person mentioned in that subsection at any time if, at that time, that person—

(*a*) has or had entered into a binding contract for its acquisition, or

(*b*) subject only to completion of the administration of a deceased person's estate, is or was entitled to it under the terms of the deceased person's will.

(3) An order under subsection (1) above shall be subject to annulment in pursuance of a resolution of either House of Parliament.

Statutory undertakers.

5.—(1) In this Act, unless the context otherwise requires, " statutory undertakers " means—

(*a*) persons authorised by any enactment to carry on any railway, light railway, tramway, road transport, water transport, canal, inland navigation, dock harbour, pier or lighthouse undertaking, or any undertaking for the supply of electricity, gas, hydraulic power or water,

(*b*) the British Airports Authority, the Civil Aviation Authority, the National Coal Board, the Post Office and any other authority, body or undertakers which by virtue of any enactment are to be treated as statutory undertakers for any of the purposes of the Act of 1971 or of the Scottish Act of 1972, and

(*c*) any other authority, body or undertakers specified in an order made by the Secretary of State under this paragraph,

and " statutory undertaking " shall be construed accordingly.

(2) In this Act " operational land " means, in relation to statutory undertakers—

(*a*) land which is used for the purpose of carrying on their undertaking, and

(*b*) land in which an interest is held for that purpose,

not being land which, in respect of its nature and situation, is comparable rather with land in general than with land which is used, or in which interests are held, for the purpose of the carrying on of statutory undertakings.

(3) In relation to any statutory undertakers specified in an order made under this subsection by the Secretary of State and the appropriate Minister acting jointly, subsection (2) above shall not apply

and in this Act " operational land " shall have the meaning given by the order as respects those undertakers.

(4) In this Act the expression " the appropriate Minister ", and any reference to the Secretary of State and the appropriate Minister—

(a) in relation to any statutory undertakers who are also statutory undertakers for the purposes of any provision of Part XI of the Act of 1971 or Part XI of the Scottish Act of 1972, shall have the same meanings as in the said Part XI, and

(b) in relation to any other statutory undertakers, shall have the meanings given by an order made by the Secretary of State under this subsection.

(5) If, in relation to anything required or authorised to be done under this Act, any question arises as to which Minister is the appropriate Minister in relation to any statutory undertakers, that question shall be determined by the Treasury; and if any question so arises whether any land is operational land of statutory undertakers, or would be such land if it were used or held by statutory undertakers for the purposes covered by planning permission, that question shall be determined by the Minister who is the appropriate Minister in relation to those undertakers.

(6) An order made under this section shall be subject to annulment in pursuance of a resolution of either House of Parliament.

Other interpretation.

6.—(1) In this Act, unless the context otherwise requires—

the " Acquisition of Land Acts " means the Acquisition of Land (Authorisation Procedure) Act 1946 and the Acquisition of Land (Authorisation Procedure) (Scotland) Act 1947, and " the Act of 1946 " and " the Scottish Act of 1947 " mean those Acts respectively,

" the Act of 1971 " means the Town and Country Planning Act 1971,

" the Scottish Act of 1972 " means the Town and Country Planning (Scotland) Act 1972,

" agriculture " has the meaning assigned to it by section 290 of the Act of 1971 or section 275 of the Scottish Act of 1972,

" building " includes any structure or erection, and any part of a building as so defined, but does not include plant or machinery comprised in a building,

" buildings or works " includes waste materials, refuse and
    other matters deposited on land, and references to the
    erection or construction of buildings or works shall be
    construed accordingly,

" charity " has the same meaning as in section 360 of the
    Income and Corporation Taxes Act 1970 and as respects
    Scotland " charitable " shall be construed as if it were
    contained in that Act,

" common " includes any land subject to be enclosed under
    the Inclosure Acts 1845 to 1882, and any town or village
    green,

" community council " means a community council in Wales,

" development " has the meaning assigned to it by section 22
    of the Act of 1971 or section 19 of the Scottish Act of
    1972, and " develop " shall be construed accordingly,

" development order " has the meaning assigned to it by
    section 24 of the Act of 1971 or section 21 of the Scottish
    Act of 1972,

" development plan " has the same meaning as in the Act of
    1971 or the Scottish Act of 1972,

" disposal " includes disposal by sale, exchange, excambion or
    lease and, in the case of a lease, by grant, assignment or
    assignation,

" easement ", in relation to Scotland, means servitude,

" enactment " includes an enactment in any local or private
    Act of Parliament, and an order, rule, regulation, byelaw
    or scheme made under an Act of Parliament,

" erection ", in relation to buildings, includes extension,
    alteration and re-erection,

" freehold ", in relation to Scotland, means the estate or
    interest of the proprietor of the *dominium utile* or in
    relation to land not held on feudal tenure the interest in
    land of the owner thereof, and " freeholder " shall be
    construed accordingly,

" fuel or field garden allotment " means any allotment set out
    as a fuel allotment, or a field garden allotment, under an
    Inclosure Act,

" functions " includes powers and duties,

" general development order " means a development order
    made as a general order applicable (subject to such

exceptions as may be specified therein) to all land in England and Wales, or to all land in Scotland,

" government department " includes any Minister of the Crown,

" land " means any corporeal hereditament, including a building and includes an interest in or right over land,

" land ", in relation to Scotland, includes land covered with water, any building, any interest in land and any servitude or right in or over land,

" land acquisition and management scheme " has the meaning given by section 16 of this Act,

" lease " includes an underlease or sublease and an agreement for a lease, underlease or sublease, but does not include an option to take a lease or a mortgage,

" local authority " means—

> (a) in relation to England, the council of a county or district, the council of a London borough, the Common Council of the City of London and the Greater London Council,

> (b) in relation to Wales, the council of a county or district,

> (c) in relation to Scotland, a regional, general or district planning authority within the meaning of Part IX of the Local Government (Scotland) Act 1973,

and this Act shall apply to the Isles of Scilly as if the Council of those Isles were the council of a county,

" material interest ", in relation to land, means the freehold or a lease the unexpired term of which at the relevant time is not less than seven years,

" minerals " has the meaning assigned to it by section 290 of the Act of 1971 or section 275 of the Scottish Act of 1972,

" Minister " means any Minister of the Crown or other government department,

" mortgagee ", in relation to Scotland, means the creditor in a heritable security,

" new town authority " means a development corporation as defined in section 2 of the New Towns Act 1965, or in section 2 of the New Towns (Scotland) Act 1968,

" open space " means any land laid out as a public garden or used for the purposes of public recreation, or land which is a disused burial ground,

" parish council " includes a parish meeting and the parish trustees of a parish,

" planning permission " means permission granted (or to be deemed or treated as granted) under Part III of the Act of 1971 or of the Scottish Act of 1972, and in construing references to planning permission to develop or to carry out development of land, or to applications for such permission, regard shall be had to section 32(2) of the Act of 1971 or section 29(2) of the Scottish Act of 1972 (permission to retain development),

" prescribed " in relation to the form of any document, means prescribed by regulations under section 53 of this Act.

(2) For the purposes of the definition of " material interest " above it shall be assumed that any option (other than one conferred by or under Act of Parliament) to renew or extend the lease, whether or not forming part of a series of options, is exercised, and that any option (other than one conferred by or under Act of Parliament) to terminate the lease is not exercised.

(3) In this Act any reference to the time when planning permission is or was granted, in the case of planning permission granted on an appeal, is a reference to the time of the decision appealed against or, in the case of planning permission granted on an appeal in the circumstances mentioned in section 37 of the Act of 1971 or section 34 of the Scottish Act of 1972, a reference to the time when in accordance with that section notification of the decision is or was deemed to have been received.

(4) In this Act any reference to planning permission for relevant development includes a reference to planning permission for development which includes relevant development.

(5) In this Act any reference to the suspension of planning permission shall be taken as a reference to suspension under sections 19 to 22 of, and Schedule 7 to, this Act, and cognate expressions shall be construed accordingly.

(6) In this Act any reference to a notice to treat shall, unless the context otherwise requires, be construed as including a reference to a notice to treat which by virtue of any enactment is deemed to have been served, and any reference to the date of service of a notice to treat shall be construed accordingly.

(7) References in this Act to any enactment shall, except where the context otherwise requires, be construed as references to that

enactment as amended or extended by or under any other enactment, including this Act.

Commencement

The appointed days, etc.

7.—(1) In this Act the "first appointed day" and "second appointed day" each mean such day as the Secretary of State may by order appoint, and "the relevant date" has the meaning given by section 18(6) of this Act.

(2) The first appointed day shall not be earlier than the first date when a draft of regulations under section 3 of this Act (excepting one or more classes of development from relevant development) has been approved by resolution of each House of Parliament.

(3) The second appointed day shall not be earlier than the first date when—

> (a) all relevant development has been designated, by orders under section 18 of this Act, in all areas of Great Britain, and

> (b) a draft of regulations under section 27 of this Act establishing one or more financial hardship tribunals, or conferring on one or more existing bodies or groups of bodies the functions of financial hardship tribunals, has been approved by resolution of each House of Parliament.

(4) The order appointing the second appointed day shall not be made unless a draft of the order has been approved by resolution of each House of Parliament.

(5) Schedule 2 to this Act concerns the provisions of this Act respectively coming into force on, or depending on,—

> (a) the first appointed day,
> (b) the relevant date, and
> (c) the second appointed day.

PART II
THE LAND AUTHORITY FOR WALES

The Authority.

8.—(1) There shall be a Land Authority for Wales who shall perform the functions assigned to them by this Act.

(2) The provisions of Schedule 3 to this Act shall have effect with respect to the Authority.

(3) The Authority, in the performance of their functions under this Act, shall comply with such directions as may be given to them by the Secretar of State.

(4) The Authority shall not be regarded as the servant or agent of the Crown or as enjoying any status, privilege or immunity of the Crown; and their property shall not be regarded as property of, or property held on behalf of, the Crown.

The initial debt.

9.—(1) The Authority shall on establishment assume a debt to the Secretary of State (in this section referred to as " the initial debt ") of such amount as the Secretary of State may with the approval of the Treasury determine by notice in writing given to the Authority.

(2) The Secretary of State may out of money provided by Parliament defray expenses incurred in establishing the Authority, and any expenses incurred before its establishment in providing for its accommodation, including the payment of any rent, and for the payment of salaries and expenses to the persons who are appointed as members and officers of the Authority.

In determining the amount of the initial debt the Secretary of State shall have regard to the expenses so incurred by him.

(3) The amount of the initial debt shall not exceed £100,000.

(4) The rate of interest payable on the initial debt, the arrangements for paying off the principal, and the other terms of the debt shall be such as the Secretary of State may with the approval of the Treasury from time to time determine.

(5) Any sums received by the Secretary of State by way of interest on or repayment of the initial debt shall be paid into the National Loans Fund.

Borrowing powers.

10.—(1) The Authority may borrow temporarily, by way of overdraft or otherwise, such sums as they may require for meeting their obligations and discharging their functions—

(*a*) in sterling from the Secretary of State, or

(*b*) with the consent of the Secretary of State, or in accordance with any general authority given by the Secretary of State, either in sterling or in a currency other than sterling from a person other than the Secretary of State.

(2) The Authority may borrow otherwise than by way of temporary loan such sums as the Authority may require—

(*a*) in sterling from the Secretary of State, or

(*b*) with the consent of the Secretary of State, in a currency other than sterling from a person other than the Secretary of State.

(3) The Authority may, with the consent of the Secretary of State, borrow (otherwise than by way of temporary loan) from the Commission of the European Communities or the European Investment Bank sums in any currency.

(4) The aggregate amount outstanding by way of the principal of—

    (*a*) the initial debt, and

    (*b*) any money borrowed by the Authority under this section,

shall not exceed £40 million or such greater amount not exceeding £60 million as the Secretary of State may specify by order.

(5) An order under this section shall not be made unless a draft of it has been laid before and approved by the House of Commons.

(6) The Authority shall not borrow money otherwise than under this section.

(7) The Secretary of State may lend to the Authority any sums which the Authority have power to borrow from him, and any such loan shall be repaid to the Secretary of State at such times and by such methods, and interest on the loan shall be paid to him at such rates and at such times, as he may from time to time determine.

(8) The Treasury may issue out of the National Loans Fund to the Secretary of State such sums as are necessary to enable him to make loans in pursuance of this section, and any sums received by the Secretary of State in pursuance of subsection (7) above shall be paid into that Fund.

(9) References in this section to the Secretary of State are references to him acting with the approval of the Treasury.

Guarantees.

11.—(1) The Treasury may guarantee, in such manner and on such conditions as they think fit, the repayment of the principal of and the payment of interest on any sums which the Authority borrow from a person other than the Secretary of State.

(2) Immediately after a guarantee is given under this section the Treasury shall lay a statement of the guarantee before each House of Parliament; and where any sum is issued for fulfilling the guarantee so given the Treasury shall, as soon as practicable after the end of each financial year (beginning with that in which the sum is issued and ending with that in which all liability in respect of the principal of the sum and in respect of interest thereon is finally discharged), lay before each House of Parliament a statement relating to that sum.

(3) Any sums required by the Treasury for fulfilling a guarantee under this section shall be charged on and issued out of the Consolidated Fund.

(4) If any sums are issued in fulfilment of a guarantee given under this section, the Authority shall make to the Treasury, at such times and in such manner as the Treasury may from time to time direct, payments of such amounts as the Treasury so direct in or towards repayment of the sums so issued and payments of interest, at such rate as the Treasury so direct, on what is outstanding for the time being in respect of sums so issued.

(5) Any sums received by the Treasury in pursuance of subsection (4) above shall be paid into the Consolidated Fund.

Accounts and audit.

12.—(1) The Authority shall—

    (a) keep proper accounts and proper records in relation to the accounts, and

    (b) prepare in respect of each accounting year a statement of accounts, in such form as the Secretary of State may with the approval of the Treasury require, showing the state of affairs and the profit or loss of the Authority, and

    (c) on or before 30th November in any year transmit to the Comptroller and Auditor General the statement of accounts of the Authority for the accounting year last ended.

(2) The Comptroller and Auditor General shall examine and certify the statement of accounts transmitted to him under subsection (1) above, and lay copies of it together with his report thereon before each House of Parliament.

(3) The Secretary of State shall for each financial year prepare, in such form and manner as the Treasury may approve, an account of—

    (a) sums issued to the Secretary of State in pursuance of section 10 of this Act, and the disposal by the Secretary of State of those sums;

    (b) sums required to be paid into the National Loans Fund in pursuance of section 9 or 10 of this Act;

and shall send a copy of the account to the Comptroller and Auditor General not later than the end of November next following that year; and the Comptroller and Auditor General shall examine, certify and report on the account and shall lay copies of it and of his report on it before Parliament.

Reports.

13.—(1) The Authority shall as soon as practicable after the end of each accounting year make to the Secretary of State a report on the exercise of their functions during that year.

(2) The report for any accounting year—

    (*a*) shall set out any direction given to the Authority under this Act, unless the Secretary of State has notified to the Authority his opinion that it should be omitted in the interests of national security, and

    (*b*) shall include such information relating to the plans, and past and present activities, of the Authority and the financial position of the Authority, as the Secretary of State may from time to time direct.

(3) There shall be attached to the report for each accounting year a copy of the statement of accounts in respect of that year.

(4) The Secretary of State shall lay before Parliament copies of each report made to him under subsection (1) above.

Management, etc. of land held by the Authority.

14.—(1) The Authority shall have the general function of managing and turning to account land acquired by them under this Act and for the time being held by them.

(2) The Authority may, with the consent of the Secretary of State, dispose of a material interest in any land held by them, and may dispose of any other interest in land so held.

(3) The Authority may execute any building, engineering or other works in respect of any land where they are of the opinion that it is expedient to do so with a view to the subsequent disposal of that or any other land.

(4) The Authority may arrange for the discharge of any of their functions by a local authority, and all local authorities in Wales shall have power to enter into such arrangements.

Any arrangements made under this subsection for the discharge of any functions by a local authority shall not prevent the Authority from discharging those functions.

(5) As soon as practicable after the making of any arrangements under subsection (4) above for the discharge of any functions of the Authority by a local authority, the local authority shall—

    (*a*) send a copy of the arrangements to every other local authority within whose area the functions are to be so discharged, and

(b) deposit a copy of the arrangements at their principal office and keep it available there at all reasonable hours for public inspection without payment.

(6) Where by virtue of subsection (4) above any functions of the Authority are to be discharged by a local authority, then, subject to the terms of the arrangements, section 101 of the Local Government Act 1972 (arrangements for discharge of functions by local authorities) shall apply is if those functions were functions of the local authority.

(7) A local authority shall have power to enter into, and carry out, an agreement with the Authority whereby the local authority will, as agents of the Authority, perform any service or execute any works which the Authority could perform or execute by virtue of this Act.

(8) The Authority shall, without prejudice to their powers apart from this subsection, have power to do anything to facilitate, or anything which is conducive or incidental to, the performance of any of the Authority's functions.

(9) Every local authority in Wales shall supply the Authority—

(a) with such information as the Secretary of State may by regulations prescribe for the purposes of this section, and

(b) with such certificates supporting the information as the Secretary of State may in the regulations specify.

PART III
COMMUNITY LAND
Acquisition and appropriation of land

Powers of acquisition and appropriation.

15.—(1) An authority—

(a) shall have power to acquire by agreement, or

(b) on being authorised to do so by the Secretary of State shall have power to acquire compulsorily,

any land which, in their opinion, is suitable for development.

(2) In subsection (1) above " development " does not include development of any class specified in Schedule 1 to this Act.

(3) Where an authority exercise their powers under subsection (1) above in relation to any land, they shall have power to acquire by agreement or on being authorised to do so by the Secretary of State shall have power to acquire compulsorily—

(a) any land adjoining that land which is required for the purpose of executing works for facilitating its development or use, or (*b*) where that land forms part of a common or open space or fuel or field garden allotment, any land which is required for the purpose of being given in exchange therefor.

In the application of this subsection to Scotland the words " or fuel or field garden allotment " shall be omitted.

(4) The Acquisition of Land Acts shall apply in relation to the compulsory acquisition of land in pursuance of this section as if—

(*a*) this section were contained in an Act in force immediately before the commencement of the Act of 1946, or as the case may be the Scottish Act of 1947,

(*b*) the Land Authority for Wales, a new town authority and the Peak Park Joint and Lake District Special Planning Boards were local authorities.

(5) Schedule 4 to this Act in which—

(*a*) Part I modifies the said Acts of 1946 and 1947 as applied by subsection (4) above,

(*b*) Part II deals with the acquisition of land by agreement,

(*c*) Part III contains supplemental provisions as respects land acquired under this section,

(*d*) Part IV deals with appropriation of land by local authorities,

shall have effect.

(6) No compulsory purchase order shall be made under this section before the first appointed day, and no land shall be appropriated for the purposes of this Part of this Act before that day.

Land acquisition and management schemes.

16.—(1) There shall be a land acquisition and management scheme for the area of each county authority.

(2) The scheme shall be made, and from time to time revised, by all the authorities in the area of the county authority acting jointly.

(3) The scheme shall be for the performance by each of the authorities in the area of the county authority of the following functions—

(*a*) the acquisition by those authorities of land with a view to—

(i) developing it themselves and disposing of a material interest in it, or

(ii) making it available for development by others,

(b) any other functions under any of the provisions of this Act other than Part IV.

(4) The scheme shall be made not later than 31st December 1975, or such later date as the Secretary of State may agree in any particular case.

(5) As respects Scotland, the scheme shall be made not later than such date as the Secretary of State may by order specify.

(6) Schedule 5 to this Act concerns the making, revision and contents of the schemes, and in that Schedule this section is called the principal section.

(7) Except if and so far as the Secretary of State, on the application of all the authorities in the area of the county authority, otherwise directs, a scheme under this section shall not create any obligation enforceable in law.

(8) Any reference in this section or Schedule 5 to this Act to the functions of any authority shall, where the context admits, include references to functions under this or any other Act passed before this Act or later.

(9) In this section and in Schedule 5 to this Act—

" county authority " means the council of a county or the Greater London Council or, as respects Scotland, a regional planning authority or a general planning authority within the meaning of Part IX of the Local Government (Scotland) Act 1973,

" local government law " means the Local Government Act 1972, or the Local Government (Scotland) Act 1973,

" planning law " means the Act of 1971 or the Scottish Act of 1972,

and in this Act a scheme under this section is referred to as a " land acquisition and management scheme ".

(10) For the purposes of this section the Peak Park Joint Planning Board shall be regarded as an authority in the areas of Derbyshire, Greater Manchester, South Yorkshire, West Yorkshire, Staffordshire and Cheshire.

(11) In the application of this section and Schedule 5 to this Act to Scotland, in relation to a regional planning authority references to all the authorities in the area of that authority acting jointly shall be construed as references to that authority acting after consultation with all the other authorities in their area, and in relation

to a general planning authority references which but for this sub-section would be references to all the authorities in the area of that authority acting jointly shall be construed as references to the general planning authority acting alone.

(12) This section shall not apply in Wales, or in the Isles of Scilly.

Duties of authorities

General duties.

17.—(1) In exercising their functions on or after the first appointed day every authority shall have regard to—

(*a*) the desirability of bringing development land into public ownership, and of developing that land themselves or of making it available for development by others, and

(*b*) the desirability of securing the proper planning of their area.

(2) In considering whether any land is development land, an authority shall have regard to—

(*a*) the provisions of the development plan, so far as material,

(*b*) whether planning permission for any relevant development on the land is in force or has been refused, and

(*c*) any other considerations which, on an application for planning permission for any relevant development on the land, would be material for the purpose of determining that application.

(3) In considering whether any land in Wales is development land, the Land Authority for Wales shall (except in a case where planning permission is in force for the carrying out of relevant development on the land) consult the council of the county, and that of the district, whose area includes the land.

(4) Schedule 6 to this Act, which imposes further duties on authorities, shall have effect.

(5) In this section and in Schedule 6 to this Act " functions " means functions under this Act and functions concerning the acquisition, management or disposal of land—

(*a*) in the case of a local authority, a new town authority or the Peak Park Joint or Lake District Special Planning Board, under the Act of 1971 or the Scottish Act of 1972, .

(*b*) in the case of a new town authority, under the New Towns Act 1965 or the New Towns (Scotland) Act 1968.

Comprehensive acquisition of development land.

18.—(1) The Secretary of State may by order—

    (a) apply this section to all, or any part, of the area of a county authority, and

    (b) designate the descriptions of relevant development as respects which the order is to apply,

and in this section " designated relevant development " means relevant development designated by such an order.

(2) Before making an order under subsection (1) above, the Secretary of State shall consult all the authorities whose areas include land to which the order applies.

(3) It shall be the duty of all the authorities whose areas include land to which the order applies to arrange between them for all outstanding material interests in land which is needed for the purposes of designated relevant development to be acquired by one of those authorities (including a local authority in Wales whose area includes the land).

(4) The authorities in acting under this section shall have regard to any relevant land acquisition and management scheme, and shall not be under any duty as respects—

    (a) land which is not needed for designated relevant development within ten years from the time at which they are acting, or

    (b) land which, by virtue of section 19(5) or section 20(2) of this Act, none of them have power to acquire compulsorily under this Part of this Act at the time at which they are acting, or

    (c) land a material interest in which has been disposed of by an authority (including a local authority in Wales whose area included the land), and in which immediately before the disposal there were no material interests outstanding, or

    (d) the operational land of statutory undertakers.

(5) The order shall designate an authority whose duty shall be to acquire all outstanding material interests in the land needed for the purposes of designated relevant development which are not acquired by any other authority (including a local authority in Wales whose area includes the land).

(6) In this Act the " relevant date " , in relation to any relevant development, means the date on which the order under this section designating that development comes into force.

(7) An order under this section—

    (*a*) shall not be made before the land acquisition and management scheme for the area of the county authority has been made;

    (*b*) shall not come into force before the first appointed day; and

    (*c*) shall be subject to annulment in pursuance of a resolution of either House of Parliament.

(8) Subsection (7)(*a*) above shall not apply in Wales, or in the Isles of Scilly.

(9) In this section " county authority " has the same meaning as in section 16 of this Act.

Planning permission for relevant development

Permission before relevant date: applications before first appointed day.

19.—(1) If an election is made under subsection (2) below, this section applies to planning permission for relevant development which is granted before the relevant date where—

    (*a*) the application was made before the first appointed day, and

    (*b*) the planning permission was granted after 12th September 1974.

(2) A person who—

    (*a*) owns a material interest in the whole of the land covered by the planning permission, and

    (*b*) as against every other owner (if any) of such an interest is entitled to possession of that land,

may make an election under this subsection by notice in the prescribed form served on any one of the authorities; and the authority on whom the notice is served shall as soon as practicable send a copy of the notice to each of the other authorities.

(3) In subsection (2) above " owner ", in relation to a material interest in land, includes a person who has entered into a binding contract for its acquisition and " owns " shall be construed accordingly; and in the application of that subsection to Scotland " material interest " includes the interest of a crofter or landholder in his croft or holding.

(4) No notice of election shall be served under subsection (2) above at a time which is—

(a) before the first appointed day, and

(b) before the grant of planning permission.

(5) If at any time one of the authorities abandon their power to purchase the land (in the sense given by paragraph 1 of Schedule 7 to this Act), that authority shall not have power to acquire the land—

(a) under this Part of this Act, or

(b) under the Act of 1971 or the Scottish Act of 1972,

in pursuance of a compulsory purchase order made before the end of the period specified in that paragraph.

(6) Planning permission to which this section applies shall be suspended from the date of service of the notice of election until the end of the period prescribed by paragraph 2 of Schedule 7 to this Act.

Permission before relevant date: applications on or after first appointed day.

20.—(1) This section applies to planning permission for relevant development which is granted before the relevant date in pursuance of an application made on or after the first appointed day.

(2) Where—

(a) planning permission is granted pursuant to the application, and

(b) at any time an authority abandon their power to purchase the land (in the sense given by paragraph 1 of Schedule 7 to this Act),

that authority shall not have power to acquire the land under this Part of this Act, or under the Act of 1971 or the Scottish Act of 1972, in pursuance of a compulsory purchase order made before the end of the period specified in that paragraph.

(3) Where planning permission to which this section applies is granted before the end of the period prescribed by paragraph 2 of Schedule 7 to this Act, it shall be suspended, when granted, until the end of that period.

Permission granted on or after relevant date.

21.—(1) This section applies to planning permission for relevant development granted on or after the relevant date in pursuance of an application (whenever made).

(2) Planning permission to which this section applies shall be suspended except—

    (*a*) where there are no outstanding material interests in the land and the development covered by the permission is carried out by or on behalf of an authority, or

    (*b*) where subsection (3) or (4) below applies.

(3) This subsection applies where—

    (*a*) an authority make a compulsory purchase order as respects the land on which the relevant development covered by the permission will be carried out, and

    (*b*) the Secretary of State serves notice on the authority that he does not intend to confirm the order as respects that land, and

    (*c*) that notice contains a direction that this subsection shall apply.

(4) This subsection applies where—

    (*a*) a material interest in the land has been disposed of by an authority and immediately before the disposal there were no material interests outstanding, and

    (*b*) the authority have for the purposes of this section approved the carrying out of the development in accordance with the planning permission, and

    (*c*) the authority have issued a certificate in the prescribed form stating that they are satisfied that paragraphs (*a*) and (*b*) apply.

(5) If the material interest was disposed of by the authority before the first appointed day, subsection (4) above shall not apply unless the authority have approved the interest as being an interest appropriate for the purposes of this section (and the certificate states that it is so approved).

(6) The certificate shall be conclusive evidence of the facts stated in it.

(7) As soon as practicable after issuing the certificate, the authority shall send a copy of the certificate to every other authority whose area includes the land.

(8) Subsection (7) above shall not apply if and so far as an authority entitled to receipt of a copy otherwise direct.

(9) In the application of this section to Wales " authority " includes a local authority whose area includes the land.

Suspension of planning permission: supplemental.

22.—(1) If relevant development covered by planning permission is carried out at a time when the planning permission is suspended under sections 19 to 21 above (in this section called " the previous sections "), the planning permission shall be disregarded in applying Part V of the Act of 1971 and Part V of the Scottish Act of 1972 (enforcement of control) to the development so carried out.

(2) If relevant development covered by planning permission is carried out at a time when the planning permission is suspended under the previous sections, then, in determining for the purpose of compensation the value of the land as at any time after any of the development is so carried out, any value attributable to the development so carried out shall be ignored.

(3) Where any development is carried out without planning permission and planning permission covering that development is subsequently granted—

(a) under section 32 of the Act of 1971 or section 29 of the Scottish Act of 1972 (planning permission for retention of development already carried out), or

(b) (by the Secretary of State on appeal against an enforcement notice) under section 88 of the Act of 1971 or section 85 of the Scottish Act of 1972,

the development shall be treated for the purposes of subsection (2) above as carried out after the grant, and while the planning permission is suspended.

(4) Where planning permission is granted under section 32 or 88 of the Act of 1971 or section 29 or 85 of the Scottish Act of 1972, the person granting the permission may, if satisfied that it is reasonable in the circumstances, direct that subsection (2) above shall not apply to the development covered by the permission.

(5) Except as provided by subsection (2) above, the previous sections shall not affect compensation in respect of a compulsory purchase, or any other compensation which depends, directly or indirectly, on the value of land.

(6) Section 192(1) of the Act of 1971 and section 181(1) of the Scottish Act of 1972 (blight notices) shall have effect as if the land specified therein included land in respect of which planning permission for relevant development is suspended under the previous sections.

(7) Any time limit imposed by a condition attached to planning permission which is suspended under the previous sections shall be extended for a period equal to the suspension.

(8) The previous sections shall not apply to planning permission granted in respect of—

    (*a*) land in which there are no material interests outstanding, or

    (*b*) land which is operational land of statutory undertakers, or would be such land if it were used or held by statutory undertakers for the purposes covered by the permission.

(9) It is hereby declared that references in the previous sections to planning permission granted on an application include planning permission treated as granted on an application deemed to have been made under section 88(7) of the Act of 1971, or section 85(7) of the Scottish Act of 1972.

Disposal notification areas

Disposal notification areas.

23.—(1) An authority may exercise the powers conferred by this section for the purpose of obtaining information about disposals of development land.

(2) An authority may pass a resolution declaring any land in their area to be a disposal notification area.

Before the Land Authority for Wales pass a resolution they shall consult each local authority whose area includes any part of the land covered by the resolution.

(3) The resolution shall specify a date as the effective date for the disposal notification area, and that date shall not be earlier than—

    (*a*) the end of the period of 3 months beginning with the passing of the resolution, or

    (*b*) the first appointed day.

(4) Part I of Schedule 8 to this Act shall apply after the passing of the resolution.

(5) A person who—

    (*a*) proposes to enter into a binding contract to dispose of a material interest in land in a disposal notification area, or

    (*b*) proposes to dispose of a material interest in land in a disposal notification area,

shall give notice to the authority in accordance with Part II of the said Schedule.

(6) Subsection (5) above shall not apply—

  (a) to a disposal in performance of a contract for that disposal of which notice has been duly given under this section,

  (b) to a transaction carried out before the effective date specified in the resolution in accordance with subsection (3) above (but can apply to a disposal in performance of a contract before that date),

  (c) to a transaction which is not for valuable consideration,

  (d) to a disposal, or a contract for a disposal, to any authority or to the Crown;

and as respects any transaction to which Part III of Schedule 8 to this Act applies notice may, but need not, be given under subsection (5) above.

(7) The authority shall serve on a person who gives notice under subsection (5) above—

  (a) a written acknowledgment of receipt stating the date of receipt, and

  (b) not later than 4 weeks after that date of receipt, a counter-notice in the prescribed form stating whether or not the authority propose to purchase the land to which the notice relates or any part of that land.

Acknowledgment shall be as soon as practicable, and shall indicate that the counter-notice will follow.

(8) Section 192(1) of the Act of 1971 and section 181(1) of the Scottish Act of 1972 (blight notices) shall have effect as if the land specified therein included land which—

  (a) is land specified in a counter-notice served in accordance with paragraph (b) of subsection (7) above as land which an authority intend to purchase, or

  (b) is land as respects which an authority have failed to serve a counter-notice in accordance with that paragraph.

(9) A person who—

  (a) without reasonable excuse fails to comply with subsection (5) above, or

  (b) knowingly or recklessly furnishes a notice which is false in a material particular in purported compliance with subsection (5) above,

shall be guilty of an offence and liable on summary conviction to a fine not exceeding £400, and on indictment to a fine.

(10) Failure to give notice under this section shall not invalidate the transaction of which notice should have been given.

Revocation of duty to notify.

24.—(1) The authority who have passed a resolution declaring a disposal notification area may at any time pass a further resolution declaring that all or part of a disposal notification area is no longer to be such an area.

(2) Before the Land Authority for Wales pass such a resolution they shall consult each local authority whose area includes any part of the land covered by the resolution.

(3) Part IV of Schedule 8 to this Act shall apply after the passing of the resolution.

Land compensation

Assumptions as to planning permission on or after second appointed day.

25.—(1) This section shall apply—

(a) to compensation in respect of every compulsory acquisition of an interest in land (whether under this or any other enactment) in pursuance of a notice to treat served on a date on or after the second appointed day, and

(b) in any other case where compensation is payable pursuant to any provision contained in or made under any enactment and the amount of the compensation depends, directly or indirectly, on the value of any interest in land as at a date on or after the second appointed day.

(2) For the purpose of assessing the compensation it shall be assumed—

(a) subject to subsections (3), (5) and (6) below, that planning permission would not be granted for any development either on the land or on any other land, and

(b) subject to subsection (6) below, that any planning permission which is suspended at the time as at which compensation is to be assessed has not been granted (but that assumption shall not be made as respects any other planning permission which may be in force at that time).

(3) The assumption in subsection (2)(a) above shall not be made as respects development of any class specified in paragraph 1 of Schedule 1 to this Act or in Schedule 8 to the Act of 1971 or Schedule 6 to the Scottish Act of 1972 (development which is not new development).

(4) For the purposes of subsections (2)(*a*) and (3) above no account shall be taken of—

(*a*) any change, effected by an order under section 22 of the Act of 1971 or section 19 of the Scottish Act of 1972, in the uses of land not involving development, or

(*b*) any change, effected by the making, variation or revocation of a general development order, in the kinds of development falling within paragraph 1 of Schedule 1 to this Act,

being (in either case) a change effected on or after the second appointed day or, if the interest in land is being compulsorily acquired and notice of the making or preparation in draft of the compulsory purchase order was first published before that day, on or after the day on which it was so published.

(5) Where during the whole of the period of seven years immediately preceding the date as at which compensation is to be assessed—

(*a*) the interest in land has been owned by a charity (but not necessarily the same charity throughout), and

(*b*) the land (as distinct from the rents and profits thereof) has not been used otherwise than wholly or mainly for charitable purposes,

then, for the purposes of assessing the compensation it shall be assumed, subject to subsection (6) below, that planning permission would be granted for any development by virtue of which the use of the land would be made to correspond with the use which prevails in the case of contiguous or adjacent land.

(6) The assumptions in subsections (2) and (5) above shall not be made where—

(*a*) during the whole of the period beginning with 12th September 1974 and ending with the date mentioned in subsection (1)(*a*) or (*b*) above, the interest in land has been owned by a charity (but not necessarily the same charity throughout), and

(*b*) that period is a period of not more than eleven years.

(7) For the purposes of subsections (5) and (6) above the interest in land shall be treated as owned by a charity at any time if, at that time, the charity—

(*a*) has or had entered into a binding contract for its acquisition, or

M

(b) subject only to completion of the administration of a deceased person's estate, is or was entitled to it under the terms of the deceased person's will.

(8) The provisions of this section have effect notwithstanding anything in any other enactment.

(9) Without prejudice to the generality of subsection (8) above, subsection (2)(a) above has effect notwithstanding anything in sections 14 to 16 and Part III of the Land Compensation Act 1961 or sections 22 to 24 and Part IV of the Land Compensation (Scotland) Act 1963.

(10) The provisions of this section shall not apply if, apart from this section, the amount of the compensation would be less than if this section applied.

Compensation payable in transactions between certain authorities.

26.—(1) This section shall apply to any compulsory acquisition of an interest in land where—

(a) notice to treat was served on or after the first appointed day;

(b) the person from whom the interest is being acquired is a body mentioned in subsection (2) below or a body specified in an order made under this paragraph by the Secretary of State;

(c) the person acquiring the interest is a Minister, a body mentioned in subsection (2) below or a body specified in an order made under this paragraph by the Secretary of State.

(2) The bodies referred to in subsection (1) above are local and new town authorities, the Land Authority for Wales, the Peak Park Joint and Lake District Special Planning Boards, and joint boards established under section 2 of this Act.

(3) For the purpose of assessing compensation in respect of a compulsory acquisition to which this section applies, section 5 of the Land Compensation Act 1961 and section 12 of the Land Compensation (Scotland) Act 1963 (rules for assessing compensation) shall have effect subject to such modifications as the Secretary of State considers it expedient to make by order under this subsection.

(4) An order under this section—

(a) shall not be made without the consent of the Treasury, and

(b) shall not be made unless a draft of the order has been approved by a resolution of each House of Parliament.

Financial hardship tribunals.

27.—(1) The Secretary of State may, for the purpose of enabling cases of hardship to be considered under this section, make regulations—

    (a) constituting one or more tribunals with the duty of discharging such functions as may be specified in the regulations, or

    (b) conferring on one or more existing bodies or groups of bodies the duty of discharging such functions as may be so specified.

Any tribunal so constituted and any existing body on which functions are so conferred is, in the following provisions of this section, referred to as a " financial hardship tribunal ".

(2) Where a financial hardship tribunal is constituted under this section regulations under this section may provide—

    (a) for the membership and chairing of the tribunal,

    (b) for regulating the appointment, tenure of office and vacation of office of members, and

    (c) for the remuneration, pensions, gratuities and allowances of members, officers and servants.

(3) The regulations shall provide that appointments are made by the Secretary of State, and that remuneration, pensions, gratuities or allowances are determined by him, subject to the approval of the Minister for the Civil Service.

(4) Where any person claims that he has suffered financial hardship as a result of any alteration made by section 25 of this Act in the amount of any compensation payable to him, or for his benefit, he may apply to a financial hardship tribunal in accordance with the provisions of the said regulations, for the award of an additional payment.

(5) Where a person has applied to a financial hardship tribunal under this section, the tribunal shall consider all the circumstances of the case and, if it is satisfied—

    (a) that the claim is justified, and

    (b) that an additional payment ought to be made to him,

the tribunal shall make an order specifying the amount of the payment which, in its opinion, ought to be made.

(6) Where a financial hardship tribunal makes an order under subsection (5) above, the amount specified in the order shall be

M2

paid by the person who is also liable for the compensation to the person who is entitled to receive the compensation.

(7) The amount so specified shall be due 3 months after service by the person to whom or for whose benefit the compensation is payable of a copy of the order on the person by whom it is to be paid, and shall carry interest from the date when it is due at the rate prescribed under section 32 of the Land Compensation Act 1961 or section 40 of the Land Compensation (Scotland) Act 1963.

(8) Regulations under this section may—

    (a) provide for the procedure of financial hardship tribunals;

    (b) make such provision as may be expedient for ensuring that in appropriate cases persons applying to financial hardship tribunals under this section may, notwithstanding anything in section 25 above or in the Land Compensation Act 1961 or the Land Compensation (Scotland) Act 1963, obtain certificates of appropriate alternative development under Part III of the said Act of 1961 or Part IV of the said Act of 1963, for the purposes of their applications;

    (c) make such provision as may be expedient for dealing with the cases of deceased persons who, if they had survived, would or might have been entitled to additional payments under this section;

    (d) prescribe the criteria by reference to which a financial hardship tribunal is to decide questions arising in relation to any application under this section.

(9) The maximum amount which a financial hardship tribunal may order to be paid as respects any one claim shall not exceed £50,000, or such higher amount as may be prescribed by regulations under this section with the approval of the Treasury.

(10) Regulations under this section—

    (a) which establish a financial hardship tribunal,

    (b) which confer on a body the functions of a financial hardship tribunal, or

    (c) which prescribe the criteria by reference to which a financial hardship tribunal is to decide questions arising in relation to any application under this section,

shall not be made unless a draft of the regulations has been approved by a resolution of each House of Parliament.

(11) Regulations under this section which do not require to be approved in draft by a resolution of each House of Parliament shall be subject to annulment in pursuance of a resolution of either House of Parliament.

(12) This section applies to compensation payable by a government department as it applies to compensation payable by any other person, and any amount due from a government department pursuant to an order of a financial hardship tribunal shall be paid out of money provided by Parliament.

(13) The expenses of a financial hardship tribunal so far as attributable to the provisions of this section, shall be defrayed by the Secretary of State out of money provided by Parliament.

(14) In Part II of Schedule 1 to the House of Commons Disqualification Act 1975 (bodies of which all members are disqualified) there shall be inserted at the appropriate place in alphabetical order the entry:

" A Financial Hardship Tribunal within the meaning of section 27(1) of the Community Land Act 1975."

This subsection shall extend to Northern Ireland.

PART IV
UNOCCUPIED OFFICE PREMISES
Powers of acquisition
Power to acquire unoccupied office premises.

28.—(1) Where any building which consists of or comprises office accommodation occupying more than 5,000 square metres of floor space (in this Part of this Act referred to as an " office building ") has been erected, whether before or after the passing of this Act, on any land, this section applies to that land and any other land used or intended for use for the purposes of the building.

(2) If the Secretary of State is satisfied as respects any office building that—

    (a) at least 75 per cent. of the office accommodation (calculated by reference to the area of floor space it occupies) has remained unoccupied for the whole of the period mentioned in subsection (3) below, and

    (b) that period is a period of not less than two years,

he may acquire the land to which this section applies either by agreement or, subject to subsection (4) below, compulsorily.

(3) The period referred to in subsection (2) above is such period as—

    (a) begins with the completion date, and

    (b) ends with the date on which the Secretary of State enters into a binding contract to purchase the land or, as the case may be, first publishes a notice stating that a compulsory purchase order for its acquisition has been prepared in draft.

294   COMMUNITY LAND ACT 1975

(4) The Secretary of State shall not acquire compulsorily under subsection (2) above—

    (*a*) the interest of any person who, in right of that interest, is occupying any part of the office building and is effectively using it for the purpose for which planning permission was given, or

    (*b*) any interest in the land to which this section applies, if he is satisfied that the person entitled to possession of the unoccupied office accommodation has tried his best to let it.

(5) In determining for the purposes of subsection (4)(*b*) above whether the person entitled to possession of the unoccupied office accommodation has tried his best to let it, the Secretary of State shall have regard to the following, as well as other relevant factors—

    (*a*) the rent sought, compared with rents of similar accommodation in the area,

    (*b*) the other covenants and conditions required by that person to be contained in any proposed lease,

    (*c*) whether or not that person indicated to prospective lessees that he was prepared to let the accommodation in parts,

    (*d*) the number and resources of the firms of estate agents retained for the purpose of letting the accommodation, and

    (*e*) the nature and extent of advertising of the accommodation by that person or those agents.

(6) In this section " floor space " means gross floor space, and the amount of any such space shall be ascertained by external measurement of that space whether the office accommodation in question is or is not bounded (wholly or partly) by external walls of the office building.

(7) In this Part of this Act " erection " , in relation to an office building, includes conversion into such a building by extension, alteration or re-erection, and " erected " shall be construed accordingly.

(8) In this section and in section 29 of this Act " completion date ", in relation to an office building, means the date on which—

    (*a*) where the office building consists only of office accommodation, the erection of the building, or

    (*b*) where it also comprises other accommodation, the erection of such part of it as consists of office accommodation,

was completed.

(9) No notice stating that a compulsory purchase order under this section has been prepared in draft shall be published before the expiration of a period of one month beginning with the passing of this Act.

Amount of compensation payable on compulsory acquisition under s. 28.

29.—(1) Where there is compulsorily acquired under section 28 of this Act an unincumbered freehold interest in the whole of any land to which that section applies, the amount of compensation payable as respects the value of that interest shall be the value of the interest assessed by reference to prices current on the completion date.

(2) Where there is compulsorily acquired under section 28 of this Act any other interest in the whole, or any interest in part, of any land to which that section applies, then, subject to subsection (3) below, the amount of compensation payable as respects the value of that interest shall be determined by the formula—

$$C = \frac{I}{A} \times F$$

where—

C is the amount of compensation payable,

I is the value of the interest in question assessed by reference to prices current on the material date,

A is the aggregate value of that interest and all other interests which subsist in the whole or any part of the land on the date on which the notice to treat is served assessed by reference to prices current on the material date, and

F is the value of an unincumbered freehold interest in the whole of the land assessed by reference to prices current on the completion date.

(3) Where the interest of a mortgagee is compulsorily acquired under section 28 of this Act, subsection (2) above shall not affect the amount payable to the mortgagee under sections 14 to 17 of the Compulsory Purchase Act 1965 or sections 99 to 106 of the Lands Clauses Consolidation (Scotland) Act 1845, except in so far as it reduces the amount of compensation payable as respects the value of the mortgaged interest.

(4) In this section—

" assessed " means assessed in accordance with the provisions of the Land Compensation Act 1961 or the Land Compensation (Scotland) Act 1963,

" land obligations " has the meaning given by section 1(2) of the Conveyancing and Feudal Reform (Scotland) Act 1970,

" material date " , in relation to the compulsory acquisition of any interest, means the date on which the Secretary of State takes possession of that interest or the date on which the amount of compensation is determined, whichever is 'he earlier, and

" unincumbered ", in relation to a freehold interest, means subject to any easements, restrictive covenants or land obligations affecting the interest on the material date but otherwise free from incumbrances.

(5) The provisions of this section shall not apply if, apart from this section, the amount of the compensation would be less than if this section applied.

(6) Nothing in this section shall affect the assessment of compensation for disturbance, severance, injurious affection or any other matter not directly based on the value of an interest which is compulsorily acquired.

Additional powers of acquisition.

30.—(1) If the Secretary of State is satisfied that, in order to facilitate the disposal of any land which he has acquired or proposes to acquire under section 28 of this Act, it is necessary to acquire any other land, he may acquire that other land either by agreement or compulsorily.

(2) No notice stating that a compulsory purchase order under this section has been prepared in draft shall be published before the expiration of a period of one month beginning with the passing of this Act.

Application of Acquisition of Land Acts, etc.

31.—(1) The Acquisition of Land Acts shall apply, as modified by subsection (2) below, to the compulsory acquisition of land under this Part of this Act as they apply to the compulsory acquisition of land in a case falling within section 1(1)(b) of the Act of 1946, or as the case may be the Scottish Act of 1947.

(2) So much of Schedule 1 to or of any regulations made under the Act of 1946, or as the case may be the Scottish Act of 1947, as requires a notice relating to a compulsory purchase order, or the order itself, to specify the purpose for which the land is required, or for which it is authorised to be compulsorily purchased, shall not have effect in relation to the compulsory acquisition of land under section 28 of this Act.

(3) The provisions of Part I of the Compulsory Purchase Act 1965 (so far as applicable), other than section 31, shall apply in relation to the acquisition of land by agreement under this Part of this Act; and in the said Part I as so applied " land " has the meaning given by section 6(1) of this Act.

(4) For the purpose of the acquisition by agreement of land in Scotland by the Secretary of State under this Part of this Act, the Lands Clauses Acts (except the provisions relating to the purchase of land otherwise than by agreement and the provisions relating to access to the special Act, and except sections 120 to 125 of the Lands Clauses Consolidation (Scotland) Act 1845) and sections 6 and 70 of the Railways Clauses Consolidation (Scotland) Act 1845 and sections 71 to 78 of that Act, as originally enacted and not as amended for certain purposes by section 15 of the Mines (Working Facilities and Support) Act 1923, shall be incorporated with this Part of this Act, and in construing those Acts for the purposes of this Part of this Act, this Part of this Act shall be deemed to be the special Act and the Secretary of State to be the promoter of the undertaking or company, as the case may require; and in those Acts as so incorporated " land " shall have the meaning given by section 6(1) of this Act.

Supplemental provisions

Assumptions as to occupation.

32.—(1) The Secretary of State shall be entitled to assume for the purposes of this Part of this Act that any office building or part of an office building as respects which the person for the time being entitled to possession was rated under Schedule 1 to the General Rate Act 1967 or section 24 of the Local Government (Scotland) Act 1966 (rating of unoccupied property) for any period remained unoccupied from the beginning of that period until—

    (*a*) the date (if any) on which notice was given to the rating authority that it had become occupied, or

    (*b*) the end of the period,

whichever is the earlier.

(2) The Secretary of State shall also be entitled to assume for the purposes of this Part that any office building or part of an office building which—

    (*a*) was unoccupied,

    (*b*) became occupied on any date, and

    (*c*) became unoccupied again on the expiration of a period of less than six months beginning with that date,

remained unoccupied on that date and during that period.

Determination of date of completion.

33.—(1) Where the erection of any office building has been treated for the purposes of Schedule 1 to the General Rate Act 1967 or Schedule 3 to the Local Government (Scotland) Act 1966 (rating of unoccupied property) as completed on any date, then, unless the Secretary of State serves a completion notice under subsection (2) below, it shall be deemed to have been completed on that date for the purposes of this Part of this Act.

(2) The Secretary of State may serve on every person entitled to possession of any part of an office building a notice (in this section referred to as a "completion notice") stating that the erection of the building is to be deemed for the purposes of this Part to have been completed on such date as may be specified in the notice.

(3) The date specified in a completion notice shall be earlier than any date on which, by virtue of subsection (1) above, the erection of the building to which the notice relates would, but for the notice, be deemed to have been completed for the purposes of this Part.

(4) If every person on whom a completion notice is served agrees in writing with the Secretary of State that the erection of the building to which the notice relates shall be deemed for the purposes of this Part to have been completed on a date specified by the agreement, it shall be deemed for those purposes to have been completed on that date and the notice shall be deemed to be withdrawn.

(5) The Secretary of State may withdraw a completion notice by a subsequent notice served on every person on whom the completion notice was served; and a notice under this subsection may be served—

 (a) at any time before an appeal in pursuance of subsection (6) below is brought against the completion notice; and

 (b) with the agreement of every person on whom the completion notice was served, at any time thereafter and before the appeal is determined.

(6) A person on whom a completion notice is served may, during the period of 21 days beginning with the date of service of the notice, appeal to the county court, or in Scotland to the sheriff, against the notice on the ground that the erection of the building to which the notice relates was not completed by the date specified in the notice.

(7) If a completion notice served in respect of a building is not withdrawn and no appeal in pursuance of subsection (6) above is brought against the notice or such an appeal is abandoned or dismissed, the erection of the building shall be deemed for the purposes of this Part to have been completed on the date specified

in the notice; and if the notice is not withdrawn and such an appeal is brought and is not abandoned or dismissed, the erection of the building shall be deemed for those purposes to have been completed on such date as the court shall determine.

(8) Where at any time the only work which remained to be done to a building to which a completion notice relates was work of a kind which was customarily done to a building of the type in question after its erection had been substantially completed, it shall be assumed for the purposes of this section that the erection of the building was completed at the expiration of such period beginning with the date of its completion apart from the work as was reasonably required for carrying out the work.

(9) In this section, unless the context otherwise requires, references to an office building include references to part of such a building.

Power to obtain information.

34.—(1) The Secretary of State may for the purposes of this Part of this Act by notice require—

(a) any person appearing to the Secretary of State to have an interest in the whole or part of any office building, or

(b) any person claiming possession of the whole or part of any such building, or

(c) any person who receives rent in respect of the whole or part of any such building, or

(d) any person who manages the whole or part of any such building as agent or otherwise,

to give such information as may be specified or described in the notice.

(2) The information which may be so specified or described is—

(a) the nature of the interest in the building belonging to the person to whom the notice is addressed (if any),

(b) the name and address of any other person known to him as having an interest in the building, and

(c) any other information which may reasonably be demanded from him for the purposes of this Part.

(3) A notice under this section shall specify the time, not being less than 14 days from service of the notice, within which it is to be complied with, and may specify the way in which it is to be complied with.

(4) A notice under this section may (in addition to or instead of asking for information) require the person to whom the notice is addressed—

    (*a*) to state whether he has in his possession or control any document which constitutes, or is evidence of, any lease or other disposition of, or of an interest in, the building, and

    (*b*) to produce to an officer of the Secretary of State, being an officer duly authorised for the purpose, any such document which is in his possession or control,

and such a notice may require that the officer of the Secretary of State be permitted to make extracts from, or take copies of, the document.

(5) Nothing in this section shall be taken to require a person who has acted as solicitor for any person to disclose any privileged communication made to him in that capacity.

(6) A person who—

    (*a*) refuses or without reasonable excuse fails to comply with a notice under this section, or

    (*b*) in furnishing any information in compliance with a notice under this section, makes any statement which he knows to be false in a material particular, or recklessly makes any statement which is false in a material particular, or

    (*c*) with intent to deceive, produces in compliance with a notice under this section a document which is false in a material particular,

shall be liable—

    (i) on summary conviction to a fine not exceeding £400, and

    (ii) on conviction on indictment, to a fine or imprisonment for a term not exceeding two years or both.

Powers of entry.

35.—(1) For the purposes of this Part of this Act a person duly authorised in writing by the Secretary of State may at any reasonable time enter any office building, or any building which he reasonably believes to be an office building, for the purpose of examining and surveying it.

(2) A person authorised under this section to enter any building shall, if so required, produce evidence of his authority before so entering, and shall not demand admission as of right to any building unless seven days' notice of the intended entry has been given to the occupier of the building.

(3) A person who wilfully obstructs a person acting in exercise of his powers under this section shall be liable on summary conviction to a fine not exceeding £100.

Service of notices.

36.—(1) Subject to subsection (2) below, any notice authorised to be served under this Part of this Act may be served either—

(*a*) by delivering it to the person on whom it is to be served; or

(*b*) by leaving it at the usual or last known place of abode of that person; or

(*c*) by sending it in a prepaid registered letter, or by recorded delivery service, addressed to that person at his usual or last known place of abode; or

(*d*) in the case of an incorporated company or body, by delivering to the secretary or clerk of the company or body at their registered or principal office, or by sending it in a prepaid registered letter or by the recorded delivery service, addressed to the secretary or clerk of the company or body at that office.

(2) Where the notice is authorised to be served on any person as having an interest in or being entitled to possession of the whole or part of any office building, and the name or address of that person cannot be ascertained after a reasonable inquiry, the notice shall be taken to be duly served if—

(*a*) being addressed to him either by name or by description of " the owner " or " the person entitled to possession ", as the case may be, of the building or the part of the building (describing it) it is delivered or sent in the manner specified in subsection (1)(*a*), (*b*) or (*c*) above, or

(*b*) being so addressed, and marked in such manner as the Secretary of State may think fit for securing that it shall be plainly identifiable as a communication of importance, it is sent to the building in a prepaid registered letter or by the recorded delivery service and is not returned to the Secretary of State, or is delivered to some person in the building, or is affixed conspicuously to some object forming part of the building.

PART V

MISCELLANEOUS

Acquisition and disposal of land by the Crown

Acquisition and disposal of land by the Crown.

37.—(1) Where, in exercise of the power conferred by section 2 of the Commissioners of Works Act 1852, section 113 of the Act of 1971 or section 103 of the Scottish Act of 1972 (acquisition of land necessary for the public service) the Secretary of State has acquired, or proposes to acquire, any land (the " public service land ") and in his opinion other land ought to be acquired together with the public service land—

(a) in the interests of the proper planning of the area concerned; or

(b) for the purpose of ensuring that the public service land can be used, or developed and used, (together with that other land) in what appears to the Secretary of State to be the best, or most economic, way; or

(c) where the public service land or any land acquired, or which the Secretary of State proposes to acquire, by virtue of paragraph (a) or (b) above, forms part of a common or open space or fuel or field garden allotment, for the purpose of being given in exchange therefor,

the said section 2 and 113, or as the case may be 103, shall apply to that other land as if its acquisition were necessary for the public service.

In the application of this subsection to Scotland the words " or fuel or field garden allotment " shall be omitted.

(2) The said section 2, 113 and 103 shall be construed and have effect as if references to land necessary for the public service included land which it is proposed to use not only for the public service but also—

(a) to meet the interests of proper planning of the area, or

(b) to secure the best, or most economic, development or use of the land,

for other purposes.

(3) The said sections 2, 113 and 103 shall be construed and have effect as if references to the public service included the service in the United Kingdom—

(a) of any international organisation or institution of which the United Kingdom, or Her Majesty's Government in the United Kingdom, is, or is to become, a member;

(b) of any office or agency established by such an organisation or institution or for its purposes, or established in pursuance of a treaty to which the United Kingdom is, or is to become, a party;

and for the purposes of paragraph (*b*) above " treaty " includes any international agreement, and any protocol or annex to a treaty or international agreement.

(4) Where the Secretary of State proposes to dispose of any of his land and is of the opinion that it is necessary, in order to facilitate that disposal, to acquire adjoining land then, notwithstanding that the acquisition of that adjoining land is not necessary for the public service, the said section 2 shall apply as if it were necessary for the public service.

(5) Where the Secretary of State is authorised by the said section 2 to acquire land by agreement for a particular purpose, he may acquire that land notwithstanding that it is not immediately required for that purpose; and any land acquired by virtue of this subsection may, until required for the purpose for which it was acquired, be used for such purpose as the Secretary of State may determine.

(6) The Secretary of State may dispose of land held by him and acquired by him or any other Minister under—

(*a*) the said section 2, 113 or 103, or

(*b*) Part IV of this Act,

to such person, in such manner and subject to such conditions as may appear to the Secretary of State to be expedient, and in particular may under this subsection dispose of land held by him for any purpose in order to secure the use of the land for that purpose.

(7) This section shall come into force at the expiration of a period of one month beginning with the passing of this Act.

(8) Any expenditure of the Secretary of State attributable to this section shall be paid out of money provided by Parliament.

Acquisition of land by Crown in Northern Ireland.

38.—(1) The provisions of the law of Northern Ireland mentioned below (acquisition of land necessary for the public service) shall be construed and have effect as if references to the public service included the service in the United Kingdom—

(*a*) of any international organisation or institution of which the United Kingdom, or Her Majesty's Government in the United Kingdom, is, or is to become, a member;

(*b*) of any office or agency established by such an organisation or institution or for its purposes, or established in pursuance of a treaty to which the United Kingdom is, or is to become, a party;

and for the purposes of paragraph (*b*) above " treaty " includes any international agreement, and any protocol or annex to a treaty or international agreement.

(2) The said provisions are section 5 of the Stormont Regulation and Government Property Act (Northern Ireland) 1933 and Article 65 of the Land Acquisition and Compensation (Northern Ireland) Order 1973.

(3) This section extends to Northern Ireland only.

(4) This section shall come into force at the expiration of a period of one month beginning with the passing of this Act.

Crown land

Application of Act to Crown land.

   39.—(1) Notwithstanding the Crown or Duchy interest—

   (*a*) a private interest in Crown land may, with the consent in writing of the appropriate authority, be acquired compulsorily under section 15 of this Act, and

   (*b*) sections 23 and 45 of this Act apply to a material interest in Crown land which is a private interest as they apply to a material interest in land which is not Crown land.

   (2) In this section " Crown land " means land in which there is a Crown interest or a Duchy interest, and—

   (*a*) " Crown interest " means an interest belonging to Her Majesty in right of the Crown, or belonging to a government department, or held in trust for Her Majesty for the purposes of a government department,

   (*b*) " Duchy interest " means an interest belonging to Her Majesty in right of the Duchy of Lancaster, or belonging to the Duchy of Cornwall,

   (*c*) " private interest " means an interest which is not a Crown interest or a Duchy interest,

and " appropriate authority " in relation to Crown land shall be determined in accordance with section 266(7) of the Act of 1971, or section 253(7) of the Scottish Act of 1972.

Grants to authorities who buy or rent Crown land.

   40.—(1) This section applies where any interest in land is acquired from the Crown on or after the first appointed day—

   (*a*) by a local or new town authority, the Land Authority for Wales, the Peak Park Joint or Lake District Special Planning Board, or a joint board established under section 2 of this Act, or

   (*b*) by a body specified in an order made under this subsection by the Secretary of State with the consent of the Treasury.

An order under this subsection shall not be made unless a draft of the order has been approved by a resolution of the Commons House of Parliament.

(2) If the Secretary of State with the approval of the Treasury considers it appropriate, he may make to the body concerned a grant of such amount as may be approved by the Treasury having regard to the purchase price, rent or other payments made by the body to the Crown in respect of the interest.

(3) Any grant under this section shall be paid out of money provided by Parliament.

Compulsory acquisition from authorities or statutory undertakers

Exclusion of special parliamentary procedure.

41.—(1) The Acquisition of Land Acts shall apply to any compulsory acquisition of an interest in land where—

(*a*) the notice of the making or preparation in draft of a compulsory purchase order is first duly published on or after the first appointed day, and

(*b*) the person acquiring the interest is a local or new town authority, the Land Authority for Wales, the Peak Park Joint or Lake District Special Planning Board, a joint board established under section 2 of this Act, any statutory undertakers or a Minister,

subject to the modification made by this section.

(2) Paragraph 9 of Schedule 1 to the Act of 1946 or, as the case may be, the Scottish Act of 1947 (special parliamentary procedure for acquisitions from local authorities, statutory undertakers and National Trust) shall not apply to the acquisition except where the interest belongs to the National Trust or the National Trust for Scotland.

Land transactions by authorities

Consent for disposals.

42.—(1) In the Local Government Act 1972 after section 123 there shall be inserted the following section—

"Consent for disposals of land by principal councils.
123A.—(1) Except with the consent of the Secretary of State, a principal council shall not dispose of a material interest in any land.

(2) This section has effect notwithstanding section 123 above, and notwithstanding any other provision of this or any other Act, whenever passed.

(3) This section shall not apply to a disposal in pursuance of a contract entered into by the principal council before the coming into force of this section.

(4) In this section " material interest " means—

    (*a*) the freehold, or

    (*b*) a lease (granted or assigned) the unexpired term of which at the relevant time is not less than seven years.

For the purposes of this subsection it shall be assumed that any option (other than one conferred by or under Act of Parliament) to renew or extend the lease, whether or not forming part of a series of options, is exercised, and that any option (other than one conferred by or under Act of Parliament) to terminate the lease is not exercised."

(2) In the Local Government (Scotland) Act 1973, after section 74 there shall be inserted the following section—

"Consent for disposals of land.

74A.—(1) Except with the consent of the Secretary of State, a local authority shall not dispose of a material interest in land.

(2) This section has effect notwithstanding section 74 above, and notwithstanding any other provision of this or any other Act, whenever passed.

(3) This section shall not apply to a disposal in pursuance of a contract entered into by a local authority before the coming into force of this section.

(4) In this section " material interest " means—

    (*a*) the estate or interest of the proprietor of the *dominium utile* or in the case of land not held on feudal tenure the interest in the land of the owner thereof, or

    (*b*) a lease (granted or assigned) the unexpired term of which at the relevant time is not less than seven years.

For the purposes of this subsection it shall be assumed that any option (other than one conferred by or under Act of Parliament) to renew or extend the lease, whether or not forming part of a series of options, is exercised, and that any option (other than one conferred by or under Act of Parliament) to terminate the lease is not exercised."

(3) This section shall come into force on the first appointed day.

Accounts and records.

43.—(1) Every authority shall—

    (a) keep such accounts and records, and

    (b) prepare and submit to the Secretary of State such statements of account,

relating to the acquisition, holding and disposal of land as the Secretary of State may with the approval of the Treasury direct.

(2) Directions under subsection (1) above may in particular relate to—

    (a) the items which are or are not to be included in the accounts, and the kinds of transactions which are to be recorded, and

    (b) the form and manner in which the statements of accounts are to be prepared and the times at which they are to be submitted to the Secretary of State.

(3) Money to be credited to an account kept under this section shall not be applied by the authority for any purpose without the consent of the Secretary of State.

(4) Where any item debited to an account kept under this section has been defrayed by borrowing, the authority shall not be required, notwithstanding anything in Schedule 13 to the Local Government Act 1972 or Schedule 3 to the Local Government (Scotland) Act 1975 or in any other enactment, to make any annual provision for the repayment of the capital.

(5) Every authority shall supply the Secretary of State—

    (a) with such information as the Secretary of State may specify to enable him to ascertain the state of any account or record kept, or to verify any statement of account submitted to him, under this section, and

    (b) with such certificates supporting the information as the Secretary of State may specify.

(6) The Secretary of State may publish in such manner as appears to him appropriate—

    (a) statements of account submitted to him under this section, and

    (b) any information obtained by him under subsection (5) above.

(7) In relation to Wales " authority " in this and the next section includes a local authority.

Community land surplus accounts.

44.—(1) The Secretary of State may, with the approval of the Treasury and after consulting such associations of authorities as appear to him to be concerned, direct that any statement of account which—

(*a*) is submitted to him under the last preceding section for any financial year, and

(*b*) is of a kind specified in the direction,

shall be a community land surplus account.

(2) So much of any surplus in a community land surplus account as the Secretary of State with the approval of the Treasury directs shall be paid by the authority to the Secretary of State.

(3) Subject to subsection (4) below, the remainder of the surplus (if any) shall be applied by the authority—

(*a*) for any purpose for which capital money may be properly applied, or

(*b*) for meeting any liability under a land acquisition and management scheme,

or in both those ways.

(4) The application of money in accordance with subsection (3)(*a*) above by an authority other than a new town authority or the Land Authority for Wales shall, subject to section 27 of the Town and Country Planning Act 1959 (which, in England and Wales, authorises the application of capital money in certain cases without consent), be effected only with the consent of the Secretary of State.

(5) The Secretary of State may, out of sums received by him under subsection (2) above, with the approval of the Treasury and after consulting such associations of authorities as appear to him to be concerned, pay such amounts to such authorities as he considers expedient.

(6) the Secretary of State shall for each financial year prepare, in such form and manner as the Treasury may approve, an account of—

(*a*) sums received by him under this section and paid out under subsection (5),

(*b*) the remaining sums received by him under this section.

(7) The Secretary of State shall, on or before 30th November in any year, transmit to the Comptroller and Auditor General the said account for the financial year last ended.

(8) The Comptroller and Auditor General shall examine and certify the account submitted to him, and lay copies of it together with his report before each House of Parliament.

Disposal of land at direction of Secretary of State.

45.—(1) The Secretary of State may direct a local authority or the Peak Park Joint or Lake District Special Planning Board to dispose of a material interest in any land which is for the time being entered in an account kept by them under section 43 of this Act, in such manner, and subject to such terms and conditions, as may be specified in the direction.

(2) Where a direction is given under this section for the disposal of a material interest in any land—

> (a) section 21 of this Act shall not apply to any planning permission in respect of that land which is specified in the direction, and

> (b) sections 20 and 21 of this Act shall not apply to any planning permission in respect of that land which is subsequently granted by the Secretary of State.

(3) Before giving a direction to an authority under this section, the Secretary of State shall consult the authority.

(4) No direction shall be given under this section before the first appointed day.

Register of land holdings.

46.—(1) The Secretary of State may by regulations provide for the keeping of registers by authorities recording their acquisitions, holdings and disposals of land.

(2) Regulations under this section may prescribe—

> (a) the kinds of land and the kinds of transactions to be registered,

> (b) the form of the registers, and the particulars to be contained in them,

> (c) the circumstances in which, and conditions subject to which, the registers are to be open to public inspection.

(3) In the application of this section to Wales " authorities " include local authorities.

Certification of appropriate alternative development

Certification of appropriate alternative development.

47.—(1) Section 17 of the Land Compensation Act 1961 and section 25 of the Land Compensation (Scotland) Act 1963 (certification of appropriate alternative development) shall each be amended in accordance with subsections (2) to (5) below and, as amended by this section, section 49(3) of the said Act of 1963 and section 172(2) of the Local Government (Scotland) Act 1973, shall have effect as set out in Schedule 9 to this Act.

(2) For subsection (3) of each section there shall be substituted the following subsection—

" (3) An application for a certificate under this section—

> (*a*) shall state whether or not there are, in the applicant's opinion, any classes of development which, either immediately or at a future time, would be appropriate for the land in question if it were not proposed to be acquired by any authority possessing compulsory purchase powers and, if so, shall specify the classes of development and the times at which they would be so appropriate;

> (*b*) shall state the applicant's grounds for holding that opinion; and

> (*c*) shall be accompanied by a statement specifying the date on which a copy of the application has been or will be served on the other party directly concerned."

(3) In subsection (4) of section 17 there shall be substituted for the words " paragraph (*b*) " the words " paragraph (*c*) ", for the words " planning permission that might have been expected to be granted " the words " grant of planning permission ", for the words " might reasonably have been expected to be " the words " would have been " and for the words " could not reasonably have been expected to be " the words " would not have been ".

(4) In subsection (4) of section 25 there shall be substituted for the words " subsection (3)(*b*) " the words " subsection (3)(*c*) ", for the words " might reasonably have been expected to be " the words " would have been " and for the words " could not reasonably have been expected to be " the words " would not have been ".

(5) In subsections (5) and (7) of each section for the words " might reasonably have been expected to be " there shall be substituted the words " would have been ".

(6) This section shall have effect only in relation to applications, and certificates issued in pursuance of applications, made after the expiration of a period of one month beginning with the passing of this Act.

PART VI
SUPPLEMENTAL
Reserve powers

Powers of Secretary of State.

48.—(1) The Secretary of State may act under this section in a case where it appears to him expedient that an authority should cease to be responsible for exercising—

(*a*) any functions under this Act, or

(*b*) any functions under any other Act, whether passed before this Act or later, being functions concerning the disposal or management of land.

(2) In such a case the Secretary of State may make an order transferring any such functions—

(*a*) to himself, or

(*b*) to another authority, or

(*c*) to a body appointed under section 50 below.

(3) The order may include among the functions transferred—

(*a*) the management and disposal of land in any account kept by the authority under section 43 of this Act, and

(*b*) so far as appears to the Secretary of State expedient functions both under this Act and (so far as they relate to the disposal or management of land) other Acts,

and may provide for the transfer from the authority of such of the property, rights, liabilities and obligations of the authority as the Secretary of State considers appropriate.

(4) The Secretary of State shall not make the order except after holding a public local inquiry unless the authority from whom the functions are to be transferred have consented to the making of the order; and an order made after such an inquiry has been held shall be subject to annulment in pursuance of a resolution of either House of Parliament.

(5) Where any functions are transferred under this section from any authority, the amount of any expenses which the Secretary of State certifies were incurred by the transferee in performing those functions shall on demand be paid to him by the first-mentioned authority.

(6) Any expenses which under the last preceding subsection are required to be paid by the authority shall be defrayed by the authority in the like manner, and shall be debited to the like account as if the functions have not been transferred, and the expenses have been incurred by the authority in performing them.

(7) The authority shall have the like powers for the purpose of raising any money required in pursuance of the last preceding subsection as the authority would have for the purpose of raising money required for defraying expenses incurred for the purposes of the functions in question.

(8) Functions of a new town authority shall not be transferred under this section (but that shall not prevent functions being transferred to a new town authority and subsequently being re-transferred).

(9) This section shall not apply in Wales.

(10) Any payment made by the Secretary of State for the purpose of this section shall be paid out of money provided by Parliament.

(11) An order under this section shall not be made before the first appointed day.

Re-transfer of functions.

49.—(1) Where any functions have been transferred from an authority under the last preceding section the Secretary of State may at any time make an order re-transferring to that authority all of the functions so transferred.

(2) The order may, in connection with the re-transfer of any functions to the authority, make such provision as the Secretary of State considers appropriate as respects any property, rights, liabilities and obligations held by the transferee for the purposes of functions transferred from the authority.

(3) The amount of any expenses which the Secretary of State certifies were incurred by the transferee in carrying out the order shall on demand be paid to the transferee by the authority to whom the functions are re-transferred, and subsections (6) and (7) of the last preceding section shall apply as respects the way that authority defray those expenses.

Bodies to exercise reserve powers.

50.—(1) The Secretary of State may by order from time to time establish one or more bodies corporate to exercise, or to be available to exercise, the functions conferred on such bodies by section 48 of this Act.

(2) An order under this section may provide—

    (*a*) for the membership and chairing of the body,

    (*b*) for regulating the appointment, tenure of office and vacation of office of members, and for regulating their meetings and proceedings, and

(c) for the remuneration, pensions, gratuities and allowances of members, officers and servants.

(3) The regulations shall provide that appointments are made by the Secretary of State, and that remuneration, pensions, gratuities or allowances are determined by him, subject to the approval of the Minister for the Civil Service.

(4) An order shall not be made under this section unless a draft of the order has been approved by a resolution of each House of Parliament.

(5) Payments made pursuant to an order under this section shall be defrayed out of money provided by Parliament.

Other supplemental provisions

Power to obtain information.

51.—(1) For the purpose of enabling the Secretary of State or an authority to make an order or serve any notice or other document which, by any of the provisions of this Act, he or they are authorised or required to make or serve, the Secretary of State or the authority may require the occupier of any premises, and any person who, either directly or indirectly, receives rent in respect of any premises, to state in writing the nature of his interest therein, and the name and address of any other person known to him as having an interest therein, whether as a freeholder, mortgagee, lessee or otherwise.

(2) Any person who, having been required in pursuance of this section to give any information fails to give that information shall be guilty of an offence and liable on summary conviction to a fine not exceeding £100.

(3) Any person who, having been so required to give any information, knowingly makes any mis-statement in respect thereof shall be guilty of an offence and liable on summary conviction to a fine not exceeding £400 or on conviction on indictment to imprisonment for a term not exceeding two years or to a fine, or both.

Service of documents.

52.—(1) Sections 231 and 233 of the Local Government Act 1972 (service of documents by local authorities, and on local authorities) shall be applied in accordance with this section.

(2) The said sections shall apply as if the Land Authority for Wales were a local authority.

(3) In relation to—

(a) any document required or authorised by or under this Act to be given to or served on a new town authority, or (*b*) any document required or authorised by or under this Act to be given to or served on any person by or on behalf of a new town authority,

the said sections shall apply as if the new town authority were a local authority.

    (4) In relation to—

    (*a*) any document required or authorised by or under this Act to be given to or served on a local authority or new town authority in Scotland, or

    (*b*) any document required or authorised by or under this Act to be given to or served on any person by or on behalf of a local authority or new town authority in Scotland,

sections 190 and 192 of the Local Government (Scotland) Act 1973 shall apply as if the local authority (within the meaning of this Act) or new town authority were a local authority within the meaning of that Act.

Regulations and orders.

53.—(1) The Secretary of State may make regulations for prescribing the form of—

    (*a*) any document required or authorised by or under this Act to be given to or served on any authority, and

    (*b*) any document authorised or required by or under this Act to be given, served, made or issued by any authority.

    (2) Any power—

    (*a*) to make orders under any provision of this Act other than paragraphs 17(4) and 19(5) of Schedule 4, and

    (*b*) to make regulations under any provision of this Act,

shall be exercisable by statutory instrument.

    (3) Any regulation or order under this Act—

    (*a*) may make different provision for different areas, different authorities or other different cases,

    (*b*) may include transitional and other supplemental and incidental provisions,

    (*c*) in the case of regulations varying the kinds of development which are relevant development, may include transitional provisions which make such adaptations or modifications of this Act as appear to the Secretary of State necessary or expedient.

(4) An order made under any provision of this Act, other than an order under section 7 appointing the first or second appointed day, may be varied or revoked by a subsequent order so made.

Directions and consents.

54. Any direction or consent given by the Secretary of State under this Act may be—

> (a) either general or limited to any particular case or class of case,
>
> (b) addressed to any particular authority or class of authority, or
>
> (c) unconditional or subject to conditions.

Local inquiries.

55. Section 250 of the Local Government Act 1972 or section 210 of the Local Government (Scotland) Act 1973 shall extend to any public local inquiry held under this Act.

Offences by corporations.

56.—(1) Where an offence under this Act which has been committed by a body corporate is proved to have been committed with the consent or connivance of, or to be attributable to any neglect on the part of, a director, manager, secretary or other similar officer of the body corporate, or any person who was purporting to act in any such capacity, he, as well as the body corporate, shall be guilty of that offence and liable to be proceeded against accordingly.

(2) Where the affairs of a body corporate are managed by its members, this section shall apply in relation to acts and defaults of a member in connection with his functions of management as if he were a director of the body corporate.

Financial provisions.

57.—(1) There shall be paid out of money provided by Parliament—

> (a) any expenses of the Secretary of State under this Act, and
>
> (b) any increase in money so payable under any other Act which is attributable to the provisions of this Act.

(2) Any sum paid to the Secretary of State under this Act shall, except as otherwise expressly provided, be paid into the Consolidated Fund.

Short title, etc.

58.—(1) This Act may be cited as the Community Land Act 1975.

(2) The consequential and minor amendments in Schedule 10 to this Act shall have effect.

(3) The enactments mentioned in Schedule 11 to this Act shall be repealed to the extent specified in the third column of that Schedule.

(4) Except as otherwise expressly provided, this Act shall not extend to Northern Ireland.

SCHEDULES

SCHEDULE 1

Section 3.

EXEMPT DEVELOPMENT

1. Development for which planning permission—

   (*a*) is granted by a general development order for the time being in force, or

   (*b*) would be so granted but for a direction given under the order,

and which is carried out so as to comply with any condition or limitation subject to which planning permission is or would be so granted.

2. The carrying out, on land which is used for the purposes of agriculture or forestry, of any building or other operations required for the purposes of that use, other than operations for the erection of dwelling-houses.

3. The winning and working, on land held or occupied with land used for the purposes of agriculture, of any minerals reasonably required for the purposes of that use, including the fertilisation of the land so used and the maintenance, improvement or alteration of buildings or works thereon which are occupied or used for those purposes.

SCHEDULE 2

Section 7.

COMMENCEMENT DATES, ETC.
PART I

1. *First appointed day*

The main provisions where it appears are—

Provision of Act	Subject matter
Section 15	Powers of acquisition and appropriation.
Section 17	General duties of authorities.
Sections 19 and 20	Planning permission for relevant development.
Sections 23 and 24	Disposal notification areas.
Section 48	Reserve powers.

2. The " relevant date "

The main provisions where it appears are—

Provision of Act	Subject matter
Section 18	Comprehensive acquisition of development land.
Section 21	Planning permission for relevant development.

3. Second appointed day

The main provision where it appears is—

Provision of Act	Subject matter
Section 25	Assessment of compensation: assumptions as to planning permission.

PART II

1.—(1) The Secretary of State shall maintain and keep up to date a register showing the orders which have been made under section 18 of this Act in such a way as enables members of the public to inform themselves as to the dates (in this Act called " the relevant date ") when they came into force, the areas to which they apply and the descriptions of relevant development to which they apply.

(2) The registers for England, Scotland and Wales shall be kept respectively in London, Edinburgh and Cardiff at the principal offices of the Secretary of State having general responsibility for planning matters in relation to those countries respectively.

(3) The registers shall be available for inspection by the public at all reasonable hours.

2. As soon as practicable after the making of an order under section 18 of this Act, each of the authorities whose areas include land to which the order applies—

(a) shall publish a notice of the effect of the order in two or more newspapers circulating in the locality, of which one shall, if practicable, be a local newspaper, and

(b) shall deposit a copy of the order at their principal office and shall keep it available there at all reasonable hours for public inspection without payment.

SCHEDULE 3

Section 8.

THE LAND AUTHORITY FOR WALES

1. The Land Authority for Wales shall by that name be a body corporate and shall consist of such number of members, not less

than six and not exceeding nine, as the Secretary of State may from time to time determine.

2.—(1) The members shall be appointed by the Secretary of State, who may appoint one of them to be chairman of the Authority and another to be deputy chairman.

(2) Four offices as members of the Authority shall be held by members appointed by the Secretary of State after consultation with such organisations as appear to him to be representative of local authorities in Wales.

3.   In Part II of Schedule 1 to the House of Commons Disqualification Act 1975 (bodies of which all members are disqualified) there shall be inserted at the appropriate place in alphabetical order the entry:

" The Land Authority for Wales ".

This paragraph shall extend to Northern Ireland.

4.—(1) Subject to the provisions of this paragraph, a member of the Authority, and the chairman and deputy chairman, shall hold and vacate office in accordance with the terms of his appointment.

(2) A member may by notice in writing addressed to the Secretary of State resign his membership and the chairman or deputy chairman may by the like notice resign his office.

(3) The Secretary of State may remove a person from membership if satisfied that he—

(a) has become bankrupt or made an arrangement with his creditors; or

(b) is incapacitated by physical or mental illness; or

(c) has been absent from more than six consecutive meetings of the Authority otherwise than for a reason approved by the Secretary of State; or

(d) is otherwise unable or unfit to discharge the functions of a member, or is unsuitable to continue as a member.

(4) A person who ceases to be a member, or ceases to be chairman or deputy chairman, shall be eligible for re-appointment.

(5) If the chairman or deputy chairman ceases to be a member of the Authority he shall also cease to be chairman or deputy chairman.

(6) A person may hold all or any of the following offices at the same time, that is secretary or other officer of the Authority, member of the Authority and deputy chairman of the Authority; and a

person holding the office of chairman of the Authority may hold any other office except that of secretary or deputy chairman.

5. The Authority, with the approval of the Secretary of State, may appoint a secretary of the Authority, and such other officers and servants as the Authority may, after consultation with the Secretary of State and with the consent of the Minister, determine.

6.—(1) The Authority shall pay to members of the Authority such remuneration and allowances as may be determined by the Secretary of State with the consent of the Minister.

(2) In the case of any such person as the Secretary of State may with the consent of the Minister determine, the Authority shall pay such pension, allowance or gratuity to or in respect of him, or make such payment towards the provision of such a pension, allowance or gratuity, as may be so determined.

(3) If a person ceases to be a member of the Authority, and it appears to the Secretary of State that there are special circumstances which make it right that that person should receive compensation, the Secretary of State may, with the consent of the Minister, require the Authority to pay to that person a sum of such amount as the Secretary of State may with the consent of the Minister determine.

(4) As soon as practicable after the making of any determination under sub-paragraph (2) or sub-paragraph (3) of this paragraph the Secretary of State shall lay a statement thereof before each House of Parliament.

Staff

7. The Authority shall pay to their officers and servants such remuneration and allowances as they may, after consultation with the Secretary of State and with the consent of the Minister, determine.

8.—(1) The Authority shall, in the case of such of the persons employed by them as may be determined by the Authority with the consent of the Secretary of State given with the approval of the Minister, pay such pensions, allowances or gratuities to or in respect of those persons as may be so determined, make such payments towards the provision of such pensions, allowances or gratuities as may be so determined or provide and maintain such schemes (whether contributory or not) for the payment of such pensions, allowances or gratuities as may be so determined.

(2) Where a person employed by the Authority and participating in a scheme for the payment of pensions, allowances or gratuities which is applicable to such persons becomes a member of the Authority, his service as a member may be treated for the purposes of the scheme as service as a person employed by the Authority.

Proceedings and instruments

9.—(1) Subject to the following provisions of this Schedule the Authority shall have power to regulate their own procedure.

(2) The quorum at meetings of the Authority shall be four.

(3) In paragraph 1 of the Schedule to the Public Bodies (Admission to Meetings) Act 1960 (which specifies the bodies in England and Wales to which that Act applies) after paragraph (*b*) there shall be inserted the following paragraph:—

" (*bb*) the Land Authority for Wales; ".

10.—(1) A member of the Authority who is in any way directly or indirectly interested in any land which is the subject of a transaction entered into or proposed to be entered into by the Authority shall disclose the nature of his interest at a meeting of the Authority; and the disclosure shall be recorded in the minutes of the Authority, and the member shall not take any part in any deliberation or decision of the Authority with respect to the transaction.

(2) For the purposes of sub-paragraph (1) above a general notice given at a meeting of the Authority by a member of the Authority to the effect that he is a member of a specified company or firm and is to be regarded as interested in any transaction which may, after the date of the notice, be entered into in relation to that company or firm, shall be regarded as a sufficient disclosure of his interest in relation to any such transaction.

(3) A member of the Authority need not attend in person at a meeting of the Authority in order to make any disclosure which he is required to make under this paragraph if he takes reasonable steps to secure that the disclosure is made by a notice which is brought up and read at the meeting.

11. The proceedings of the Authority shall not be invalidated by any vacancy in the number of their members or by any defect in the appointment of any person as a member or chairman or deputy chairman or by any failure to comply with the requirements of paragraph 10 above.

12. The seal of the Authority shall be authenticated by the signature of the secretary or of any person authorised by the Authority to act in that behalf.

13. A certificate signed by the secretary that any instrument purporting to be made or issued by or on behalf of the Authority was so made or issued shall be conclusive evidence of that fact.

14. Every document purporting—

(*a*) to be an instrument made or issued by or on behalf of the Authority and to be sealed with the seal of the Authority authenticated in the manner provided by paragraph 12 above, or to be signed or executed by the secretary or any person authorised by the Authority to act in that behalf, or

(b) to be such a certificate as is mentioned in paragraph 13 above,

shall be received in evidence and be deemed without further proof to be so made or issued or to be such a certificate, unless the contrary is shown.

Supplemental

15.—(1) A person dealing with the Authority, or with a person claiming under the Authority, shall not be concerned to inquire—

(a) whether any directions have been given to the Authority under this Act or whether any directions so given have been complied with, or

(b) whether the consent or approval of the Secretary of State or the Minister required for any of the purposes of this Act has been given, or whether any condition or limitation subject to which any such consent or approval was given has been complied with,

and, in favour of any such person, the validity of anything done by the Authority shall not be affected by anything contained in any such direction, consent or approval or by reason that any such pirection, consent or approval has not been given.

(2) Without prejudice to sub-paragraph (1) above, the validity of a compulsory purchase order made by the Authority shall not be affected by anything contained in a direction given under section 8(3) of this Act or by reason that any such direction has not been complied with.

16. In this Schedule " the Minister " means the Minister for the Civil Service.

SCHEDULE 4

Section 15.

ACQUISITION AND APPROPRIATION OF LAND
PART I
MODIFICATIONS OF ACQUISITION OF LAND ACTS

1.—(1) Subject to sub-paragraph (2) below, the Acquisition of Land Acts shall apply in relation to the compulsory acquisition of land under section 15 of this Act with the modifications made by the following provisions of this Part of this Schedule.

N

(2) The modifications made by paragraphs 2 and 3 below shall not have effect unless—

(*a*) there are no material interests comprised in the compulsory purchase order other than outstanding material interests in development land, and

(*b*) the order contains a certificate to that effect.

(3) A certificate under sub-paragraph (2) above shall not be questioned in any legal proceedings whatsoever.

2.—(1) For paragraph 4 of Schedule 1 there shall be substituted the following paragraph:—

" 4.—(1) If no objection is duly made by any such owner, lessee or occupier as aforesaid or if all objections so made are withdrawn, the confirming authority, upon being satisfied that the proper notices have been published and served, may, if it thinks fit, confirm the order with or without modifications.

(2) If any objection duly made as aforesaid is not withdrawn, then, before confirming the order, the confirming authority may if it considers it expedient to do so, and shall if sub-paragraph (3) below applies—

(*a*) cause a public local inquiry to be held, or

(*b*) afford to any person by whom an objection has been duly made as aforesaid and not withdrawn, an opportunity of appearing before and being heard by a person appointed by the confirming authority for the purpose.

(3) This sub-paragraph applies unless the confirming authority is satisfied either—

(*a*) that planning permission for relevant development is in force in respect of the land comprised in the order, and that the planning permission was granted by the confirming authority after a public local inquiry; or

(*b*) where a local plan for the district in which the land is situated has been adopted or approved under Part II of the Town and Country Planning Act 1971, that the grant of planning permission for relevant development in respect of the land comprised in the order would be in accordance with the provisions of that plan; or

(*c*) where no such plan has been so adopted or approved, that the grant of planning permission for relevant development in respect of the land comprised in the order would be in accordance with the provisions of the development plan.

(4) After considering any objection duly made as aforesaid and, in a case where there has been an inquiry or hearing under sub-paragraph (2) above, the report of the person who held the inquiry or the person appointed to conduct the hearing, the confirming authority may confirm the order with or without modifications.

(5) If any person by whom an objection has been made is given, and avails himself of, the opportunity of being heard, the confirming authority shall afford to the acquiring authority, and to any other persons to whom it appears to the confirming authority expedient to afford it, an opportunity of being heard on the same occasion.

(6) Notwithstanding anything in sub-paragraphs (2) to (5) above, the confirming authority may require any person who has made an objection, within such period (not being less than 28 days from the date of the requirement) as the confirming authority may specify, to state in writing, the grounds thereof, and may disregard the objection for the purposes of this paragraph if satisfied that the objection—

(a) relates exclusively to matters which can be dealt with by the tribunal by whom the compensation is to be assessed, or

(b) is made on the ground that the acquisition is unnecessary or inexpedient.

(7) If the objector fails to state the grounds of his objection as required within the time specified by the confirming authority, the confirming authority may disregard the objection.

(8) Where an objection has been duly made as aforesaid and not withdrawn, and the confirming authority do not hold an inquiry or hearing, then, as soon as may be after it has determined either to confirm or not to confirm the order, the authority shall send to any person who—

(a) is such an owner, lessee or occupier as is mentioned in paragraph 3(1)(b) above, and

(b) has specified an address for the purposes of this paragraph,

a notification of its decision, which shall be addressed to that person and sent by registered post or the recorded delivery service to the address so specified.

(9) In this paragraph—

(a) any reference to a plan includes a reference to any alteration to that plan;

(b) ' development plan ' and ' planning permission ' have the same meanings as in the Town and Country Planning Act 1971;

(c) ' relevant development ' has the same meaning as in the Community Land Act 1975."

(2) In relation to the Scottish Act of 1947, the paragraph 4 of Schedule 1 set out above shall have effect as if for references to the Act of 1971 there were substituted references to the Scottish Act of 1972 and for the reference to paragraph 3(1)(b) of Schedule 1 there were substituted a reference to paragraph 3(b) of Schedule 1.

3.—(1) If the Secretary of State considers it necessary to do so in the public interest, he may from time to time by order direct that for such period (not exceeding five years) as may be specified in the order the paragraph 4 of Schedule 1 set out above shall have effect as if the references in sub-paragraph (3)(b) to a local plan adopted or approved under Part II of the Act of 1971 included references—

(a) to any local plan which has been prepared by the local planning authority and as respects which the purposes of paragraphs (a) to (c) of section 12(1) of the Act of 1971 (publicity in connection with the preparation of plans) have, in the opinion of the confirming authority, been adequately achieved by the steps taken by the local planning authority, and

(b) to any other plan which has been so prepared and as respects which, if it had been a local plan, those purposes would, in the opinion of the confirming authority, have been adequately achieved by the steps so taken.

(2) Where the land comprised in a compulsory purchase order consists of a dwelling-house and the occupier of the dwelling-house duly objects to the order and that objection is not withdrawn, the Secretary of State shall not rely on the modification made by an order under this paragraph.

(3) Where the land comprised in a compulsory purchase order comprises a dwelling-house together with other land and the occupier of the dwelling-house duly objects to the order and that objection is not withdrawn, then, if the Secretary of State relies on the modification made by an order under this paragraph, he shall not confirm the compulsory purchase order without a modification excluding the dwelling-house from that order.

(4) In this paragraph " dwelling-house " means any building or part of a building in which a person is residing, and includes any other building or part of a building in which a person normally resides but from which he is temporarily absent.

(5) In relation to the Scottish Act of 1947, this paragraph shall have effect as if, in sub-paragraph (1) above, for the references to Part II and section 12(1) of the Act of 1971 there were substituted references to Part II and section 10(1) of the Scottish Act of 1972, and for the references to the local planning authority there were substituted references to the regional planning authority, the general planning authority or the district planning authority, as the case may require.

(6) An order under this paragraph shall not be made unless a draft of the order has been approved by a resolution of each House of Parliament.

4.—(1) Where a compulsory purchase order authorising the acquisition of any land is submitted to the Secretary of State in accordance with Part I of Schedule 1 then, if the Secretary of State—

(a) is satisfied that the order ought to be confirmed so far as it relates to part of the land comprised therein, but

(b) has not for the time being determined whether it ought to be confirmed so far as it relates to any other such land,

he may confirm the order so far as it relates to the land mentioned in paragraph (a) above, and give directions postponing the consideration of the order, so far as it relates to any other land specified in the directions, until such time as may be so specified.

(2) Where the Secretary of State gives directions under sub-paragraph (1) above, the notices required by paragraph 7 of Schedule 1 to be published and served shall include a statement of the effect of the directions.

5.—(1) Notwithstanding anything in paragraph 10 of Schedule 1, a compulsory purchase order under Part III of this Act authorising the acquisition of land which has been acquired by statutory undertakers for the purposes of their undertaking may be confirmed without a certificate under that paragraph.

In this sub-paragraph " statutory undertakers " has the meaning given by the relevant Acquisition of Land Act, and includes any authority, body or undertakers which by virtue of any enactment are to be treated as statutory undertakers for any of the purposes of that Act.

(2) Except where the appropriate Minister's certificate is given, a compulsory purchase order to which this paragraph applies shall be of no effect unless it is confirmed by the appropriate Minister jointly with the Minister or Ministers who would apart from this sub-paragraph have power to confirm it.

In this sub-paragraph "the appropriate Minister's certificate" means such a certificate as is mentioned in paragraph 10 of Schedule 1.

(3) Sections 238 to 240 of the Act of 1971 and sections 227 to 229 of the Scottish Act of 1972 (measure of compensation for statutory undertakers) shall apply in respect of a compulsory acquisition which is effected by a compulsory purchase order which by virtue of this paragraph is confirmed without a certificate.

Compulsory purchase by Land Authority for Wales

6. Where the compulsory purchase order was made by the Land Authority for Wales—

> (*a*) a notice under paragraph 3(1)(*b*) of Schedule 1 (notice specifying the time for making objections) shall be served on the local authorities within whose areas the land is situated,
>
> (*b*) those local authorities shall have a right to object in accordance with the notice,
>
> (*c*) the references in paragraph 4 of that Schedule to objections made by an owner, lessee or occupier shall include references to an objection made by such a local authority.

PART II
ACQUISITION OF LAND BY AGREEMENT

7.—(1) The provisions of Part I of the Compulsory Purchase Act 1965 (so far as applicable), other than section 31, shall apply in relation to the acquisition of land by agreement under section 15 of this Act; and in the said Part I as so applied " land " shall have the meaning given by section 6(1) of this Act.

(2) For the purpose of the acquisition by agreement of land in Scotland by an authority under section 15 of this Act, the Lands Clauses Acts (except the provisions relating to the purchase of land otherwise than by agreement and the provisions relating to access to the special Act, and except sections 120 to 125 of the Lands Clauses Consolidation (Scotland) Act 1845) and sections 6 and 70 of the Railway Clauses Consolidation (Scotland) Act 1845 and sections 71 to 78 of that Act, as originally enacted and not as amended for certain purposes by section 15 of the Mines (Working Facilities and Support) Act 1923, shall be incorporated with section 15 of this Act, and in construing those Acts for the purpose of that section, that section shall be deemed to be the special Act, and the authority to be promoters of the undertaking or company, as the case may require; and in those Acts as so incorporated " land " shall have the meaning given by section 6(1) of this Act.

PART III
SUPPLEMENTAL PROVISIONS
Extinguishment of rights over land compulsorily acquired

8.—(1) Subject to the provisions of this paragraph, upon the completion by an authority of a compulsory acquisition of land under Part III of this Act, all private rights of way and rights of laying down, erecting, continuing or maintaining any apparatus on, under or over the land shall be extinguished, and any such apparatus shall vest in the authority.

(2) Sub-paragraph (1) above shall not apply to any right vested in, or apparatus belonging to, statutory undertakers for the purpose of the carrying on of their undertaking.

(3) In respect of any right or apparatus not falling within sub-paragraph (2) above, sub-paragraph (1) above shall have effect subject—

    (*a*) to any direction given by the authority before the completion of the acquisition that sub-paragraph (1) above shall not apply to any right or apparatus specified in the direction; and

    (*b*) to any agreement which may be made (whether before or after the completion of the acquisition) between the authority and the person in or to whom the right or apparatus in question is vested or belongs.

(4) Any person who suffers loss by the extinguishment of a right or the vesting of any apparatus under this paragraph shall be entitled to compensation from the authority.

(5) Any compensation payable under this paragraph shall be determined in accordance with the Land Compensation Act 1961 or the Land Compensation (Scotland) Act 1963.

Development of land acquired under Part III of this Act

9.—(1) An authority acquiring any land under Part III of this Act shall, in relation to that land, have power (notwithstanding any limitation imposed by law on the capacity of the authority by virtue of their constitution) to erect, construct or carry out any buildings or works, not being a building or work for the erection, construction or carrying out of which, whether by that authority or by any other person, statutory power exists by virtue of, or could be conferred under, an alternative enactment.

(2) The consent of the Secretary of State shall be requisite to any exercise by an authority of the power conferred on them by sub-paragraph (1) above; and any such consent may be given either in respect of a particular operation or in respect of operations of any class, and either subject to or free from any conditions or limitations.

(3) Where an authority propose to carry out any operation which they would have power to carry out by virtue only of sub-paragraph (1) above, they shall notify the Secretary of State of their proposal, and the Secretary of State may direct such advertisement by the authority as appears to him to be requisite for the purposes of this paragraph.

(4) The functions of an authority shall include power for the authority (notwithstanding any such limitation as is mentioned in sub-paragraph (1) above) to repair, maintain and insure any building or works on land acquired under Part III of this Act, and generally to deal therewith in a proper course of management.

(5) An authority may, with the consent of the Secretary of State, enter into arrangements with an authorised association for the carrying out by the association of any operation which, apart from the arrangements, the authority would have power under this paragraph to carry out, on such terms (including terms as to the making of payments or loans by the authority to the association) as may be specified in the arrangements.

(6) Nothing in this paragraph shall be construed as authorising such an association to carry out any operation which they would not have power to carry out apart from sub-paragraph (5) above.

(7) Nothing in this paragraph shall be construed as authorising any act or omission on the part of an authority which is actionable at the suit, or in Scotland the instance, of any person on any ground other than such a limitation as is mentioned in sub-paragraph (1) above.

(8) In this paragraph " alternative enactment " means any enactment which is not contained in—

(a) this Act,

(b) the Act of 1971 or the Scottish Act of 1972,

(c) section 2, 5, or 6 of the Local Authorities (Land) Act 1963, or

(d) section 5, 8, 13(1) or 14 of the Local Employment Act 1972.

(9) In this paragraph " authorised association " means any society, company or body of persons approved by the Secretary of State whose objects include the promotion, formation or management of garden cities, garden suburbs or garden villages, and the erection, improvement or management of buildings for the working classes and others, and which does not trade for profit or whose constitution forbids the issue of any share or loan capital with interest or dividend exceeding the rate for the time being fixed by the Treasury.

Power to override easements and other rights

10.—(1) The erection, construction or carrying out, or maintenance, of any building or work on land which has been acquired by an authority under Part III of this Act, whether done by the authority or by a person deriving title under them, is authorised by virtue of this paragraph if it is done in accordance with planning permission notwithstanding that it involves interference with an interest or right to which this paragraph applies, or involves a breach of a restriction as to the user of land arising by virtue of a contract.

(2) Nothing in this paragraph shall authorise interference with any right of way or right of laying down, erecting, continuing or maintaining apparatus on, under or over land, being a right vested in or belonging to statutory undertakers for the purpose of the carrying on of their undertaking.

(3) This paragraph applies to the following interests and rights, that is to say, any easement, liberty, privilege, right or advantage annexed to land and adversely affecting other land, including any natural right to support.

(4) In respect of any interference or breach in pursuance of sub-paragraph (1) above, compensation shall be payable under—

(*a*) section 7 or 10 of the Compulsory Purchase Act 1965, or

(*b*) section 61 of the Lands Clauses Consolidation (Scotland) Act 1845 and section 6 of the Railways Clauses (Consolidation) (Scotland) Act 1845,

and shall be assessed in the same manner and subject to the same rules as in the case of other compensation under those sections in respect of injurious affection where the compensation is to be estimated in connection with a purchase to which the said Act of 1965 or the said Acts of 1845 apply, or the injury arises from the execution of works on land acquired by such a purchase.

(5) Where a person deriving title under the authority by whom the land in question was acquired is liable to pay compensation by virtue of sub-paragraph (4) above, and fails to discharge that liability, the liability shall, subject to sub-paragraph (6) below, be enforceable against the authority.

(6) Nothing in sub-paragraph (5) above shall be construed as affecting any agreement between the authority and any other person for indemnifying the authority against any liability under that sub-paragraph.

(7) Nothing in this paragraph shall be construed as authorising any act or omission on the part of any person which is actionable at the suit, or in Scotland the instance, of any person on any grounds

other than such an interference or breach as is mentioned in sub-paragraph (1) above.

(8) In this paragraph—

(a) a reference to a person deriving title from another person includes a reference to any successor in title of that other person,

(b) a reference to deriving title is a reference to deriving title either directly or indirectly.

Use and development of consecrated land and burial grounds

11.—(1) Any consecrated land, whether or not including a building, which has been acquired by an authority under Part III of this Act may, subject to the following provisions of this paragraph, be used by any person in any manner in accordance with planning permission, notwithstanding any obligation or restriction imposed under ecclesiastical law or otherwise in respect of consecrated land.

(2) Sub-paragraph (1) above does not apply to land which consists or forms part of a burial ground.

(3) Any use of consecrated land authorised by sub-paragraph (1) above, and the use of any land (not being consecrated land) acquired by an authority under Part III of this Act which at the time of acquisition included a church or other building used or formerly used for religious worship or the site thereof, shall be subject to compliance with the requirements of regulations made by the Secretary of State for the purposes of this paragraph with respect to the removal and re-interment of any human remains, and the disposal of monuments and fixtures and furnishings.

(4) Any use of consecrated land authorised by sub-paragraph (1) above shall be subject to such provisions as may be prescribed by such regulations for prohibiting or restricting the use of the land, either absolutely or until the prescribed consent has been obtained, so long as any church or other building used or formerly used for religious worship, or any part thereof, remains on the land.

(5) Any regulations made for the purposes of this paragraph—

(a) shall contain such provisions as appear to the Secretary of State to be requisite for securing that any use of land which is subject to compliance with the regulations shall as, nearly as may be, be subject to the like control as is imposed by law in the case of a similar use authorised by an enactment not contained in this Act or by a Measure, or as it would be proper to impose on a disposal of the land in question otherwise than in pursuance of an enactment or Measure;

(*b*) shall contain requirements relating to the disposal of any such land as is mentioned in sub-paragraphs (3) and (4) above such as appear to the Secretary of State requisite for securing that the provisions of those sub-paragraphs shall be complied with in relation to the use of the land; and

(*c*) may contain such incidental and consequential provisions (including provision as to the closing of registers) as appear to the Secretary of State to be expedient for the purposes of the regulations.

(6) Any land consisting of a burial ground or part of a burial ground, which has been acquired as mentioned in sub-paragraph (1) above, may be used by any person in any manner in accordance with planning permission, notwithstanding anything in any enactment relating to burial grounds or any obligation or restriction imposed under ecclesiastical law or otherwise in respect of burial grounds.

(7) Sub-paragraph (6) above shall not have effect in respect of any land which has been used for the burial of the dead until the requirements prescribed by regulations made under this paragraph with respect to the removal and re-interment of human remains, and the disposal of monuments, in or upon the land have been complied with.

(8) Provision shall be made by any regulations made for the purposes of this paragraph—

(*a*) for requiring the persons in whom the land is vested to publish notice of their intention to carry out the removal and re-interment of any human remains or the disposal of any monuments;

(*b*) for enabling the personal representatives or relatives of any deceased person themselves to undertake the removal and re-interment of the remains of the deceased, and the disposal of any monument commemorating the deceased, and for requiring the persons in whom the land is vested to defray the expenses of such removal, re-interment and disposal, not exceeding such amount as may be prescribed;

(*c*) for requiring compliance with such reasonable conditions (if any) as may be imposed, in the case of consecrated land, by the bishop of the diocese, with respect to the manner of removal, and the place and manner of re-interment of any human remains, and the disposal of any monuments, and with any directions given in any case by the Secretary of State with respect to the removal and re-interment of any human remains.

(9) Subject to the provisions of regulations made under this paragraph, no faculty shall be required for the removal and re-interment in accordance with the regulations of any human remains, or for the removal or disposal of any monuments, and the provisions of section 25 of the Burial Act 1857 (prohibition of removal of human remains without the licence of the Secretary of State except in certain cases) shall not apply to a removal carried out in accordance with the regulations.

(10) Regulations under this paragraph shall be subject to annulment by a resolution of either House of Parliament.

(11) Nothing in this paragraph shall be construed as authorising any act or omission on the part of any person which is actionable at the suit of any person on any grounds other than contravention of any such obligation, restriction or enactment as is mentioned in sub-paragraph (1) or (6) above.

(12) In this paragraph " burial ground " includes any churchyard, cemetery or other ground, whether consecrated or not, which has at any time been set apart for the purposes of interment, and " monument " includes a tombstone or other memorial.

(13) This paragraph shall not apply in Scotland.

Use and development of churches and burial grounds in Scotland

12. Section 118 of the Scottish Act of 1972 shall have effect in relation to land in Scotland which is acquired by a local authority under Part III of this Act as it has effect in relation to land acquired by a planning authority as mentioned in subsection (1) of that section.

13. The provisions of section 20 of the New Towns (Scotland) Act 1968 and any regulations made thereunder shall have effect in relation to land in Scotland which is acquired by a new town authority under Part III of this Act as they have effect in relation to land acquired by a development corporation as mentioned in subsection (1) of that section.

Use and development of land for open spaces

14.—(1) Any land being, or forming part of, a common or open space or fuel or field garden allotment, which has been acquired by an authority under Part III of this Act may be used by any person in any manner in accordance with planning permission, notwithstanding anything in any enactment relating to land of that kind, or in any enactment by which the land is specially regulated.

In the application of this sub-paragraph to Scotland, the words " or fuel or field garden allotment " shall be omitted.

(2) Nothing in this paragraph shall be construed as authorising any act or omission on the part of any person which is actionable at the suit, or in Scotland the instance, of any person on any grounds other than contravention of any such enactment as is mentioned in sub-paragraph (1) above.

Saving for paragraphs 11 to 14

15.—(1) This paragraph applies as respects paragraphs 11 to 14 above.

(2) In relation to any authority or body corporate, nothing in the said paragraphs shall be construed as authorising any act or omission on their part in contravention of any limitation imposed by law on their capacity by virtue of the constitution of the authority or body.

(3) Any power conferred by the said paragraphs to use land in a manner therein mentioned shall be construed as a power to use the land, whether it involves the erection, construction or carrying out of any building or work, or the maintenance of any building or work, or not.

Construction of the Compulsory Purchase Acts in relation
to this Act

16.—(1) In construing the Compulsory Purchase Act 1965 in relation to any of the provisions of Part III of this Act—

(a) references to the execution of works shall be construed as including references to any erection, construction or carrying out of buildings or works authorised by paragraph 10 of this Schedule;

(b) in relation to the erection, construction or carrying out of any buildings or works so authorised, references in section 10 of the said Act of 1965 to the acquiring authority shall be construed as references to the persons by whom the buildings or works in question are erected, constructed or carried out.

(2) As respects Scotland, in construing the Lands Clauses Acts and section 6 of the Railways Clauses Consolidation (Scotland) Act 1845, as incorporated by virtue of paragraph 1 of Schedule 2 to the Scottish Act of 1947, in relation to any of the provisions of this Act—

(a) references to the execution of works shall be construed as including references to any erection, construction or carrying out of buildings or works authorised by paragraph 10 of this Schedule; and

(b) in relation to the erection, construction or carrying out of any buildings or works so authorised, references in section

6 of the said Act of 1845 to the company shall be construed as references to the person by whom the buildings or works in question are erected, constructed or carried out.

Extinguishment of rights of way, and rights as to apparatus, of statutory undertakers

17.—(1) Where any land has been acquired by an authority under Part III of this Act and—

(*a*) there subsists over that land a right vested in or belonging to statutory undertakers for the purpose of the carrying on of their undertaking, being a right of way or a right of laying down, erecting, continuing or maintaining apparatus on, under or over that land; or

(*b*) there is on, under or over the land apparatus vested in or belonging to statutory undertakers for the purpose of the carrying on of their undertaking,

the authority, if satisfied that the extinguishment of the right or, as the case may be, the removal of the apparatus, is necessary for the purpose of carrying out any development, may serve on the statutory undertakers a notice stating that, at the end of the period of 28 days from the date of service of the notice or such longer period as may be specified therein, the right will be extinguished or requiring that, before the end of that period, the apparatus shall be removed.

(2) The statutory undertakers on whom a notice is served under sub-paragraph (1) above may, before the end of the period of 28 days from the service of the notice, serve a counter-notice on the authority stating that they object to all or any provisions of the notice and specifying the grounds of their objection.

(3) If no counter-notice is served under sub-paragraph (2) above—

(*a*) any right to which the notice relates shall be extinguished at the end of the period specified in that behalf in the notice; and

(*b*) if, at the end of the period so specified in relation to any apparatus, any requirement of the notice as to the removal of the apparatus has not been complied with, the authority may remove the apparatus and dispose of it in any way they may think fit.

(4) If a counter-notice is served under sub-paragraph (2) above on an authority, the authority may either withdraw the notice (without prejudice to the service of a further notice) or may apply to the Secretary of State and the appropriate Minister for an order under this paragraph embodying the provisions of the notice with or without modification.

(5) Where by virtue of this paragraph any right vested in or belonging to statutory undertakers is extinguished, or any requirement is imposed on statutory undertakers, those undertakers shall be entitled to compensation from the authority.

(6) Sections 238 and 240 of the Act of 1971, or as the case may be sections 227 and 229 of the Scottish Act of 1972 (measure of compensation for statutory undertakers) shall apply to compensation under sub-paragraph (5) above as they apply to compensation under section 237(2) of the Act of 1971, or as the case may be section 226(2) of the Scottish Act of 1972.

Orders under paragraph 17

18.—(1) Before making an order under paragraph 17(4) above the Ministers proposing to make the order—

    (*a*) shall afford to the statutory undertakers on whom notice was served under paragraph 17(1) above an opportunity of objecting to the application for the order; and

    (*b*) if any objection is made, shall consider the objection and afford to those statutory undertakers and to the authority on whom the counter-notice was served, an opportunity of appearing before, and being heard by, a person appointed by the Secretary of State and the appropriate Minister for the purpose,

and may then, if they think fit, make the order in accordance with the application either with or without modification.

(2) Where an order is made under paragraph 17(4) above—

    (*a*) any right to which the order relates shall be extinguished at the end of the period specified in that behalf in the order; and

    (*b*) if, at the end of the period so specified in relation to any apparatus, any requirement of the order as to the removal of the apparatus has not been complied with, the authority may remove the apparatus and dispose of it in any way they may think fit.

Notice for same purposes as paragraph 17 but given by statutory undertakers to authority

19.—(1) Subject to the provisions of this paragraph, where any land has been acquired by an authority under Part III of this Act and—

    (*a*) there is on, under or over the land apparatus vested in or belonging to statutory undertakers; and

(b) the undertakers claim that development to be carried out on the land is such as to require, on technical or other grounds connected with the carrying on of their undertaking, the removal or re-siting of the apparatus affected by the development,

the undertakers may serve on the authority a notice claiming the right to enter on the land and carry out such works for the removal or re-siting of the apparatus or any part of it as may be specified in the notice.

(2) Where, after the land has been acquired as mentioned in sub-paragraph (1) above, development of the land is begun to be carried out, no notice under this paragraph shall be served later than 21 days after the beginning of the development.

(3) Where a notice is served under this paragraph, the authority on whom it is served may, before the end of the period of 28 days from the date of service, serve on the statutory undertakers a counter-notice stating that they object to all or any of the provisions of the notice and specifying the grounds of their objection.

(4) If no counter-notice is served under sub-paragraph (3) above, the statutory undertakers shall, after the end of the said period of 28 days, have the rights claimed in their notice.

(5) If a counter-notice is served under sub-paragraph (3) above, the statutory undertakers who served the notice under this paragraph may either withdraw it or may apply to the Secretary of State and the appropriate Minister for an order under this paragraph conferring on the undertakers the rights claimed in the notice or such modified rights as the Secretary of State and the appropriate Minister think it expedient to confer on them.

(6) Where by virtue of this paragraph or an order of Ministers made under it, statutory undertakers have the right to execute works for the removal or re-siting of apparatus, they may arrange with the authority for the works to be carried out by the authority, under the superintendence of the undertakers, instead of by the undertakers themselves.

(7) Where works are carried out for the removal or re-siting of statutory undertakers' apparatus, being works which the undertakers have the right to carry out by virtue of this paragraph or an order of Ministers made under it, the undertakers shall be entitled to compensation from the authority.

(8) Sections 238 and 240 of the Act of 1971, or as the case may be sections 227 and 229 of the Scottish Act of 1972 (measure of compensation for statutory undertakers) shall apply to compensation under sub-paragraph (7) above as they apply to compensation under section 237(3) of the Act of 1971, or as the case may be section 226(3) of the Scottish Act of 1972.

Rights of entry

20.—(1) Any person, being an officer of the Valuation Office of the Inland Revenue Department or a person duly authorised in writing by an authority, may at any reasonable time enter any land for the purposes of surveying it, or estimating its value, in connection with any proposal to acquire that land or any other land, under Part III of this Act, or in connection with any claim for compensation in respect of any such acquisition.

(2) Any person duly authorised in writing by the Land Authority for Wales may at any reasonable time enter upon any land for the purpose of surveying it in order to enable the Land Authority for Wales to determine whether to make an application for planning permission for the carrying out of relevant development of that land.

(3) Subject to the provisions of paragraph 21 below, any power conferred by this paragraph to survey land shall be construed as including power to search and bore for the purpose of ascertaining the nature of the subsoil or the presence of minerals therein.

21.—(1) A person authorised under the last preceding paragraph to enter any land shall, if so required, produce evidence of his authority before so entering, and shall not demand admission as of right to any land which is occupied unless twenty-four hours' notice of the intended entry has been given to the occupier.

(2) Any person who wilfully obstructs a person acting in the exercise of his powers under the last preceding paragraph shall be guilty of an offence and liable on summary conviction to a fine not exceeding £20.

(3) If any person who, in compliance with the provisions of the last preceding paragraph, is admitted into a factory, workshop or workplace discloses to any person any information obtained by him therein as to any manufacturing process or trade secret, he shall, unless the disclosure is made in the course of performing his duty in connection with the purpose for which he was authorised to enter the premises, be guilty of an offence and liable on summary conviction to a fine not exceeding £400 or on conviction on indictment to imprisonment for a term not exceeding two years or a fine, or both.

(4) Where any land is damaged in the exercise of a right of entry conferred under the last preceding paragraph or in the making of any survey for the purpose of which any such right of entry has been so conferred, compensation in respect of that damage may be recovered by any person interested in the land from the Secretary of State or authority on whose behalf the entry was effected.

(5) Except in so far as may be otherwise provided by regulations made by the Secretary of State under this sub-paragraph, any question of disputed compensation under sub-paragraph (4) above shall be referred to and determined by the Lands Tribunal or, as the case may be, by the Lands Tribunal for Scotland.

In relation to the determination of any question under this sub-paragraph, the provisions of sections 2 and 4 of the Land Compensation Act 1961 and sections 9 and 11 of the Land Compensation (Scotland) Act 1963 shall apply, subject to any necessary modifications and to the provisions of any regulations under this sub-paragraph.

(6) Where under the last preceding paragraph a person proposes to carry out any works authorised by sub-paragraph (3) of that paragraph—

(a) he shall not carry out those works unless notice of his intention to do so was included in the notice required by sub-paragraph (1) of this paragraph, and

(b) if the land in question is held by statutory undertakers, and those undertakers object to the proposed works on the grounds that the carrying out thereof would be seriously detrimental to the carrying on of their undertaking, the works shall not be carried out except with the authority of the appropriate Minister.

Displacement of Rent Acts

22.   If the Secretary of State certifies that possession of a house which has been acquired by an authority under Part III of this Act, and is for the time being held by the authority for the purposes for which it was acquired, is immediately required for those purposes, nothing in—

(a) the Rent Act 1968, or

(b) the Rent (Scotland) Act 1971 or Part III of the Housing (Scotland) Act 1974,

shall prevent the acquiring authority from obtaining possession of the house.

PART IV
APPROPRIATION OF LAND

23.—(1) A local authority and the Peak Park Joint and Lake District Special Planning Boards shall have power to appropriate land under section 122 of the Local Government Act 1972 or section 73 of the Local Government (Scotland) Act 1973—

(a) for the purposes of Part III of this Act notwithstanding that the land is still required for the purpose for which it was held immediately before the appropriation, and (*b*) for any other purpose notwithstanding that it was held immediately before the appropriation for the purposes of Part III of this Act, and is still required for those purposes.

(2) All the provisions of Part III of this Schedule, other than paragraph 8, shall apply to land appropriated for the purposes of Part III of this Act as they apply to land acquired under Part III of this Act.

SCHEDULE 5

Section 16.

LAND ACQUISITION AND MANAGEMENT SCHEMES

1. In making or revising a land acquisition and management scheme the matters to be considered shall include—

(*a*) the resources available to the respective authorities concerned, and in particular the services of persons qualified and experienced in the acquisition, management, planning, development and disposal of land which are so available,

(*b*) any previous experience of any authority in the exercise of functions relating to the acquisition of land with a view to either—

(i) developing it themselves and disposing of a material interest in it, or

(ii) making it available for development by others,

(*c*) the provisions of planning law or local government law relating to the discharge of functions, and particularly the function of determining applications for planning permission,

(*d*) any existing arrangements (including arrangements contained in development plans or development plan schemes) for the division of functions under planning law between the authorities,

(*e*) any functions of the authorities, and in particular their functions under the law relating to the provision of housing accommodation, and

(*f*) such other matters as the Secretary of State may direct.

Contents of schemes

2.—(1) Each land acquisition and management scheme shall contain arrangements for the execution of the authorities' functions in connection with the acquisition of land with a view to—

(*a*) developing it themselves and disposing of a material interest in it, or

(*b*) making it available for development by others.

(2) This paragraph applies in particular to arrangements as respects the service of notices under Part II of Schedule 7 to this Act.

3.—(1) Each scheme shall contain—

(a) arrangements for the co-ordination of action by the authorities, including action under this Act,

(b) arrangements, where appropriate, for the use by one authority of officers or servants employed by another authority,

(c) where appropriate, provisions for the transfer of sums between authorities,

(d) arrangements for determining matters of dispute between the authorities,

(e) provisions for the periodic review of the scheme, and

(f) such other matters as the Secretary of State may direct,

and may contain such transitional and other supplemental and incidental provisions as appear expedient to the authorities making the scheme.

(2) Heads (a), (c) and (d) of sub-paragraph (1) above shall not apply to a scheme made by a general planning authority in Scotland.

Supervision by Secretary of State

4.—(1) As soon as practicable after a scheme has been made or revised (by all the authorities in the area of the county authority acting jointly) the county authority shall send a copy of the scheme (or the scheme as revised) to the Secretary of State.

(2) Where it appears to the Secretary of State that a scheme should be revised he may after consulting all the authorities direct those authorities (acting jointly) to revise it in accordance with the direction, and before the date specified in the direction.

(3) Where there is a failure to make a scheme within the time allowed by the principal section, or to comply with a direction under this paragraph, the Secretary of State may himself make a scheme (or revise one); and the scheme or revision shall have effect as if made by all the authorities acting jointly.

Public inspection

5.—(1) As soon as practicable after a scheme has been made or revised, each of the authorities in the area of the county authority shall deposit a copy of the scheme (or the scheme as revised) at their principal office and shall keep it available there at all reasonable hours for public inspection without payment; and each of those authorities shall, on application, furnish copies of the scheme (or the scheme as revised) to any person on payment of a reasonable sum for each copy.

(2) As soon as practicable after a scheme has been made or revised, the county authority shall send a copy of the scheme (or the scheme as revised) to every parish council whose area comprises any part of the area of the county authority.

(3) As respects Scotland sub-paragraph (2) above shall not apply but, in the case of a scheme made or revised for the area of a general planning authority, that authority shall send as soon as practicable a copy of the scheme (or the scheme as revised) to every district council whose district comprises any part of that area.

6. The provisions of paragraph 5 above shall apply in relation to any direction given by the Secretary of State under section 16(7) of this Act as they apply in relation to a scheme which has been made or revised.

SCHEDULE 6
Section 17.
GENERAL DUTIES OF AUTHORITIES

1.—(1) Every authority in exercising their functions on or after the first appointed day, and in particular in deciding—

  (a) whether development land acquired by them should be developed by them, or made available for development by others, or

  (b) what use should be made of such land until it is so developed or made so available,

shall have regard to the following matters—

  (i) the needs of persons living or carrying on business or other activities in the area, or wishing to do so;

  (ii) the needs of builders and developers engaged in, or wishing to engage in, the carrying out of development in the area;

  (iii) the needs of agriculture and forestry;

  (iv) the needs and obligations of other authorities, local and new town authorities and parish or community councils;

  (v) the needs and obligations of charities;

  (vi) the needs and obligations of statutory undertakers; and

  (vii) such other matters as the Secretary of State may direct.

(2) In Scotland a general planning authority, in acting as described in sub-paragraph (1) above, shall also have regard to the needs and obligations of district councils within their area.

2.—(1) Where an authority decide that land acquired by them as development land should be made available for development by persons other than any authority, they shall proceed as follows.

(2) Before disposing, or entering into a binding contract to dispose, of any material interest in the land to any person who has not made an application within sub-paragraph (3) below, the authority shall have regard to any application which has been so made.

(3) The relevant applications to the authority are those made in the prescribed form before all outstanding material interests in the land had been acquired by the authority—

(*a*) by a person who owned a material interest in the land immediately prior to its acquisition by the authority; or

(*b*) by an applicant for planning permission for development of the same class as the development for which the land is being made available,

being in either case an application for an opportunity—

(i) to negotiate the purchase of a material interest in the land in order to carry out the development for which the land is being made available on terms acceptable to the authority, or

(ii) to negotiate to carry out that development on terms acceptable to the authority.

(4) Sub-paragraph (3)(*b*) only applies where the application was accompanied by the written consent of the owner of every outstanding material interest in the land which had not been acquired by the authority.

SCHEDULE 7

Sections 19 to 22.

PLANNING PERMISSION FOR RELEVANT DEVELOPMENT
PART I
Abandonment of power to purchase

1.—(1) An authority shall be regarded as abandoning their power to purchase the land in the circumstances and at the time set out in the following Table.

(2) The period for which the authority abandon their power to purchase the land ends at the expiration of a period of five years from that time unless the authority served notice stating that they did not intend to acquire the land, but subject to conditions which are not complied with.

(3) If the authority served such a notice, the period ends with the failure (or the first failure) to comply with the conditions.

TABLE

Kind of notice	Time of abandonment of power to purchase
1. Notice stating that the authority do not intend to purchase the land (whether or not subject to conditions).	Date of service of the notice.

Planning permission to which section 19 applies

2. Notice stating that the authority intend to purchase the land, where section 19 of this Act applies.	The expiration of a period of twelve months beginning with the service of the notice unless the authority have completed the first step towards acquisition of the land before the end of that period.

Planning permission to which section 20 applies

3. Notice stating that the authority intend to purchase the land, where section 20 of this Act applies.	The expiration of— (*a*) a period of twelve months beginning with the service of the notice, or (*b*) if the applicant appeals against refusal of planning permission, twelve months beginning with the date on which a copy of the notice of appeal was duly served on the Secretary of State, unless the authority have completed the first step towards acquisition of the land before the end of the period or later period.

Making of compulsory purchase order

4. Completion of first step towards acquisition of the land by making and publishing notice of a compulsory purchase order.	The expiration of a period of twelve months beginning with the date on which the compulsory purchase order becomes operative, unless the authority have served notice to treat in respect of all outstanding material interests in the land before the end of that period.

(4) In this paragraph "notice" means notice under Part II of this Schedule served on—

    (*a*) where section 19 of this Act applies, the person making the election, and

    (*b*) where section 20 of this Act applies, the applicant for planning permission.

(5) For the purposes of this Schedule an authority complete the first step towards acquisition of the land when—

    (*a*) they enter into a binding contract to purchase the land, or

    (*b*) notice is duly published of the making of a compulsory purchase order for the acquisition of the land by the authority.

End of suspension of planning permission

2.—(1) The suspension of planning permission to which section 19 or section 20 of this Act applies ends at the time when—

    (*a*) all the authorities have abandoned their power to purchase the land, or

    (*b*) any authority purchase the land,

whichever is the earlier.

(2) If an authority complete the first step towards acquisition of the land by making and publishing notice of a compulsory purchase order and at any time—

    (*a*) the Secretary of State serves notice on the authority that he does not intend to confirm the compulsory purchase order as respects the land on which the relevant development covered by the planning permission will be carried out, or

    (*b*) the compulsory purchase order is quashed by a court as respects the said land,

then for the purposes of this paragraph (but not for the purposes of paragraph 1 above) the authority shall be treated as abandoning their power to purchase at that time.

(3) In sub-paragraph (1)(*b*) above "authority" includes a local authority in Wales whose area includes the land.

Interpretation

3. Subject to paragraph 9(3) below, references in this Schedule to purchase or acquisition of land shall, unless the context otherwise requires, be taken as references to purchase or acquisition of all outstanding material interests in the land on which the relevant development covered by the planning permission will be carried out.

PART II
NOTICES BY AUTHORITIES
Planning permission to which section 19 applies

4.—(1) It shall be the duty of each of the authorities to serve on the person making an election under section 19 of this Act a notice stating that the authority intend, or do not intend, to acquire the land to which the planning permission relates.

(2) A notice under this paragraph shall be in the prescribed form and shall be served not later than three months from service of the notice of election.

(3) An authority who fail to comply with this paragraph shall be treated for the purposes of this Schedule as having served notice (on the latest date allowed for giving notice) stating that they do not intend to acquire the land.

Planning permission to which section 20 applies

5.—(1) It shall be the duty of each of the authorities to serve—

(a) on the applicant for planning permission to which section 20 of this Act applies, and

(b) on any other person named in any certificate which in accordance with section 27 of the Act of 1971 or section 24 of the Scottish Act of 1972 is submitted with the application for planning permission,

a notice stating that the authority intend, or do not intend, to acquire the land to which the application relates if planning permission is granted in accordance with the application.

(2) A notice under this paragraph shall be in the prescribed form and shall be served within the time allowed for giving notice to the applicant for planning permission of the manner in which his application has been dealt with, being the time prescribed by order under section 31(1)(d) of the Act of 1971 or section 28(1)(d) of the Scottish Act of 1972.

(3) If the application for planning permission is one deemed to have been made under section 88 of the Act of 1971 or section 85 of the Scottish Act of 1972 (appeal against enforcement notice), a notice under this paragraph shall be served only if planning permission is granted in accordance with the application; and the notice—

(a) shall be served within three months of the grant on the applicant and on any other person on whom the enforcement notice was served, and

(b) shall state that the authority intend, or do not intend, to acquire the land.

(4) An authority who fail to comply with the provisions of this paragraph relating to the service of notice on the applicant shall be treated for the purposes of this Schedule as having served notice (on the latest date allowed for giving notice) stating that they do not intend to acquire the land.

Duty of authority to notify change of intention

6.—(1) If an authority, after serving notice under the preceding provisions of this Part of this Schedule of intention to acquire the land, decide not to acquire the land, it shall be the duty of the authority to serve a notice to that effect—

(a) on the persons on whom that notice was required to be served, and

(b) where the authority have, before serving all the notices under paragraph (a), made a compulsory purchase order for the acquisition of the land, on the persons on whom notice of the making of the order was required to be served.

(2) A notice under this paragraph shall be in the prescribed form and shall be served as soon as practicable after the authority have decided not to acquire the land.

Notices subject to conditions

7.—(1) A notice under the preceding provisions of this Part of this Schedule stating that the authority do not intend to acquire the land may be expressed to be subject to a condition.

(2) If the condition does not comply with the requirements of the next following paragraph, the authority shall be treated for the purposes of this Schedule as if the notice stated unconditionally that the authority did not intend to acquire the land.

(3) A person seeking to question a condition on the ground that it does not comply with the requirements of the next following paragraph may, within six weeks of the day on which the notice is first served, make an application to the High Court or, as the case may be, to the Court of Session to determine the question.

(4) Except as so provided a condition shall not be questioned on that ground in any legal proceedings whatsoever.

Kinds of conditions

8.—(1) The conditions which may be imposed are as follows:—

1. A condition that no relevant development is carried out on the land except in accordance with the originating planning permission.

2. A condition that no relevant development is carried out on the land except in accordance with a planning permission specified in the notice (being permission granted before service of the notice).

3. A condition that the development is begun not later than the expiration of a period specified in the notice.

4. In the case of an outline planning permission, a condition that application for approval of all reserved matters is made within a period specified in the notice.

5. A condition that the development permitted by the originating planning permission or other planning permission specified in the notice is completed within a period specified in the notice, or such extended period as the authority may agree.

6. Any other condition specified in regulations made by the Secretary of State under this paragraph.

(2) A condition requiring the carrying out of the originating planning permission or other planning permission specified in the notice implies a requirement that it be begun within the time prescribed by sections 41 and 42 of the Act of 1971, or sections 38 and 39 of the Scottish Act of 1972 (unless the condition prescribes a shorter period).

(3) Any period prescribed by the notice shall be a reasonable period.

(4) The condition may be one combining two or more of those allowed by this paragraph.

(5) A condition may at any time be relaxed by a subsequent notice served in the same manner as the previous notice, but—

(a) the condition as relaxed must be one allowed by this paragraph,

(b) a condition cannot be relaxed after a failure to comply with the condition.

(6) Regulations under this paragraph shall be subject to annulment in pursuance of a resolution of either House of Parliament.

(7) In this paragraph—

" originating planning permission " means the planning permission mentioned in section 19, or as the case may be section 20, of this Act, and

" outline planning permission " and " reserved matters " have the same meanings as in sections 41 and 42 of the Act of 1971 or sections 38 and 39 of the Scottish Act of 1972.

Notices for parts of the land

9.—(1) A notice under this Part of this Schedule may be one relating to part only of the land.

(2) A notice under this Part of this Schedule, other than one which states unconditionally that the authority do not intend to acquire any part of the land, shall be accompanied by a plan indicating the land to which the notice relates.

(3) Accordingly, it follows that both paragraph 1 and paragraph 2 of this Schedule may apply differently to different parts of the land.

(4) This paragraph shall not absolve an authority from the duty to serve notices under this Part of this Schedule as respects all the land.

Registration of notices

10.—(1) A notice under paragraph 4 or 5 above stating that the authority intend to acquire the land shall be a local land charge.

(2) If the authority subsequently serve a notice under paragraph 6 above stating that they have decided not to acquire the land, then, if they are not a local authority keeping a local land charges register, they shall, as soon as practicable thereafter, send a copy of the notice to every local authority keeping such a register whose area comprises any part of the land.

11.—(1) In relation to any time before the coming into force of the Local Land Charges Act 1975, paragraph 10 above shall have effect subject to the following modifications.

(2) For sub-paragraph (1) there shall be substituted—

" (1) As soon as practicable after serving a notice under paragraph 4 or 5 above stating that they intend to acquire the land, the authority shall send a copy of the notice to the proper officer (for the purposes of section 15 of the Land Charges Act 1925) of every local authority whose area comprises any part of the land; and as soon as practicable after receiving the copy of the notice, the proper officer shall register the notice in the local land charges register in such manner as may be prescribed by rules under section 19 of that Act."

(3) In sub-paragraph (2) the words " then, if they are not a local authority keeping a local land charges register " shall be omitted and for the words " every local authority keeping such a register " there shall be substituted the words " the proper officer (for the purposes of section 15 of the Land Charges Act 1925) of every local authority ".

(4) At the end there shall be added the following sub-paragraph—

" (3) In this paragraph ' local authority ' does not include a county council or the Greater London Council.".

12. As respects Scotland, paragraph 10 above shall not apply but any notice referred to in that paragraph shall be registered by the authority as soon as practicable in the register kept by them by virtue of section 31(2) of the Scottish Act of 1972 in accordance with the provisions of that section, but where the authority are not an authority responsible for keeping such a register they shall as soon as practicable send a copy of the notice to the local authority responsible for keeping the register for the area concerned, and that local authority shall register the notice accordingly.

PART III
TRANSMISSION OF INFORMATION
Copies of applications for planning permission

13.—(1) This paragraph applies to applications for planning permission (for development of any description) made on or after the first appointed day.

(2) If an authority in column 1 of the following Table receive an application for planning permission to which this paragraph applies, the authority shall as soon as practicable after receipt send a copy of the application to the authority specified in column 2 of that Table.

(3) This paragraph shall not apply if and so far as the authority entitled to receipt of a copy otherwise direct.

TABLE

Application made to	Copy to be transmitted to
Council of a London borough ...	Greater London Council.
Common Council of City of London.	Greater London Council.
District Council in Wales	Land Authority for Wales.
District Council, in England or Wales, where the application relates to land in the area of a new town authority.	The new town authority.
District planning authority in Scotland.	Regional planning authority.
District planning authority or a general planning authority in Scotland, where the application relates to land in the area of a new town authority.	The new town authority.

Planning permissions in Wales

14.—(1) In Wales on any grant on or after the first appointed day of planning permission (for development of any description), the local planning authority, or as the case may be the Secretary of State, shall as soon as practicable send a copy of the notification of the planning permission to the Land Authority for Wales.

(2) This paragraph shall not apply if and so far as the Land Authority for Wales otherwise direct.

SCHEDULE 8

Sections 23 and 24.

DISPOSAL NOTIFICATION AREAS
PART I

Procedure on passing a resolution

1.—(1) As soon as practicable after passing a resolution declaring an area to be a disposal notification area, the authority shall—

(a) publish a notice of the resolution identifying the area and naming a place or places where a copy of the resolution, and a map on which the area is defined, may be inspected at all reasonable times, and

(b) send a copy of the resolution, and of the map, to every parish or community council whose area comprises any part of the disposal notification area.

(2) The resolution shall be a local land charge.

Functions of the Secretary of State

2.—(1) As soon as practicable after passing the resolution the authority shall send to the Secretary of State a copy of the resolution, and a copy of the map.

(2) If it appears to the Secretary of State appropriate he may, at any time, send a notification to the authority—

(a) that the area declared to be a disposal notification area is no longer to be such an area, or

(b) that land in the area, being land defined on a map accompanying the notification, is to be excluded from the disposal notification area.

(3) A notification under sub-paragraph (2)(a) or (b) above shall take effect on the date on which it is received by the authority, and the authority shall as soon as practicable after receipt—

(a) publish a notice of the effect of the Secretary of State's notification and naming a place or places where a copy of the notification and, in the case of a notification affecting a part only of the area, a map on which that part of the area is defined, may be inspected at all reasonable times, and

(b) send a copy of the notification, and of any map, to every parish or community council, and (if they are not a local authority keeping a local land charges register) to every local authority keeping such a register, whose area comprises any part of the disposal notification area affected by the notification.

PART II
Notification of disposals

3.—(1) This paragraph applies to a notice under section 23(5) of this Act.

(2) The notice shall be in the prescribed form and shall be given not less than 4 weeks, and not more than 6 months, before the date of the carrying out of the transaction to which it relates.

(3) The notice shall contain—

(a) the name and address of the person by whom it is furnished,

(b) the address of, and any further information necessary to identify, the land to which the notice relates, and

(c) the interest in that land which the person serving the notice has at the time of service.

(4) The reference in sub-paragraph (3)(a) above to a person's address is a reference to his place of abode or his place of business or, in the case of a company, its registered office.

(5) To the extent that it is capable of being so given, the information required by sub-paragraph (3)(b) above may be given by reference to a plan accompanying the notice.

(6) The notice shall also indicate whether or not, when the transaction (including performance of any contract) has been carried out, the person giving the notice will retain any material interest in the land, or any part of the land, and shall specify—

(a) the nature of that interest, and

(b) the land in which the interest will subsist.

PART III
Disposals of which notice may, but need not, be given

4.—(1) This paragraph applies to a disposal by an individual of a material interest in land which is the whole or any part of his private residence.

(2) This paragraph also applies to a disposal by trustees of a material interest in land held in trust where—

(*a*) that land is the whole or any part of a person's private residence, and

(*b*) that person is entitled, under the terms of the trust to occupy that residence or to receive the whole of the income derived from, or from the proceeds of sale of, the material interest.

(3) In this paragraph—

(*a*) " disposal " includes a contract for a disposal,

(*b*) " dwelling-house " includes part of a dwelling-house,

(*c*) an individual's " private residence " means—

(i) land comprising a dwelling-house which, at the date of the disposal, is that individual's only or main residence, and

(ii) land which at that date he has for his own occupation and enjoyment with that dwelling-house as its garden or grounds up to an area which, when aggregated with the area of the site of the dwelling-house, does not exceed one acre;

and a person's " private residence " shall be construed accordingly.

PART IV
Termination of all or part of a disposal notification area

5.—(1) This paragraph applies where an authority pass a resolution declaring that all or part of a disposal notification area is no longer to be a disposal notification area.

(2) As soon as practicable after passing the resolution, the authority shall—

(*a*) publish a notice of the effect of the resolution and naming a place or places where a copy of the resolution, and, in the case of a resolution affecting a part only of the area, a map on which that part of the area is defined, may be inspected at all reasonable times, and

(*b*) send a copy of the resolution, and of any map, to every parish or community council, and (if they are not a local authority keeping a local land charges register) to every local authority keeping such a register, whose area comprises any part of the disposal notification area affected by the resolution.

(3) As soon as practicable after passing the resolution the authority shall send to the Secretary of State a copy of the resolution, and a copy of any map.

PART V
Publication

6. Any reference in this Schedule to publication of a notice is a reference to publication in the London Gazette or the Edinburgh Gazette, as the case may require, and in two or more newspapers circulating in the locality, of which at least one shall, if practicable, be a local newspaper.

Savings

7. The passing of a resolution declaring that all or part of a disposal notification area is no longer to be such an area, and any notification within paragraph 2(3) of this Schedule, shall not affect—

(*a*) liability for any offence committed, or

(*b*) the operation of any notice served under section 193(1) of the Act of 1971 or section 182(1) of the Scottish Act of 1972 (power to serve blight notice),

before the resolution or notification.

Transitory provisions

8.—(1) In relation to any time before the coming into force of the Local Land Charges Act 1975, paragraphs 1(2), 2(3)(*b*) and 5(2)(*b*) above shall have effect subject to the following modifications.

(2) For paragraph 1(2) there shall be substituted—

" (2) As soon as practicable after passing the resolution the authority shall send a copy of the resolution and of the map to the proper officer (for the purposes of section 15 of the Land Charges Act 1925) of every local authority whose area comprises any part of the disposal notification area; and as soon as practicable after receiving the copy of the resolution the proper officer shall register the resolution in the local land charges register in such manner as may be prescribed by rules under section 19 of that Act.

In this sub-paragraph and in paragraphs 2(3)(*b*) and 5(2)(*b*) below ' local authority ' does not include a county council or the Greater London Council."

(3) In paragraphs 2(3)(*b*) and 5(2)(*b*) for the words from " (if " to " a register " there shall be substituted the words " to the proper officer (for the purposes of section 15 of the Land Charges Act 1925) of every local authority ".

Scotland

9. As respects Scotland, paragraphs 1(1)(*b*) and (2) and 2(3)(*b*) and paragraph 5(2)(*b*) above shall not apply, but—

   (*a*) the resolution or notification referred to in paragraph 1, paragraph 2(3) or paragraph 5 above shall be registered by the authority as soon as practicable in the register kept by them by virtue of section 31(2) of the Scottish Act of 1972 in accordance with the provisions of that section, but where the authority are not an authority responsible for keeping such a register, they shall as soon as practicable send a copy of the resolution and map or notification to the local authority responsible for keeping the register for the area concerned, and that local authority shall register the resolution or notification accordingly, and

   (*b*) in the case of a resolution passed by or notification received by a general planning authority, that authority shall send as soon as practicable a copy of such resolution or notification and of any map to every district council whose district comprisés any part of the disposal notification area or any part thereof affected by the resolution, or as the case may be, notification.

SCHEDULE 9

Section 47.

LAND COMPENSATION ACTS AS AMENDED
PART I
SECTION 17 OF LAND COMPENSATION ACT 1961

Certification of appropriate alternative development.

17.—(1) Where an interest in land is proposed to be acquired by an authority possessing compulsory purchase powers, and that land or part thereof does not consist or form part of—

   (*a*) an area defined in the development plan as an area of comprehensive development, or

   (*b*) an area shown in the development plan as an area allocated primarily for a use which is of a residential, commercial or industrial character, or for a range of two or more uses any of which is of such a character,

then, subject to subsection (2) of this section, either of the parties directly concerned may apply to the local planning authority for a certificate under this section.

(2) If, in the case of an interest in land falling within subsection (1) of this section, the authority proposing to acquire it have served a notice to treat in respect thereof, or an agreement has been made

for the sale thereof to that authority, and a reference has been made to the Lands Tribunal to determine the amount of the compensation payable in respect of that interest, no application for a certificate under this section shall be made by either of the parties directly concerned after the date of that reference except either—

(a) with the consent in writing of the other of those parties, or

(b) with the leave of the Lands Tribunal.

(3) An application for a certificate under this section—

(a) shall state whether or not there are, in the applicant's opinion, any classes of development which, either immediately or at a future time, would be appropriate for the land in question if it were not proposed to be acquired by any authority possessing compulsory purchase powers and, if so, shall specify the classes of development and the times at which they would be so appropriate;

(b) shall state the applicant's grounds for holding that opinion; and

(c) shall be accompanied by a statement specifying the date on which a copy of the application has been or will be served on the other party directly concerned.

(4) Where an application is made to the local planning authority for a certificate under this section in respect of an interest in land, the local planning authority shall, not earlier than twenty-one days after the date specified in the statement mentioned in paragraph (c) of subsection (3) of this section, issue to the applicant a certificate stating either of the following to be the opinion of the local planning authority regarding the grant of planning permission in respect of the land in question, if it were not proposed to be acquired by an authority possessing compulsory purchase powers that is to say—

(a) that planning permission for development of one or more classes specified in the certificate (whether specified in the application or not) would have been granted; or

(b) that planning permission would not have been granted for any development other than the development (if any) which is proposed to be carried out by the authority by whom the interest is proposed to be acquired.

(5) Where, in the opinion of the local planning authority, planning permission would have been granted as mentioned in paragraph (a) of subsection (4) of this section, but would only have been granted subject to conditions, or at a future time, or both subject to conditions and at a future time, the certificate shall specify those conditions, or that future time, or both, as the case may be, in

addition to the other matters required to be contained in the certificate.

(6) For the purposes of subsection (5) of this section, a local planning authority may formulate general requirements applicable to such classes of case as may be described therein; and any conditions required to be specified in the certificate in accordance with that subsection may, if it appears to the local planning authority to be convenient to do so, be specified by reference to those requirements, subject to such special modifications thereof (if any) as may be set out in the certificate.

(7) In determining, for the purposes of the issue of a certificate under this section, whether planning permission for any particular class of development would have been granted in respect of any land, the local planning authority shall not treat development of that class as development for which planning permission would have been refused by reason only that it would have involved development of the land in question (or of that land together with other land) otherwise than in accordance with the provisions of the development plan relating thereto.

(8) Where an application for a certificate under this section relates to land of which part (but not the whole) consists or forms part of such an area as is mentioned in paragraph (a) or paragraph (b) of subsection (1) of this section, any certificate issued under this section in pursuance of that application shall be limited to so much of that land as does not fall within any such area.

(9) On issuing to one of the parties directly concerned a certificate under this section in respect of an interest in land, the local planning authority shall serve a copy of the certificate on the other of those parties.

PART II
SECTION 25 OF LAND COMPENSATION (SCOTLAND) ACT 1963

Certification of appropriate alternative development.

25.—(1) Where an interest in land is proposed to be acquired by an authority possessing compulsory purchase powers, and that land or part thereof does not consist or form part of—

(a) an area defined in the development plan as an area of comprehensive development, or

(b) an area shown in the development plan as an area allocated primarily for a use which is of a residential, commercial or industrial character, or for a range of two or more uses any of which is of such a character, then, subject to subsection (2) of this section, either of the parties directly concerned may apply to the planning authority for a certificate under this section.

(2) If, in the case of an interest in land falling within subsection (1) of this section, the authority proposing to acquire it have served a notice to treat in respect thereof, or an agreement has been made for the sale thereof to that authority, and a reference has been made to the Lands Tribunal for Scotland to determine the amount of the compensation payable in respect of that interest, no application for a certificate under this section shall be made by either of the parties directly concerned after the date of that reference except either—

(a) with the consent in writing of the other of those parties, or

(b) with the leave of the Lands Tribunal for Scotland.

(3) An application for a certificate under this section—

(a) shall state whether or not there are, in the applicant's opinion, any classes of development which, either immediately or at a future time, would be appropriate for the land in question if it were not proposed to be acquired by any authority possessing compulsory purchase powers and, if so, shall specify the classes of development and the times at which they would be so appropriate;

(b) shall state the applicant's grounds for holding that opinion; and

(c) shall be accompanied by a statement specifying the date on which a copy of the application has been or will be served on the other party directly concerned.

(4) Where an application is made to the planning authority for a certificate under this section in respect of an interest in land, the planning authority shall, not earlier than twenty-one days after the date specified in the statement mentioned in subsection (3)(c) of this section, issue to the applicant a certificate stating that, in the opinion of the planning authority in respect of the land in question, either—

(a) planning permission for development of one or more classes specified in the certificate (whether specified in the application or not) would have been granted; or

(b) planning permission would not have been granted for any development other than the development (if any) which is proposed to be carried out by the authority by whom the interest is proposed to be acquired.

(5) Where, in the opinion of the planning authority, planning permission would have been granted as mentioned in subsection (4)(*a*) of this section, but would only have been granted subject to conditions, or at a future time, or both subject to conditions and at a future time, the certificate shall specify those conditions, or that future time, or both, as the case may be, in addition to the other matters required to be contained in the certificate.

(6) For the purposes of subsection (5) of this section, a planning authority may formulate general requirements applicable to such classes of case as may be described therein; and any conditions required to be specified in the certificate in accordance with that subsection may, if it appears to the planning authority to be convenient to do so, be specified by reference to those requirements, subject to such special modifications thereof (if any) as may be set out in the certificate.

(7) In determining, for the purposes of the issue of a certificate under this section, whether planning permission for any particular class of development would have been granted in respect of any land, the planning authority shall not treat development of that class as development for which planning permission would have been refused by reason only that it would have involved development of the land in question (or of that land together with other land) otherwise than in accordance with the provisions of the development plan relating thereto.

(8) Where an application for a certificate under this section relates to land of which part (but not the whole) consists or forms part of such an area as is mentioned in subsection (1)(*a*) or subsection (1)(*b*) of this section, any certificate issued under this section in pursuance of that application shall be limited to so much of that land as does not fall within any such area.

(9) On issuing to either of the parties directly concerned a certificate under this section in respect of an interest in land, the planning authority shall serve a copy of the certificate on the other of those parties.

SCHEDULE 10

Section 58(2).

MINOR AND CONSEQUENTIAL AMENDMENTS
General

1.—(1) Subject to sub-paragraph (2) below, a body corporate which has made application under paragraph 2(3)(*a*) of Schedule 6 to this Act shall have power to acquire a material interest in the land in order to carry out the development for which the land is being made available, notwithstanding any limitation imposed by law (whether by virtue of any enactment or of its constitution or otherwise) on the capacity of the body corporate to acquire the land in order to carry out the development.

(2) Sub-paragraph (1) above does not apply where any limitation is imposed by law (whether by virtue of any enactment or of its constitution or otherwise) on the capacity of the body corporate to carry out the development on its own land.

(3) Nothing in this paragraph shall be construed as authorising any act or omission on the part of a body corporate which is actionable at the suit, or in Scotland the instance, of any person on any ground other than such a limitation as is mentioned in sub-paragraph (1) above.

The Commissioners of Works Act 1894

2.—(1) For subsection (1) of section 1 of the Commissioners of Works Act 1894 (which applies the Lands Clauses Acts to acquisitions under the Commissioners of Works Act 1852), there shall in relation to England and Wales be substituted the following subsection—

" (1) For the purpose of the purchase of land by the Secretary of State under the Commissioners of Works Act 1852, the provisions of Part I of the Compulsory Purchase Act 1965 (so far as applicable), other than section 31, shall apply.

In the said Part I as so applied the word " land " means (except where the context otherwise requires) any corporeal hereditament, including a building, and, in relation to the acquisition of land under the said Act of 1852, includes any interest in or right over land.".

(2) For subsection (1) of section 1 of the said Act of 1894 there shall in relation to Scotland be substituted the following subsection—

" (1) For the purpose of the purchase of land by the Secretary of State under the Commissioners of Works Act 1852, the Lands Clauses Acts (except so much thereof as relates to the acquisition of land otherwise than by agreement, and the provisions relating to access to the special Act, and except sections 120 to 125 of the Lands Clauses Consolidation (Scotland) Act 1845), and sections 6 and 70 of the Railways Clauses Consolidation (Scotland) Act 1845 and sections 71 to 78 of that Act (as originally enacted and not as amended by section 15 of the Mines (Working Facilities and Support) Act 1923) are hereby incorporated with the said Act of 1852, and, in construing those Acts for the purposes of the said Act of 1852, that Act shall be deemed to be the special Act and the Secretary of State shall be deemed to be the promoter of the undertaking or company, as the case may require.

In relation to the acquisition of land under the said Act of 1852, ' land ' includes any interest in or right over land.".

(3) This paragraph shall have effect only in relation to agreements entered into after the expiration of a period of one month beginning with the passing of this Act.

The Lands Tribunal Act 1949

3.—(1) In section 3 of the Lands Tribunal Act 1949 (rules regulating proceedings before the Lands Tribunal) after subsection (6) there shall be inserted the following subsections—

" (6A) It is hereby declared that this section authorises the making of rules which allow the Tribunal to determine cases without an oral hearing.

(6B) The rules shall require that the determination without an oral hearing of any disputed claim for compensation which—

(*a*) is payable in respect of a compulsory acquisition of land, or

(*b*) depends directly or indirectly on the value of any land,

shall require the consent of the person making the claim.

(6C) Wnere the Tribunal determine a case without an oral hearing, subsection (3) of this section shall apply subject to such modifications as may be prescribed by the rules."

(2) In sections 3(6)(*b*) of the Lands Tribunal Act 1949 (provision for the Tribunal to sit with assessors) for " sit with " there shall be substituted " be assisted by ".

The Land Compensation Act 1961

4.—(1) At the end of section 2(2) of the Land Compensation Act 1961 (tribunal to sit in public) there shall be added—

" Provided that this subsection shall not prevent the determination of cases without an oral hearing pursuant to rules under section 3 of the Lands Tribunal Act 1949 ".

(2) In section 15(5) of the Land Compensation Act 1961 (assumptions as to planning permission) for the words " might reasonably have been expected to be " there shall be substituted the words " would have been " and after the word " thereof " there shall be inserted the words " if it were not proposed to be acquired by any authority possessing compulsory purchase powers ".

(3) In section 19(3) of the Land Compensation Act 1961 (extension of sections 17 and 18 to special cases) there shall be substituted for the words " paragraph (*a*) " the words " paragraphs (*a*) and (*b*) " and for the words " paragraph (*b*) " the words " paragraph (*c*) ".

(4) In Schedule 2 to the Land Compensation Act 1961 (acquisition of houses as being unfit for human habitation), at the end of paragraph 2(1)(*h*) there shall be added the words " or

(i) an acquisition under Part III of the Community Land Act 1975.".

(5) Sub-paragraphs (2) and (3) above shall have effect only in relation to applications, or certificates issued in pursuance of applications, made after the expiration of a period of one month beginning with the passing of this Act.

The Land Compensation (Scotland) Act 1963

5.—(1) At the end of section 9(2) of the Land Compensation (Scotland) Act 1963 (tribunal to sit in public) there shall be added—

" Provided that this subsection shall not prevent the determination of cases without an oral hearing pursuant to rules under section 3 of the Lands Tribunal Act 1949 ".

(2) In section 23(5) of the Land Compensation (Scotland) Act 1963 (assumptions as to planning permission) for the words " might reasonably have been expected to be " there shall be substituted the words " would have been " and after the word " thereof " there shall be inserted the words " if it were not proposed to be acquired by any authority possessing compulsory purchase powers ".

(3) In section 27(5) of the Land Compensation (Scotland) Act 1963 (extension of sections 25 and 26 to special cases) there shall be substituted for the words " section 25(3)(*a*) " the words " subsection (3)(*a*) and (*b*) of section 25 " and for the words " subsection (3)(*b*) " the words " subsection (3)(*c*) ".

(4) In Schedule 2 to the Land Compensation (Scotland) Act 1963 (acquisition of houses as being unfit for human habitation), at the end of paragraph 1(1)(*f*) there shall be added the words " or

(*g*) an acquisition under Part III of the Community Land Act 1975 ".

(5) Sub-paragraphs (2) and (3) above shall have effect only in relation to applications, or certificates issued in pursuance of applications, made after the expiration of a period of one month beginning with the passing of this Act.

The Town and Country Planning Act 1971

6.—(1) In section 27 of the Act of 1971 (notification of applications for planning permission to owners and agricultural tenants)—

(*a*) in subsection (1)(*a*) (no notification if applicant is the estate owner or entitled to a tenancy) for the words from " that " to the end there shall be substituted the words " at the beginning of the period of twenty-one days ending with the date of the application, no person (other than the applicant) was the owner of any of the land to which the application relates ", and

(b) in subsection (7) (definition of " owner ") for the words from " who " to " unexpired " there shall be substituted the words " entitled to any material interest (within the meaning of section 6 (1) and (2) of the Community Land Act 1975) in the land ".

This sub-paragraph applies to every application for planning permission made on or after the first appointed day.

(2) In section 34 of the Act of 1971 (registers of planning applications and decisions), after subsection (1) there shall be inserted the following subsection—

" (1A) Where information concerning the grant of planning permission is entered in a register kept by virtue of subsection (1) above, there shall also be entered details of any certificate relating to that planning permission and given under section 21 of the Community Land Act 1975.".

(3) In section 194(2) of the Act of 1971 (grounds of objection to blight notice), in paragraph (d), the words " (in the case of land falling within paragraph (a) or (c) but not (d), (e) or (f) of section 192(1) of this Act) " shall be omitted and for the word " fifteen " there shall be substituted the word " ten ".

This sub-paragraph applies to every counter-notice served under the said section 194 on or after the first appointed day.

The Town and Country Planning (Scotland) Act 1972

7.—(1) In section 24 of the Scottish Act of 1972 (notification of applications to owners and agricultural tenants)—

(a) in subsection (1)(a) (no notification if applicant is estate owner or a tenant) for the words from " that " to the end there shall be substituted the words " at the beginning of the period of twenty-one days ending with the date of the application, no person (other than the applicant) was the owner of any of the land to which the application relates ", and

(b) in subsection (7) (definition of " owner ") for the words from " who " to " years " there shall be substituted the words " entitled to any material interest (within the meaning of section 6(1) and (2) of the Community Land Act 1975) in the land ".

This sub-paragraph applies to every application for planning permission made on or after the first appointed day.

(2) In section 31 of the Scottish Act of 1972 (registers of planning applications and decisions), at the end of subsection (2) there shall be added the words " and with respect of resolutions and notifications under Schedule 8 to the Community Land Act 1975 " and after that subsection there shall be inserted the following subsection—

" (2A) Where information concerning the grant of planning permission is entered in a register kept by virtue of subsection (2) above, there shall also be entered details of any certificate relating to that planning permission given under section 21 of the Community Land Act 1975."

(3) In section 183(2) of the Scottish Act of 1972 (grounds of objection to blight notice), in paragraph (d), the words " in the case of land falling within paragraph (a) or (c) but not (e), (f) or (h) of section 181(1) of this Act) " shall be omitted and for the word " fifteen " there shall be substituted the word " ten ".

This sub-paragraph applies to every counter-notice served under the said section 183 on or after the first appointed day.

The Local Government Act 1972

8.—(1) Section 123A of the Local Government Act 1972 (inserted by this Act) shall apply to the Peak Park Joint and Lake District Special Planning Boards as if they were principal councils.

(2) In paragraph 55 of Schedule 16 to the Local Government Act 1972 (which makes provision as to the exercise of functions under section 17 of the Land Compensation Act 1961 elsewhere than in Greater London) for the words " might reasonably have been expected to be granted ", in both places where they occur, there shall be substituted the words " would have been granted if the land in question were not proposed to be acquired by any authority possessing compulsory purchase powers."

This sub-paragraph shall have effect only in relation to applications made after the expiration of a period of one month beginning with the passing of this Act.

The Local Government Act 1974

9.—(1) In section 25(1) of the Local Government Act 1974 (authorities subject to investigation) after paragraph (a) there shall be inserted the following paragraph—

" (aa) the Land Authority for Wales and any body corporate established by an order made by the Secretary of State under section 50 of the Community Land Act 1975."

(2) In section 30 of the Local Government Act 1974 (reports on investigations), after subsection (2) there shall be inserted the following subsection—

" (2A) Where the complaint related to the Land Authority for Wales, the Local Commissioner shall also send the report or statement to the Secretary of State.".

The Local Government (Scotland) Act 1975

10. In section 23(1) of the Local Government (Scotland) Act 1975 (authorities subject to investigation), after paragraph (a) there shall be inserted the following paragraph—

" (aa) any body corporate established by an order made by the Secretary of State under section 50 of the Community Land Act 1975."

SCHEDULE 11

Section 58(3).

REPEALS

Chapter	Short Title	Extent of Repeal
1971 c. 78.	The Town and Country Planning Act 1971.	In section 194(2), the words " (in the case of land falling within paragraph (a) or (c) but not (d), (e) or (f) of section 192(1) of this Act) ".
1972 c. 52.	The Town and Country Planning (Scotland) Act 1972.	In section 183(2), the words " (in the case of land falling within paragraph (a) or (c) but not (e), (f) or (h) of section 181(1) of this Act) ".

These repeals take effect on the first appointed day.

D.—THE COMMUNITY LAND (EXCEPTED DEVELOPMENT) REGULATIONS 1976[1]

Draft regulations laid before Parliament under the Community Land Act 1975, s. 3(4), for approval by resolution of each House of Parliament.

Made - - - - - - 1976

Coming into Operation - - *6th April* 1976

The Secretary of State for the Environment, in relation to England, the Secretary of State for Scotland, in relation to Scotland, and the Secretary of State for Wales, in relation to Wales, in exercise of the powers conferred on them by sections 3(2) and 53(2) of the Community Land Act 1975, and of all other powers enabling them in that behalf, hereby make the following regulations in the terms of a draft which has been laid before and approved by a resoultion of each House of Parliament:—

Citation and commencement

1. These regulations may be cited as the Community Land (Excepted Development) Regulations 1976 and shall come into operation on 6th April 1976.

Interpretation

2.—(1) In these regulations, unless the context otherwise requires—

" the Act " means the Community Land Act 1975;

" builder or developer of residential or industrial property " means any person carrying on a business which—

(*a*) consists wholly or mainly of the carrying out of building operations or of building and engineering operations and includes the building of dwelling-houses or industrial buildings, or

(*b*) consists wholly or mainly of building, or arranging for the building of, dwelling-houses or industrial buildings, and of selling, feuing or letting them;[2]

---

[1] The effect of these regulations will be to take the prescribed classes of excepted development outside the duties of authorities under the Act (ss. 17 and 18), the procedures for the suspension of planning permission (ss. 19-22) and the modified compulsory purchase procedures (Sched. 4, paras. 1-3).

[2] In this definition sub-paragraph (*a*) deals primarily with builders, whereas sub-paragraph (*b*) principally covers developers and builder-developers. These definitions are qualified by the provisions relating to groups of companies in Regulation 2(5).

" building " includes part of a building[1];

" industrial building " has in relation to England and Wales the meaning assigned to it by section 66 of the Act of 1971 and in relation to Scotland the meaning assigned to it by section 64 of the Scottish Act of 1972;

" industrial undertaker " in relation to England and Wales means any person carrying on any such process or research as is mentioned in section 66(1) of the Act of 1971 and in relation to Scotland means any person carrying on any such process or research as is mentioned in section 64(1) of the Scottish Act of 1972.

(2) Any expression not referred to in paragraph (1) above which is used in these regulations and which is also used in the Act shall, unless the context otherwise requires, have the same meaning as it has in the Act.

(3) In these regulations any reference to the time when planning permission is or was granted, in the case of planning permission granted on an appeal, is a reference to the time of the decision appealed against or, in the case of planning permission granted on an appeal in the circumstances mentioned in section 37 of the Act of 1971 or section 34 of the Scottish Act of 1972, a reference to the time when in accordance with that section notification of the decision is or was deemed to have been received.[2]

(4) For the purposes of these regulations a material interest in land shall be treated as owned by any person at any time if, at that time, that person has or had entered into a binding contract for its acquisition.

(5) For the purposes of these regulations if at any time a company is

    (a) a member of a group of companies for any of the purposes of the Income and Corporation Taxes Act 1970, and

    (b) a building or developer of residential or industrial property or, as the case may be, an industrial undertaker,

then all the companies who are (at that time) members of that group of companies shall, at that time, be deemed to be builders or developers of industrial or residential property or, as the case may be, industrial undertakers.

---

[1] In this Regulation, " building " has been assigned a different meaning from that in section 6 of the Community Land Act. Regulation 2(2) makes this clear by stating that the definitions in the Act do not apply to cases where a specific definition is given in the Regulations. The new definition ensures that " building " has its ordinary meaning (e.g. for the purpose of class 11 of the Schedule) and is not extended to include " any structure or erection " as in the Act.

[2] Regulation 2(3) follows the terms of section 6(3) of the Act.

(6) For the purposes of these regulations the amount of the gross floor space in or to be comprised in a building shall be ascertained by external measurement of that space whether or not the building is to be bounded (wholly or partly) by external walls.

(7) References in these regulations to any enactment shall, except where the context otherwise requires, be construed as references to that enactment as amended or extended by or under any other enactment.

(8) The Interpretation Act 1889 shall apply for the interpretation of these regulations as it applies for the interpretation of an Act of Parliament.

Excepted Development

3. The classes of development described in the Schedule to these Regulations are prescribed for the purposes of section 3(2)(c) of the Act so that development of such classes is excepted from the definition of " relevant development " contained in section 3(2) of the Act.

SCHEDULE

PART I

EXCEPTED DEVELOPMENT

Class 1

Any development the carrying out of which is authorised by planning permission granted on or before 12th September 1974.

Class 2

Development consisting wholly or mainly of the building of dwelling-houses or industrial buildings on any land so long as—

(a) during the whole of the period beginning with 12th September 1974 and ending with the relevant time, the freehold of that land has been owned by a builder or developer of residential or industrial property (but not necessarily the same builder or developer of residential or industriar property throughout), and

(b) notice in the appropriate form as set out in Part II of this Schedule (or in a form substantially to the like effect) was given to any one of the authorities whose areas include the land by a builder or developer of residential or industrial property who, at the time of giving such notice, owned the freehold of the land described in that notice, and the notice was received by that authority not later than 5th October 1976, or where application is made before that date for planning permission to carry out the development not later than whichever of the following dates is appropriate (if it is earlier than 5th October 1976)—

(i) if it appears from a certificate under section 27 of the Act of 1971 or section 24 of the Scottish Act of 1972 that notices have been served or published under either of those sections, the date of expiration of a period of 21 days beginning with the date appearing from the certificate to be the latest of the dates of service of notices as mentioned in the certificate, or with the date of publication of a notice as therein mentioned, whichever is the later, or

(ii) if it appears from the certificate mentioned in (i) above that no such notices as therein mentioned have been served or published, the date of the application.

Class 3

The erection of any number of industrial buildings on any land so long as during the whole of the period beginning with 12th September 1974 and ending with the relevant time, a material interest in that land has been owned by an industrial undertaker (but not necessarily the same industrial undertaker throughout).

Class 4

The erection of one or more industrial buildings so long as the gross floor space or the aggregate of the gross floor space to be comprised in that building or those buildings does not exceed 1,500 sq. metres.

Class 5

The erection of one or more buildings other than any industrial building so long as the gross floor space or the aggregate of the gross floor space to be comprised in that building or those buildings does not exceed 1,000 sq. metres.

Class 6

The erection on any land of one or more buildings to be used for agriculture.

Class 7

The rebuilding or the enlargement, improvement or other alteration of any building which was in existence at the relevant time, or of any building which was in existence in the period of 10 years immediately preceding the relevant time but was destroyed or demolished before that time, so long as the gross floor space to be comprised in the building as proposed to be rebuilt, enlarged, improved or altered under this class does not exceed by more than 10 per cent. the gross floor space comprised in the building before rebuilding, enlargement, improvement or alteration.

For the purposes of this class—

(a) the erection, on land within the curtilage of a building, of an additional building to be used in connection with that building, shall be treated as the enlargement of that building, and

(b) where any two or more buildings comprised in the same curtilage are used as one unit for the purposes of any institution or undertaking, the reference in this class to the gross floor space comprised in the building shall be construed as a reference to the aggregate of the gross floor space comprised in those buildings.

Class 8

Any development on any land the freehold in which is owned by the Scottish Development Agency or the Welsh Development Agency.

Class 9

Any development on any land which is operational land of statutory undertakers or would be such land if it were used or held by statutory undertakers for the purposes of the development.

Class 10

Any development for which planning permission would be granted by a general development order for the time being in force but for a condition imposed in any planning permission granted or deemed to be granted otherwise than by such an order, and which is carried out so as to comply with any condition or limitation subject to which planning permission would be so granted.

Class 11

Any development so long as—

(a) it does not include the erection of a building, and

(b) it is not wholly or mainly connected with and ancillary to the use of one or more buildings not in existence at the relevant time and whose erection would constitute relevant development.

Class 12

Any development consisting of development in any two or more of classes 1-11 inclusive so long as it does not include any development solely in class 4 or class 5.

Class 13

Any development consisting of development in any two or more of classes 1-11 inclusive so long as it does not include any development solely in class 7.

Part II

Forms of Notice by Builder or Developer of Ownership of Land on 12th September 1974

NOTES ON THE SCHEDULE

In Class 1 of Part I of the Schedule development is excepted only if its carrying out is **authorised** by planning permission granted on or before 12 September 1974. If, however, the development is carried out after the date by which conditions under sections 41 or 42 of the Town and Country Planning Act 1971 (ss. 38 and 39 Scotland Act 1972) require it to be carried out, by virtue of section 43(7) of the 1971 Act (s. 40(7) of the Scottish Act) such development is not authorised by the planning permission. It does not therefore constitute excepted development.

Class 2(*b*) of the Schedule prescribes certain dates by which notice has to be given to an authority of the ownership of the freehold of land of the kind described in class 2(*a*) by a builder or developer of residential or industrial property. Generally notice has to be given by 5th October 1976, but if a planning application is made before that date notice has to be given either before the date of the application or, if later, before the end of the period within which representations can be made by owners. This formula is adopted to give builders the maximum time (within the overall limit) whilst still ensuring that authorities know whether the application is for relevant development or not when they consider it.

In classes 2, 3 and 7 the expression " the relevant time " occurs. This is used in the same way as in the Act itself (*e.g.* s. 4(1)(*b*) and the definition of " material interest " in s. 6(1)) and simply means any time at which it is necessary to establish whether development is " relevant " or not.

In Class 7 the reference is to the excess over the gross floor space comprised in the building before rebuilding, enlargement, improvement or alteration takes place and not to the gross floor space at any specified date. This means that successive enlargements of the same building could take place within this class, but this must not be used as a means of evasion by fragmentation of development. *See* Circular 121/75 para. 17.

Class 10 is complementary to paragraph 1 of Schedule 1 to the Act which makes development permitted by a general development order (GDO) into exempt development in certain cases. The Act covers the case where, in a specific locality, permissions under a GDO have been withdrawn by a direction under the GDO but does not deal with cases where the GDO permission has been withdrawn by a specific condition on a planning permission. This class extends excepted status to such cases.

Class 11 covers **any** development other than the erection of a building and other than development so closely connected with (and ancillary to) buildings whose erection would constitute relevant development that the development needs to be considered as a whole. " Development " has the same meaning as in section 22 of the Town and Country Planning Act 1971 (s. 19 Scotland Act 1972). Subject to the qualifications mentioned above the class therefore includes the carrying out of any building, engineering, mining or other operations in, on, over or under land, or the making of any material change in the use of any buildings or other land.

Classes 12 and 13 allow any development covered by two or more of the other classes to be treated as excepted development but exclude any aggregation of the floor space limit permitted under class 4 or class 5 with that permitted under class 7.

INDEX

A

E

I

J

L

382   INDEX

M

P

R

U